INTRODUCTION TO EVANGELISM

INTRODUCTION TO EVANGELISM

ALVIN REID

ACADEMIC

NASHVILLE, TENNESSEE

© 1998
by Alvin L. Reid
All rights reserved
Printed in the United States of America

ISBN: 978-0-8054-1143-0

Published by B&H Publishing Group,
Nashville, Tennessee

Dewey Decimal Classification: 269
Subject Heading: EVANGELISTIC WORK
Library of Congress Card Catalog Number: 98–13631

Unless otherwise noted, quotations are from New King James Version,
copyright © 1979, 1980, 1982, Thomas Nelson, Inc., Publishers;
quotations marked NIV are from the Holy Bible, New International Version,
copyright © 1973, 1978, 1984 by International Bible Society;
quotations marked NASB are from the New American Standard Bible,
© the Lockman Foundation, 1960, 1962, 1963, 1968,
1971, 1972, 1973, 1975, 1977. Used by permission.

Library of Congress Cataloging-in-Publication Data
Reid, Alvin L.
Introduction to evangelism/by Alvin L. Reid.
    p.   cm.
Includes bibliographical references.
ISBN 0–8054–1143–7
1. Evangelistic work.   2. Evangelistic work—Biblical teaching.
I. Title.
BV3770.R45   1998
269'.2—dc21

98-13631
CIP

27 28 29 30 31   14 13 12 11 10

To my precious wife, Michelle.
Your name means "Godly Woman."
No other expression could
better describe you.

Contents

PART 1

WHAT WE MUST KNOW: THE CONVICTIONAL BASIS OF EVANGELISM

PART 2

HOW WE MUST LIVE: THE SPIRITUAL BASIS OF EVANGELISM

PART 3

WHAT WE MUST DO: THE METHODOLOGICAL BASIS OF EVANGELISM

Preface

Children have a knack for cutting to the heart of an issue. One Sunday our four-year-old daughter Hannah noticed me getting ready to preach. "Daddy," she asked, "why do you always go to tell people about Jesus?" I knew her question emerged out of her desire to have Daddy go to church with her instead of preaching somewhere else. But her question is relevant to more than a four-year-old. Why should anyone tell another person about Jesus?

This book was written to remind the church why and how we must tell others about Jesus. We live in a nation blessed with unprecedented resources: Christian schools, bookstores, radio stations, churches, camps—on and on we could go. Yet the Christian faith seems to be losing ground in our culture. The easy way to confront this dilemma is to cast stones at the darkness that surrounds us, or to call the darkness names, or to retreat from it. But the Bible tells us that the way to remove darkness is to turn on the light. The pure, unadulterated gospel of the Lord Jesus Christ is still the greatest deterrent to the darkness in this present evil age.

This book flows along three fronts, all of which are vitally linked. The first deals with *conviction,* or the facts of evangelism. There are certain truths that are essential, including key biblical, theological, and historical issues. Second, there is the vital role of *passion,* fueled by the spiritual resources linked to evangelism. Most texts deal with the matters of theory and practice but hardly mention the vital role of spiritual resources. A critical feature of this book is a survey of those matters that help to develop the spiritual life of a believer or church. A believer's spiritual life leads naturally to a passion for God and thus a passion for the things that matter to God. Finally, there is the issue of *methodology*. Key methods and approaches that will aid churches and leaders in evangelism will be examined.

Introductory texts for Old or New Testament courses are legion; theological and church history texts abound. But introductory texts for evangelism courses are few, although evangelism is taught in virtually all evangelical seminaries and in many evangelical colleges. This text attempts to fill that void. I hope it will also be of help to interested church leaders and laity as well.

This text is written primarily for pastors and students in North America who seek to lead congregations to fulfill the Great Commission. However, it is also intended for anyone who wants to be a Great Commission Christian.

This book is more than a personal journey. It presents information gathered from the most significant resources and people in the field of evangelism. Still, this information comes to you through the filter of my own Christian pilgrimage. Thus, I want the readers to know how our great God has privileged me to learn the discipline of evangelism.

I came to Christ in 1970 as an eleven-year-old boy at a church in Alabama touched by the Jesus Movement; thus, I know at least in a small way how the work of God in revival can bring many people to a radical transformation in a brief time. A strong youth ministry showed me the impact youth can have on a church.

In college, I spent a summer as an itinerant evangelist, and I have preached at almost two hundred such meetings in the years since. I learned to share my faith in college by doing street evangelism.

My pilgrimage has included time as a pastor, interim pastor, and in denominational staff positions in two states. Evangelism has always played a critical role in these areas of service. My wife and I served as home missionaries in Indiana. As a consultant in evangelism, I have spoken or preached in about five hundred churches across this great nation and in several foreign countries.

As a denominational leader, I experienced great joy by serving first as associate, then as director of evangelism for the state convention of Baptists in Indiana. I taught evangelism at a university and now teach at one of the fastest growing seminaries in the world.

I have also been privileged to serve on a number of interdenominational committees and organizations.

I never dreamed of becoming an author. During my freshman year in college, I received a B+ on every theme paper I wrote, convincing me I would never excel as a writer. Then a seminary professor wrote a comment on a term paper: "You are a very good writer." That statement changed my perspective. I soon enrolled in a writer's conference held at my seminary and published an article soon thereafter. I have been writing ever since.

I share this little glimpse about my writing for three reasons. First, it illustrates the power of words. The things we read do affect our lives. We can make a difference through what we say! Second, it shows an individual can change. My perspective about my ability to write changed through a simple comment. I pray that the words of this book will convince you that you *can* make a difference in evangelism—and, if you are not confident in your ability, that you can change. Third, we can misjudge our abilities. I do not consider myself a great writer, but I believe I can write. I had misjudged myself. Whether you are a pastor or a deacon, minister or layman, student or teacher, if you have doubts about your ability to make an impact for the kingdom of God, read on. You might discover that you too have misjudged yourself.

We learn either by contrast—facing opposing views to our own—or through confirmation—by being encouraged to stand on what we believe. My primary focus in this book is the latter. Most people who read this book will already know more than enough to be effective in evangelism. My primary concern is to give you a vision that you can do that to which God has called you. Here are some convictions you can stand on with confidence.

1. *Men and women are lost until they receive salvation through Jesus.* Therefore, we must evangelize *urgently.* People apart from Christ are lost (Luke 15), dead in sins (Eph. 2:1), under sin (Rom. 3:9), and under condemnation (John 3:18). Immanuel Kant once declared that David Hume, the skeptic, awoke him from his dogmatic slumber. Surely a skeptical

world, living in fear, often without hope, should awaken us from our apathy!

2. *Many people are ready to respond to the gospel.* Therefore, we must evangelize *regularly.* Paul told Timothy to preach the word in season and out of season—or when we feel like it and when we don't! In 1995, I had the privilege of joining the faculty at Southeastern Baptist Theological Seminary. Prior to that I taught at Houston Baptist University. Before leaving the university, I made an appointment with several students, including some whom I felt needed to hear the gospel. One was a young lady named Audra. I shared Christ with her. This was new to her, although she had gone to church at times. I gave her an *Eternal Life* booklet, asking her to read it again.

The first week after beginning my work at Southeastern, I got a letter from Audra. She wrote, "On August 9, I opened my heart to Christ. . . . A big thanks goes to you." She even photocopied the tract to give it to another person who needed Christ. This point is that Audra needed someone to tell her how to be saved. The reason many people aren't Christians is that no one has told them how to be saved.

3. *Believers are commanded by the Bible to evangelize.* Therefore, we must evangelize *obediently.* Billy Graham has said the number one reason we should witness is because God says we should. In our day of consumer Christianity focused on our needs, obedience has become low on the priority list of many believers.

4. *Most believers want to witness but do not.* Therefore, we must evangelize *purposefully.* Statistics indicate that only 3 to 5 percent of believers consistently share their faith. However, as I have been in hundreds of churches over the past decade, I am amazed at the number of believers who want to witness. They are afraid, or do not know how, or have been too busy doing good things to participate in the best thing—winning people to Christ.

5. *The gospel is the greatest message we could ever tell.* Therefore, we must evangelize *confidently.* As a student in a Baptist university, I was discipled by a Presbyterian. One day Curtis asked

me a simple question that changed my life. "Alvin," he said, "what is the best thing that ever happened to you?" "The day I was saved," I heartily replied, with my Sunday school smile. "Then, Alvin," he continued, "what is the best thing you can do for someone else?" The answer was obvious. Yet I was immediately embarrassed at it because I knew my life did not reflect the joy of introducing others to the Jesus whom I knew so well.

Do you really believe the greatest thing you can tell another person is the good news about Jesus? Then tell someone!

On my next birthday after the publication of this book, I will turn forty years old. I remember thinking how old I would be when we reached the year 2000! Now that we are at the dawn of only the second new millennium since Jesus walked on the earth, I would like you to sense the wonderful privilege we have to proclaim the glorious gospel at such a unique time in history. I feel younger than I expected! May this book encourage and challenge you to fulfill the Great Commission.

By the way, my first answer to my daughter Hannah's question was a bit of a joke. "Well, Hannah," I asked, "would you prefer that I talk to them about something like *dirt*?" "No, Daddy," she replied with a smile. "Tell them about Jesus."

Acknowledgments

This book is a bit ironic. My first three books were coedited or coauthored, making this the first book written solely by me. Yet in no other book have I been more dependent on others than in this one. Certain people have played an especially important role.

First, I want to thank our great God for the glorious gospel, without which we would be hopeless and this book would be unnecessary. Further, I want to thank people who have played a prominent role in my journey through writing.

Lisa Estes, who serves several faculty members in the circus we call Broyhill Hall, typed and retyped the manuscript with skill surpassed only by her gentle, Christlike spirit. Thank you, Lisa!

My colleague, Danny Forshee, and student, Victor Lee, read the manuscript in its entirety, adding helpful comments. Doctoral students Larry McDonald and Bill Brown also read portions of the book. Many other colleagues added insights to specific parts of the book. I would especially like to thank my students at Houston Baptist University and Southeastern Baptist Theological Seminary for allowing me to present much of the material in courses over the past six years. Southeastern students are the greatest on earth! It is an honor to stand before these men and women to teach the unsearchable riches of Christ. They have taught me far more than I have taught them. Although many have influenced me, I am responsible for any shortcomings of the book.

This book could never have happened without the impact of the men of God who taught me evangelism. The influence of Roy Fish, my doctoral supervisor and my hero, will be recognized throughout the book by his students. Malcolm McDow has been my tireless encourager from the time he convinced me to do a Ph.D. until recent days as we have labored together on writing projects. Jim Eaves, for whom I was a grader and a teaching fellow, offered me numerous opportunities to teach while in the Southwestern Seminary doctoral program. Dan Crawford, whom I assisted in teaching the spring evangelism practicum, deepened my love for prayer and for students.

Several others must be thanked: John Avant, Tim Beougher, Steve Gaines, Doug Munton, Preston Nix, Thom Rainer, Mike Landry, and David Wheeler. Pastors Wayne Watts, Jerry Sutton, Fenton Moorhead, Johnny Hunt, and John Bisagno, the wonderful state evangelism directors across the Southern Baptist Convention, and the evangelism staff at the North American Mission Board have been great influences in my life. John Landers of Broadman & Holman has been tireless in his encouragement.

I want especially to thank my president, Paige Patterson, for his conviction, his example as a personal soul winner, and his leadership at Southeastern Seminary. Bailey Smith, one of the most effective pastors and evangelists in this generation, has been a dear friend and encourager. It is an honor to hold the chair named for him. References throughout this book note resources that have helped me. Certain insights and resources have been especially useful, including the writings of Delos Miles, Bill Bright, Darrell Robinson, Steve Sjogren, Roy Fish, and Rick Warren.

My family means more to me than life itself. Austin H. Reid Sr. and Margaret Reid are the greatest parents on earth. Joshua and Hannah love their Daddy, and the feeling is mutual! I really like my students, but I *love* my family!

Finally, and most precious of all, I thank God for Michelle. For over sixteen years, she has put up with a type-A, hyperactive, driven husband. There is no greater joy on earth than a family who loves and supports you. I am a blessed man.

Part 1

WHAT WE MUST KNOW: THE CONVICTIONAL BASIS OF EVANGELISM

Philip Simelvise was born in 1818 into a world of dying women. In Simelvise's day, one in six women died in childbirth. His desire to know the reason for the high death rate led him to become a physician. He discovered that these women were dying of something called "childbed fever." He decided to find out what was causing it. Studying the way the doctors worked in his day, he discovered something that we would consider appalling. When the doctors began their shift, they often went first to the morgue to do autopsies. Because they did not understand germs and bacteria, they did not wash their hands as they moved to the maternity ward. As they delivered children, they were killing the mothers.

Simelvise began to experiment with washing his hands. He encouraged his colleagues to wash their hands in a chlorine solution. Immediately the maternal death rate dropped from one in six to one in fifty among their patients.

Many physicians remained skeptical of this simple solution. Finally, Simelvise spoke to a convention of his colleagues: "This fever is caused by decomposed material conveyed to a wound. I have shown how it could be prevented. I have proven all I have said. But while we talk, talk, talk, gentlemen, women are dying. I'm not asking you to do anything world shaking, I'm asking you only to wash. For God's sake, wash your hands." But they laughed him to scorn. Philip Simelvise died insane at the age of 47 with the death rattle of a thousand women ringing in his ears.[1]

Could it be that our Lord is saying to the church today, "You are so busy talking, talking, talking about secondary issues. While you talk, the world is dying." We have a message whose truth is even more valuable than the news that could save a generation of mothers. We have the Good News that can change lives for eternity!

Part 1 surveys foundational issues that are necessary to rescue the world from hell. We must build an altar upon which the light of the gospel can burn. We dare not hold up a faint flicker in the face of the yawning darkness of our day. Instead, we must raise up a blazing inferno of biblical truth, stoked by the fuel of biblical fidelity, theological orthodoxy, and the perspective of church history.

1

Make the Message Plain: What Is Evangelism?

L*ost.*

This word shattered the peacefulness of our family vacation at Myrtle Beach in late July 1997. We had finished our first day's swim and were sitting at a restaurant on a pier. As I ordered, I noticed my wife watching a large group of people who had gathered on the beach—rescue vehicles, lifeguards, and bystanders.

A thirteen-year-old girl had been caught in a vicious riptide. Her eighteen-year-old cousin and her father tried to save her. The girl was rescued, but the father suffered serious injury. He died the following evening. The eighteen-year-old was missing. Lost.

The lifeguards formed a human chain, walking through the pounding surf, searching urgently for the lost young man. Boats were launched, and the search continued for hours. Finally, darkness stopped the search. The young man's body washed ashore two days later, fifteen miles north of where he was last seen. This event reminded me of the stark reality of the word *lost.*

Evangelism is critical because people apart from Christ are lost. They are swimming in a riptide of sin that will yank them into the abyss of hell for all eternity—unless they meet the One who is the lifeline for all mankind: the Lord Jesus Christ. Just as confusion

3

reigned when the young man was first missing, the church is confused about evangelism because the message has been diluted.

Appearances are deceptive. Adding to a church roll does not in itself indicate biblical evangelism. Talking about evangelism does not mean effective evangelism is occurring. What is evangelism? How can a person or church tell whether evangelism is biblical?

Karl Marx once said that the person who gives the definitions controls the movement. Evangelism means many things to many people in our day. Before we can go into any substantive discussion of evangelism, we must discover what the term means.

MISCONCEPTIONS ABOUT EVANGELISM

Before we can examine what evangelism is, let's consider what it is not.

THE MUTE APPROACH

People with this view suggest that evangelism is simply living a good, moral life. I call this the "mute" approach. Certainly an effective witness should live a moral life, a life worthy of our calling. But some believers go so far as to say that their lives will reflect Christ, so their words are not needed.

But if people look at you and see you are a good, moral person, how will they know Jesus is the reason? Might not a good Buddhist appear the same? They might think you just got a raise. Or that you won the big sweepstakes. How will they know if we don't tell them? "How shall they hear without a preacher" (Rom. 10:14). Evangelism includes who we are, but it is more.

THE SCALP HUNTING APPROACH

Some people see evangelism as church membership recruitment. This is the "scalp hunting" or the "sheep stealing" approach. "Scalp hunting" is more accurate because I am not sure that churches steal sheep as much as they grow greener grass! But we must admit that some folks are more interested in getting a notch on their evangelistic gun belt than they are in people's lives. They are more interested in recognition for their numbers than faithfulness to God.

Years ago a pastor told me as the evangelism leader that his goal was to lead his church to be the biggest church with the most baptisms in the state. I was not impressed, and I am convinced God was not impressed. To seek to be the biggest or the best often springs from a heart of pride rather than obedience to God.

THE PROFESSIONAL FISHERMAN APPROACH

According to this view, evangelism is a job for specialists only. Many believers who are convinced of the importance of evangelism are equally impressed that the pastor, staff, and itinerant evangelists are to accomplish the task. This familiar story reminds us of the need for all to fish:

> Now it came to pass that a group existed who called themselves fishermen. And lo, there were many fish in the waters all around. In fact, the whole area was surrounded by streams and lakes filled with fish. And the fish were hungry.

> Week after week, month after month, and year after year, these who called themselves fishermen met in meetings and talked about their call to fish, the abundance of fish, and how they might go about fishing. Year after year they carefully defined what fishing means, defended fishing as an occupation, and declared that fishing is always to be a primary task of fishermen.

> Continually, they searched for new and better methods of fishing and for new and better definitions of fishing. Further they said, "The fishing industry exists by fishing as fire exists by burning." They loved slogans such as "Fishing is the task of every fisherman." They sponsored special meetings called "Fishermen's Campaigns" and "The Month for Fishermen to Fish." They sponsored costly nationwide and worldwide congresses to discuss fishing and to promote fishing and hear about all the ways of fishing such as the new fishing equipment, fish calls, and whether any new bait had been discovered.

These fishermen built large, beautiful buildings called "Fishing Headquarters." The plea was that everyone should be a fisherman and every fisherman should fish. One thing they didn't do, however. They didn't fish.

In addition to meeting regularly, they organized a board to send out fishermen to other places where there were many fish. The board hired staffs and appointed committees and held many meetings to define fishing, to defend fishing, and to decide what new streams should be thought about. But the staff and committee members did not fish.

Large, elaborate, and expensive training centers were built whose original and primary purpose was to teach fishermen how to fish. Over the years courses were offered on the needs of fish, the nature of fish, where to find fish, the psychological reactions of fish, and how to approach and feed fish. Those who taught had doctorates in "fishology," but the teachers did not fish. They only taught fishing. Year after year, after tedious training, many were graduated and were given fishing licenses. They were sent to do full-time fishing, some to distant waters which were filled with fish.

Many who felt the call to be fishermen responded. They were commissioned and sent to fish. But like the fishermen back home, they never fished. Like the fishermen back home, they engaged in all kinds of other occupations. They built power plants to pump water for fish and tractors to plow new waterways. They made all kinds of equipment to travel here and there to look at fish hatcheries. Some also said that they wanted to be part of the fishing party, but they felt called to furnish fishing equipment. Others felt their job was to relate to the fish in a good way so the fish would know the difference between good and bad fishermen. Others felt that simply letting the fish know they were nice, land-loving neighbors and how loving and kind they were was enough.

After one stirring meeting on "The Necessity for Fishing," one young fellow left the meeting and went fishing. The next day he reported that he had caught two outstanding fish. He was honored for his excellent catch and scheduled to visit all the big meetings possible to tell how he did it. So he quit his fishing in order to have time to tell about the experience to the other fishermen. He was also placed on the Fishermen's General Board as a person having considerable experience.

Now it's true that many of the fishermen sacrificed and put up with all kinds of difficulties. Some lived near the water and bore the smell of dead fish every day. They received the ridicule of some who made fun of their fishermen's clubs and the fact that they claimed to be fishermen yet never fished. They wondered about those who felt it was of little use to attend the weekly meetings to talk about fishing. After all, were they not following the Master who said, "Follow me, and I will make you fishers of men"?

Imagine how hurt some were when one day a person suggested that those who don't catch fish were really not fishermen, no matter how much they claimed to be. Yet it did sound correct. Is a person a fisherman if, year after year, he never catches a fish? Is one following if he isn't fishing?[1]

Evangelism involves everyone in the work.

THE COP-OUT APPROACH

Evangelism is not everything we do in church. Not everything in the church has to be explicitly evangelistic. In fact, many things won't be. However, I have seen too many churches call certain events or emphases evangelistic when they are not. Churches should give attention to explicitly evangelistic emphases and distinguish between those activities that are designed for evangelism and those that are not.

The worst example of this was a church where I preached years ago. The small rural church had baptized no one in years. The pastor showed me the crowning glory of his ministry—they had added a steeple! He called it "church growth." There is nothing wrong with a steeple, but the adding of a physical structure enhances evangelism only when it leads to the evangelization of lost people!

Evangelism is the communication of the gospel by saved people to lost people. It is not inviting people to church or getting people to be religious. Evangelism, in its essence, is none of the above.

While pastor of the First Baptist Church of Pasadena, Texas, Darrell Robinson told the congregation he could not reach the masses for Christ; instead, it would take all the members' involvement. He particularly challenged the leadership, including the Sunday school director, Women's Missionary Union director, and others to participate in a lay witness training seminar. The WMU director told Robinson, "Pastor, I will come to the WIN Lay Evangelism School. I will learn how to teach our women to witness. But you must know this. I cannot witness myself. I have tried and failed. But I will learn how to teach others."

After the four nights of training, this woman's team and all the others went into the community to witness. She did not have the opportunity to witness. But God had given her a burden through the training for her beautician. At her next appointment she sat in the chair, flipping through an evangelistic tract.

The hairdresser asked, "What are you reading?"

"I'm reading a little booklet about Jesus. May I share it with you?"

They read through the booklet, and the hairdresser was interested, expressing her desire to be saved. How did the WMU director respond? She freaked out! She left, drove to the church, and rushed into Robinson's office in tears. She told her pastor the situation, pleading with him to go draw the net. Robinson said he would go, but only if she went as well. The two plus another man from the church visited the hairdresser and her husband. Within thirty minutes, both had given their lives to Christ! Then the new believer said something that changed the WMU director's life.

"You have invited me to church," the hairdresser said. "You have invited me to Sunday school. You have asked me to come hear your pastor preach. But you have never told me about Jesus. Why?"

The WMU director made a commitment to Christ at that moment to tell others about Christ. She eventually led her hairdresser's son, a neighbor, then her own father to Jesus. From that time on, she continued to share Christ faithfully. She later noted three reasons she had failed to witness. First, she did not know God expected every Christian to witness, thinking it was a job for specialists. Second, she didn't think she had a valid testimony. It was not sensational, so she thought no one would be interested. Finally, she simply did not know how. She needed someone to teach her.[2]

This story epitomizes the story of many who have misconceptions about evangelism. Scripture is where we must go to find out the true meaning of evangelism.

BIBLICAL TERMS FOR EVANGELISM

The Green Bay Packers had just lost to a team they should have easily defeated. Coach Vince Lombardi, football in hand, told his players, "Men, today we will get back to the basics—this is a football." Understanding the basics in evangelism begins with, and never moves past, the Word of God. A variety of terms demonstrate fully the New Testament teaching about evangelism.

COMMUNICATE GOOD NEWS

The basic word for *evangelism* in the New Testament is the term transliterated into the English as "evangel" (noun) or "evangelize" (verb). The verb form is seen several ways. The term *euangelizo* means "I communicate good news." You can see the prefix *eu*, which means "good." Think of other words that begin with *eu*: *eulogy*—a good word spoken of someone at a funeral; *eureka*—a good discovery; *euphoria*—a good feeling. The main part of the word *evangelism* contains the English term *angel*, a messenger. So to evangelize is to tell a good message. In the New Testament, the term implies a good message, as in a victory. While some people might attempt to make us feel as though evangelism imposes on the privacy of others, let us never forget we are telling the Good News—Jesus has conquered sin, death, and the grave!

This verb form is found thirty-three times in the New Testament and is common in Luke's Gospel, the Acts, and Paul's epistles. Often it is translated as "preach the gospel!" It is normally in the middle voice, which means "I, myself, tell the gospel." Some examples of this verb:

- "The Spirit of the Lord is on me, because he has anointed me to *preach good news* to the poor" (Luke 4:18 NIV).

- "For Christ did not send me to baptize, but to *preach the gospel*" (1 Cor. 1:17 NIV).

The noun form is *euangelion* and is found seventy-six times in the New Testament. It can be translated "gospel," "good news," or "evangel." It emphasizes not just any good news but a specific message. Paul particularly used this term a great deal. Our primary message is the specific news that Jesus died and rose again. Paul told the Corinthians: "Morever, brethren, I declare to you the gospel which I preached to you" (1 Cor. 15:1 KJV). He then summarized the gospel with the death, burial, and resurrection. There are two essential issues that confront every person: sin and death. On the cross Jesus dealt with the sin problem; in the empty tomb he defeated death. We have good news to share!

We see the verb and noun forms in Romans 1:15–16 KJV: "So, as much as is in me, I am ready to preach the gospel [*evangelize,* verb] to you who are in Rome also. For I am not ashamed of the gospel [*evangel,* noun] of Christ; for it is the power of God unto salvation to everyone who believes, for the Jew first and also for the Greek."

Another interesting use of this term is the expression *evangelistes*. It is found three times in the New Testament and is translated "evangelist." Philip is called the evangelist (Acts 21:8). Ephesians 4:11 calls the evangelist (note, not *evangelism*) one of the spiritual gifts. Paul exhorted Timothy (and all ministers) to do "the work of an evangelist" (2 Tim. 4:5). So evangelism means we have a specific, victorious message to tell.

PROCLAIM AS A HERALD

A second term is *kerusso* and its related forms. This verb form means "to proclaim in the manner of a herald." It implies the declaration of an event. The verb form is found sixty-one times in the New Testament. While not always referring to proclaiming the gospel, often it is used in that regard. In fact, at times *kerusso* and *evangelizomai* are based as synonyms, as in Romans 10:14–15. On twelve occasions the expression *kerussein to euaggelion,* "preach the gospel," is found in the New Testament, showing the close relation between the terms.

The noun *kerygma* is found eight times in the New Testament. It means "the proclamation." This term has received special attention in the modern era due particularly to C. H. Dodd's book, *The Apostolic Preaching and Its Development.* More will be said about the *kerygma* in chapter 4.

BEAR WITNESS

Notice the words translated *martureo* (verb) and *marturion* (noun). Today we think of a martyr as someone who died for the faith. The Greek word for *martyr* literally means "a witness." The term is similar to the English word, for a witness was someone who gave testimony to things they had experienced. Peter declared, "We cannot help but speak the things we have seen and heard" (Acts 4:20). But a witness gave testimony through words and actions. Many early believers died because of their commitment to Christ, leading to the expression *martyr* to describe such faithful witnesses. For many early Christians, it was better to die than to stop testifying about Christ.

The reason many believers today do not attempt to share their faith is because they have gotten over their salvation! The early believers did not—indeed they could not—get past the radical transformation they experienced through the gospel.

MAKE DISCIPLES

Matheteusate is the main verb in the Great Commission passage, Matthew 28:19–20: "Go . . . and *make disciples.*" The verb in this passage is an imperative, a command. The Great Commission is not the Great Suggestion! We are not merely to proclaim good news; we are to make disciples.

It is interesting that these terms can be seen in Great Commission passages in the Gospels and Acts.

- good news, gospel (Mark 16:15)
- preach (Mark 16:15; Luke 24:47)
- witness (Luke 24:48; Acts 1:8)
- make disciples (Matt. 28:19)

There are other words used at times in regard to evangelism, such as *laleo*, "I speak," but the above are central to understanding the New Testament meaning of evangelism.

Other expressions give insight into the message of the early church also. Followers of Christ were called to be fishers of men (Mark 1:16–20; Matt. 4:18–22); salt of the earth (Matt. 5:13); light of the world (Matt. 5:14); fruit-bearers (John 15:8); and ambassadors (2 Cor. 5:20).

SOME DEFINITIONS OF EVANGELISM

On the basis of these biblical terms, and considering the practice of the early church and of our Lord, we can determine a succinct definition of evangelism. Several important definitions have been offered.

1. THE ANGLICAN DEFINITION

"To evangelize is so to present Christ Jesus in the power of the Holy Spirit, that men shall come to put their trust in God through Him, to accept Him as their Saviour, and serve Him as their Lord in the fellowship of His Church."[3] The last phrase was originally "serve Him as their *King*" but has been changed since its inception in 1918.

2. LEWIS DRUMMOND

Lewis Drummond gives an excellent definition of *evangelism:* "a concerted effort in the power of the Holy Spirit to confront unbelievers with the truth about Jesus Christ and the claims of our Lord with a view to leading unbelievers into repentance toward God and faith in our Lord Jesus Christ and, thus, into the fellowship of His church so they may grow in the Spirit."[4]

3. D. T. NILES

One of the most familiar, simple definitions came from D. T. Niles: One beggar telling another where to get food [or bread, as some put it]. This definition is helpful in that it emphasizes the humility necessary for the believer to have when witnessing. We are not better than those to whom we witness; we have met Jesus, and He has changed us. The reason many unsaved people think those of us in the church *are* "holier than thou" in our attitude is because too many of us are holier than thou. However, this definition is weak in that it says nothing about the content of the bread that we share. Taken in its larger context in Niles's book, the definition is stronger; left alone, this comprises an incomplete definition.[5]

4. THE CHURCH GROWTH MOVEMENT

The church growth movement offers a three-tiered look at the process of evangelism.[6] The three components are these:

- 1-P, *Presence.* For example, agricultural, medical missions.

- 2-P, *Proclamation.* Presenting the gospel in an understandable manner.

- 3-P, *Persuasion.* Second Corinthians 5:11 encourages hearers to respond.

An analogy for this definition is a house. In *presence evangelism,* people's needs are met, they see a demonstration of the gospel, and, therefore, a foundation is built on which the gospel can be communicated. Because the church growth movement began on the mission field, its importance is obvious. Cross-cultural issues must be considered in a viable presentation of the gospel. Increasingly, in a post-Christian or even an anti-Christian culture in America, presence evangelism has a place. Servanthood evangelism (covered later) fits in nicely in our context.

Proclamation evangelism, to continue the house analogy, allows the light of the gospel to penetrate through the windows. People not only need a foundation, but they also need direction. The gospel can never be presented by a demonstration only; there must also be a proclamation.

Finally, *persuasion evangelism* leads people into the relationship they need with Christ. One can live in a house and not be family; by persuading people to follow Christ, we are inviting them to join God's family.

There are strengths and weaknesses to this definition. The weakness comes when believers define evangelism at the 1-P level only.

We must build bridges, but we must also do more. Still others stop at the 2-P level. This definition is complete when we see it as a whole. That being said, it is positive in that when we are stopped short of a complete presentation of the gospel, we know we have at least provided some aspect of the gospel that the Holy Spirit can use. In other words, we should always seek to present Christ through presence, proclamation, and persuasion; but when we cannot, we can be thankful that on some level we have presented Christ.

5. Bill Bright and Campus Crusade for Christ

This group's definition of *evangelism* is: "Presenting Jesus Christ in the power of the Holy Spirit and leaving the results to God." For many years, this definition has guided the witness of Campus Crusade for Christ, the largest parachurch organization on earth and one of the most evangelistic groups in Christian history. More recently, Darrell Robinson, in his book and seminar, *People Sharing Jesus*, has used this definition.

This simple definition has been liberating for a generation of witnesses. It emphasizes the vital role of the Holy Spirit in the witnessing encounter. It also recognizes that our job is to share Christ; God alone converts people. Too many believers fail to witness because they define successful witnessing as harvesting only, yet the New Testament says a great deal about planting and watering as well. As a friend once said to me, we must get people as excited about *fishing* as they are about *catching*. While our ultimate goal is always to win people to Christ, this definition reminds us that God expects us to be faithful. This is something that every believer can do.

I am convinced that God is less concerned about the number of people we win than the number of times we share the gospel. We cannot control the response of those to whom we witness; in fact, if a person is saved, it is because God saves them, not us! But we do have control over the number of times we share our faith. It is certainly appropriate for a church to set evangelism or baptismal goals; however, in the case of the individual believer, a better goal to set is the number of times to share the gospel with others.

This takes the pressure off of us to win a certain number and allows us to share the pure gospel without compromise. But there is a better reason: *If* we share Christ often enough, we *will* lead someone to Christ! I have seen this over and over again in the lives of students who are required to do witness reports. *The reason many Christians have never won anyone to Christ is because they have witnessed very little.*

THE PRIORITY OF EVANGELISM

If the message of evangelism is indeed what we are saying, then the urgency of sharing it is obvious. Yet too few believers consistently share their faith.

GOD'S PRIORITY

One need only to turn to John 3:16 to see that our Father in heaven wants lost people to be saved. The need of a lost world resulted in the death of the Son of God.

Delos Miles reminds us of the place of evangelism in the plan of God: "Evangelism is not an isolated side show of history. On the contrary, it is the main event!"[7] Evangelist D. L. Moody imagined every person he met as though that person had a large "L" in the midst of his forehead. Moody considered people lost until he knew they were saved!

The Greek word for "lost" is *apollumi.* It describes a thing not used or claimed. Luke 15 describes what it means to be lost. The lost sheep, the lost coin, the lost son—all signify value, something worth finding. In the case of the sheep, lostness meant being subjected to being taken by a wild beast or stolen by a thief, or wandering away and starving. In the case of the coin, it meant that it would not be able to fulfill its purpose for being created. In the case of the lost son, it meant wasting his inheritance, wasting his life, missing the intimate relationship of his family.

Miles noted the progressive nature of the son's lostness. First, he rebelled against his father and sold his birthright for money. Second, he left home for a faraway country. Third, he wasted his money in a riotous life. Fourth, he faced a severe famine. Fifth, he became more like the hogs that he fed than the man that he was.[8] When the New Testament refers to people as lost, it is not a derogatory term. It means people are of value. In fact, people are worth the life of Jesus the Son of God (Luke 19:10).

Personal evangelism is primary in the plan of God to reach lost people. This is obvious in the practice of the early church. Jesus won Andrew, who told Peter (John 1:40–42). Jesus won the woman at the well, who told others in the city (John 4:29). Therefore, personal evangelism is the single most effective way to reach the world for Christ. Every class taught at our seminary in the field of evangelism places personal evangelism at the heart of all we do. In our required courses, we actually go out as a class each semester to share Christ one-on-one.

GOD'S PASSION

God desires that people be saved (Luke 15; 2 Pet. 3:9). During my first year in Wake Forest, we had one of the most severe winters in decades. Snow and ice were our constant companions. One week, after days of no first-grade classes for my son, Joshua, he and I sought to rescue our family from cabin fever by renting a video. While I searched for a tape, Joshua perused the video games. Unknown to me, Joshua saw a man through the window walking up the sidewalk in a coat like mine. He left the store in pursuit of the person he thought was me.

Realizing the man was not his dad, Joshua panicked. He walked further up the sidewalk, so afraid that I had disappeared that he forgot to consider going back to the video store. By this time, I realized he was not in the store, and I got nervous. Several minutes passed, and Joshua was nowhere to be found. I prayed for my son's safety. Joshua was outside a store, crying and praying as well. About that time, two ministers from our church found Joshua. God answered our prayers! We were so glad to be reunited.

Why was I so concerned about Joshua? Because he is my son, and he means more than life to me. His lostness hurt me deeply because I love him so much.

Why is evangelism important? Because it is important to God. He did not spare his Son for you and me! Should not our priorities be similar to his?

> *William Booth,* founder of the Salvation Army, to the king of England: "Sir, some men's passion is for gold, other men's passion is for fame, but my passion is for souls."

A. T. Pierson: "There is a secret fellowship with God where we get His heavenly fire kindled within. . . . To linger in God's presence until we see souls, as through His eyes, makes us long over them with a tireless longing."

Oswald J. Smith: "Never will I be satisfied until God works in convicting power and men and women weep their way to the cross. . . . Oh that He would break me down and cause me to weep for the salvation of souls."[9]

EVANGELISM AND BELIEVERS

EVANGELISM AND OBEDIENCE

The God we serve expects his children to fulfill his purposes. In our consumer culture, where even the church has a "what's-in-it-for-me?" attitude, we must raise the standard of serving God out of a heart of obedience.

Andrew Murray said there are two kinds of Christians: soul-winners and backsliders. A born-again child of God cannot take seriously his or her relationship to Christ without dealing with the issue of evangelism. Evangelism is important to those of us who follow Jesus because of the critical role that obedience plays in our spiritual growth.

James Eaves, one of my evangelism professors at Southwestern Seminary, used to say that two barriers keep many Christians from going further in their walk with God: tithing and soul-winning. Why? Because they affect two things that matter so much—our comfort in material things and our reputation. Crossing these barriers requires faith, without which it is impossible to please God (Heb. 11:6).

Remember Samuel's conversation with Saul? Saul disobeyed God and spared the king. Then he kept some of the livestock as well. When Samuel confronted Saul, what did Saul do? He blamed the people for his own disobedience. How did Samuel reply? "To obey is better than sacrifice" (1 Sam. 15:22). But he went further: "For *rebellion* is like the sin of divination" (1 Sam. 15:23 NIV). Unfortunately, we consider really bad sins those that other people commit. But Samuel said disobedience puts us in the same boat with those involved in the occult. Is any sin worse than disobedience of God?

But there is a positive side to this. I believe many believers want to obey Christ. They want to grow spiritually. Many don't witness because of their sense of inadequacy. The good news is that any believer can be obedient. We may be varied in gifts, abilities, and time, but we can all obey. And only God knows the impact we can make.

Let me give you a little quiz.

- Who was the theological adviser to Martin Luther, inspiring him to translate the New Testament into German?

- Who was the Sunday school teacher who led Dwight L. Moody to Christ?

- Who was the elderly woman who prayed faithfully for Billy Graham for over twenty years?

- Who funded William Carey's ministry in India?

- Who encouraged the apostle Paul in a Roman dungeon as he wrote his last letter to Timothy?

- Who discovered the Dead Sea Scrolls?

Okay, did you pass? Had it not been for those unknown people, church history might tell a different story.

Jim Elliot, the martyred messenger of the gospel to the Auca Indians, once called missionaries "a bunch of nobodies trying to exalt Somebody." If God uses you as a Melanchthon (not Luther), as a Kimball (not a Moody), as Onesiphorus (rather than a Paul), it's okay. The bottom line: God will use you if you make yourself usable.

It's the "nobodies" whom Somebody chooses so carefully. And when He has selected you for a task, you are somebody, never a nobody.[10]

Be encouraged? You can obey God, and this book will offer many insights into how he will empower you to do so.

My hunch is that you came to Christ because of the impact of other people. While only the death of Jesus can provide for our salvation, we owe a debt to those who shared the message with us.

Paul declared, "I am a debtor both to Greeks and to barbarians, both to wise and to unwise. So, as much as is in me, I am *ready* to preach the gospel to you who are in Rome also" (Rom. 1:14–15). "Ready," *prothumon*, literally means "on fire." Roy Fish says Paul had "holy heartburn." Our own sense of gratitude for the witness of others should encourage us to have that same impact in the lives of others. The Lord warned the prophet Ezekiel that he was accountable to warn others of their sin (see Ezek. 33:8).

EVANGELISM AND SPIRITUAL GROWTH

When we witness, we take giant steps toward spiritual maturity. Christian growth is linked to discipline and surrender. We need Sea of Galilee Christians. The Sea of Galilee flows into the Jordan River. It is beautiful, filled with fish. The Jordan flows into the Dead Sea but not out. The Dead Sea is stagnant, lifeless, self-contained. Nothing is more pathetic than a Christian whose lives are characterized by spiritual navel-gazing—totally introverted.

Sharing Christ motivates a person to study Scripture because of the issues raised by lost people. It burns with a burden for people blinded by the gods of this world, eliciting a desire to pray. In my experience, some of the most exciting, dynamic, and evangelistic believers are those who began witnessing soon after conversion. One of the best things you can do for a new believer is to involve him immediately in sharing his faith.

EVANGELISM AND ETERNAL REWARDS

Christians will be rewarded at judgment based on our service to God (1 Cor. 3:11–15). Paul also tells us we will all stand before the judgment seat *(bema)* of Christ (2 Cor. 5:10–11). In this judgment of believers, we will give an account of how we served God. This is a judgment of service, not salvation. Paul writes that the things we have done will be judged to be good or evil. The word translated "evil" can also mean "worthless" or "trivial."

I like to use the analogy of standing before the Lord with a videotape of my life. First, the Lord shows a documentary of my life, demonstrating how I served him. Then, a second tape is viewed. This tape depicts what my life *would have been* had I served the Lord with all my heart. My aim is that the two tapes will not be too different! This thought motivates me almost daily to faithfulness.

Further, the rewards we receive are not measured by human accounting. Greatness is related to serving the Lord, especially when no one is looking. That's really the test of greatness.

On a cold, wintry night, Paul Keating was walking home in Manhattan's Greenwich Village. The twenty-seven-year-old saw two armed men assaulting a college student. A much-admired photographer for *Time* magazine, Keating had every reason to avoid trouble. He was outmanned, the student was a stranger, and he had nothing to gain. Yet he tried to rescue the young student. The victim escaped and ran to call for help. Paul Keating was found dead on the pavement from two gunshot wounds.

The city of New York posthumously awarded Keating a medal of heroism. Mary Egg Cox authored an apt eulogy at the ceremony: "Nobody was watching Paul Keating on the street that night, nobody made him step forward in the time of crisis. He did it because of who he was."[11] If we are faithful in witnessing, who we are transcends the things that we do. The reward for such a life cannot be measured in this life alone.

EVANGELISM AND THE LOST

THE WORTH OF PERSONS

People are the objects of divine love: "For when we were still without strength, in due time Christ died for the ungodly. For scarcely for a righteous man will one die; yet perhaps for a good man someone would even dare to die. But God demonstrates His own love toward us, in that while we were still sinners, Christ died for us" (Rom. 5:6–8).

Christopher Hancock is vicar of the Holy Trinity Church, Cambridge, England. In the 1980s, Chris was a member of the faculty at Magdalene College, Cambridge. When he moved into his office, one formerly occupied by a theology professor, he noticed a dull, brown rug. The bookshelves were a wretched pale green. He had the shelves repainted, but the awful rug remained. He asked that the rug be removed, but the request was repeatedly denied. One day he saw the theology professor who had used the office earlier. Chris commented about the wretched rug. "It belonged to

C. S. Lewis," the professor remarked. Suddenly the carpet's value increased! Then a rug expert valued the Persian rug at $250,000!

Do we treat lost people for whom Christ died like an old rug? Is there anything more valuable than a soul?

If you were to bring together auditors to compute all the wealth of the earth, the figure would be astronomical. But according to Scripture, *one person* is worth more than all that wealth. Jesus said, "What value . . . if one gains the world, yet loses his soul?"

POTENTIAL SERVICE FOR CHRIST

Billy Graham was converted under the ministry of evangelist Mordecai Ham in a crusade in Graham's hometown of Charlotte, North Carolina. Before his conversion, Billy's father and a group of godly businessmen prayed that "out of Charlotte the Lord would raise up someone to preach the Gospel to the ends of the earth."[12]

Evangelist D. L. Moody is another example. How could Edward Kimball, the Sunday school teacher who led Moody to Christ, have ever known the potential of the uneducated young shoe salesman? How could that preacher, a stand-in on a frozen winter day at the little Methodist chapel, have known the impact of the young Charles Spurgeon when he challenged the youth to "look to Jesus"?

Not everyone we lead to Christ will have the impact of these men, but some will. Never underestimate the impact an individual can make for Christ. Every person was created for a purpose—a purpose that will never be realized apart from a relationship with God through Christ. The most significant aspect of that purpose is stated in the Westminister Catechism: "to glorify God and enjoy Him forever."

Mike Woody gave his testimony at the 1997 meeting of the Southern Baptist Convention in Dallas, Texas. Woody had spent years in jail and had basically wasted his life. At one point he prayed, "God, show me you are real." A Christian cellmate tore his Bible in half and gave it to Woody. Ultimately he came to Christ and began to win others. Now, released from prison, he leads a significant ministry to street people and others in Fort Worth. Listen to his discovery: "I never dreamed I could be part of something good in the lives of other people." Mike Woody has learned the potential of one lost soul.

THE REALITY OF HELL AND JUDGMENT

Hell seems so far from our culture, but it is close to the heart of Scripture. The most consistent preacher on the subject of hell in the Bible was Jesus himself. He taught, preached, and ministered with an awareness of the lostness of people and the reality of judgment.

Lostness means emptiness. Lillian Veles, who also gave her testimony at the 1997 Southern Baptist Convention, came to Christ from a life of sin. "Every time I spoke to myself," she recorded of her life before Christ, "I only heard myself. But after I came to Christ, there was God in my life." The emptiness, the lostness, was replaced by intimacy with God.

A little boy's mom was facing a terminal disease. They were in a rural town where the doctor made house calls. The doctor had known the family for years and knew the situation. She was a single mom, and she asked the doctor to tell her son that she would soon die. The little boy was playing in the backyard, so the doctor went out to talk to him.

"Tommy, I need to talk to you about your mom."

"Okay, doctor."

"See that tree there, Tommy?"

"Yes, doctor."

"Your mom's going to take a trip, Tommy, and when she goes on that trip, she's not going to come back, son."

"When is she going to take that trip, doctor?"

"When the leaves are all off this tree, about that time, your mom's going to take this long trip." Time passed, the fall came, and the mother got worse and worse. Finally, she was near death, and the doctor went to see her. She said, "Would you go talk to Tommy again, let him know what's happening. He stays outside most of the time." So the doctor went outside and looked for Tommy.

"Tommy, where are you?"

"Up here."

"Tommy, what are you doing up in the tree?"

"You said when all the leaves come off this tree, my mommy's gonna take that long trip. The leaves have been falling off pretty fast lately so I've been getting them and taking some string and tying the leaves back on the tree."

Little Tommy was trying to stop the inevitable. We try to ignore the reality of hell, try to explain it away, try to pretend it's not there.

But it's there, and it's real, and we need to be telling people—warning them to avoid the yawning chasm of hell.

APPLICATION

Jim Eaves taught me a simple exercise that has helped me to demonstrate the lostness of people. We have lost that sense of utter lostness a person faces apart from Christ. Let me encourage you to try this in your place of ministry. It is best done in a Wednesday or Sunday evening service or in a small-group study.

Have the group turn to Ephesians 2. Then divide them into two groups. If you have a large number, make several small groups and divide them into two categories. Have the first group read Ephesians 2 to note every reference related to this statement: "What It Means to Be Lost." It is staggering to see all the references in only one chapter in the Bible. Have the second group examine the same text to discover "What It Means to Be Saved." After giving the groups ten to fifteen minutes to study the text, have them report their results, using an overhead, marker board, or a chalkboard to report the findings so all can see them. Draw two columns to compare the groups. Make a list of the statements, which will include the following:

- Dead in trespasses
- Walked according to the world
- Disobedient
- Lust of the flesh
- Children of wrath
- Others

As they do this, note the stark, destitute state of lost people. Remind them that their neighbor, who may be a good, decent person, is "without hope," "at enmity with God," "far off," etc. That family member who seems so moral is "dead in sin," those coworkers who give to charitable causes are "without God" unless they have met Christ. I have used this many times, and it has proven to be very effective in raising people's awareness about the lostness of people.

Then list "What It Means to be Saved." The difference between the two lists is striking. Remind the people that there should be just such a difference between saved and lost people today—not because we are better but because God has changed us! This should result in a greater sense of gratitude for salvation.

BIBLIOGRAPHY

Miles, Delos. *Introduction to Evangelism*. Nashville: Broadman Press, 1981.

Salter, Darius. *American Evangelism: Its Theology and Practice*. Grand Rapids: Baker, 1996.

2

A Clear Voice
in a Confused World:
The Biblical Standard
for Evangelism

A pastor search committee interviewed a recent seminary graduate. The candidate was young, and the committee wondered about his level of Bible knowledge. The chairman of the committee asked the student, "Do you know the Bible?"

"Of course," he replied, "I just graduated from seminary!"

"Then tell us a story of the Bible—how about the 'Good Samaritan,'" replied the chairman.

"No problem," said the pastoral candidate.

"There was a man of the Samaritans named Nicodemus. He went down to Jerusalem by night, and he fell among the stony ground, and the thorns choked him half to death.

"So he said, 'What shall I do? I will arise and go to my father's house.' So he arose and climbed up into a sycamore tree. The next day the three wise men came and got him and carried him to the ark for Moses to take care of him. But, as he was going into the eastern gate into the ark, he caught his hair in a limb, and he hung there for forty days and forty nights. Afterward he was hungry, and the ravens came and fed him.

"The next day he caught a boat and sailed down to Jerusalem. When he got there he saw Delilah sitting on a wall, and he said, 'Chunk her down, boys!' They said, 'How many times shall we chunk her down, until 7 times 7?' 'No, not until 7, but 70 times 7.'

"So they threw her down 490 times, and she burst asunder in their midst, and they picked up 12 baskets of the fragments that were there. In the resurrection, whose wife will she be?"

The committee sat stunned. They conferred briefly, then the chairman spoke to the seminary graduate. "Well, young man, we are going to recommend you as our next pastor. You may be young, but you sure know your Bible!"

The frightening thing is that I have told this story in churches, and they didn't get it! Faithful understanding of the Bible is critical to evangelism.

The Bible is our authority for evangelism. Drummond notes the close relationship between redemption in the Bible and contemporary evangelism. "If redemption truly is the heartbeat of the Bible, the church's responsibility of sharing the message of salvation rests right at the center of her ministry."[1] There is a direct correlation between one's view of Scripture and one's commitment to evangelism.[2] A high view of Scripture leads to a deep commitment to evangelism! We must acknowledge and obey the Word of God. Some neglect the authority of Scripture with tragic results. Some who respect the Bible neglect its teaching.

EVANGELISM IN THE PENTATEUCH

While the Great Commission is given by Jesus in the New Testament, evangelism's song rings throughout Scripture. The theme of redemption is the melody of the Word of God.

The Book of Genesis demonstrates our need for a Savior. The first question in the Bible demonstrates the evangelistic heart of God: "Adam, where are you?" Genesis 3:9 shows a redeeming God seeking his estranged creation. The first eleven chapters of Genesis reveal why man is so important to God and why the salvation of humanity becomes the dominant theme of Scripture.

Even when God judged Adam and Eve for their sin, we see his grace. The *protoevangelium,* Genesis 3:15, shows the early sign of the gospel: "And I will put enmity between you and the woman, And between your seed and her seed; he shall bruise your head, And you shall bruise his heel." This singular verse is pregnant with New Testament truth. The passage relates to evangelism in at least five ways:

1. The expression "he shall bruise your head" shows the grace of God in that the Father gave a promise to Eve that her seed would triumph.

2. The same phrase initiates the promise of the ultimate defeat of Satan, remembering that one of the reasons for Jesus' incarnation was to "destroy the works of the devil" (1 John 3:8).

3. Salvation comes through a mediator. This mediator will be directly related to humanity, being the "seed of woman."

4. This salvation comes through the suffering of the seed of woman, whose heel will be bruised.

5. Salvation is available to the whole race, for Eve is the mother of all living. All racial prejudices and bigotry should end with this passage, for if Eve is the mother of all living, then we are all kin. In the earliest pages of the Bible, we find ample evidence for the necessity of cross-cultural evangelism.

The flood gives us another picture of evangelism. In the midst of a godless people, Noah lived righteously. The ark is a picture of God's desire to save the world, for the righteous were not taken in the deluge. Further, the Hebrew word for *pitch* (Gen. 6:14) means "atonement." Beyond this, the grace of God shines in the brightness of the rainbow. God delivered the righteous, even as He will deliver any person made righteous through the atoning work of Christ. What a glorious gospel we share!

By the end of Genesis 11, the reader can see the devastation of sin: murder, intrigue, idolatry, rampant ungodliness, and the judgment of God. Beginning with Genesis 12, we read of God's unfolding plan to redeem humanity. Abraham is told all humanity will be blessed through his seed. The Gospel writer tells us succinctly that Jesus is "the Son of Abraham" (Matt. 1:1). Certain themes resound with the redemptive intent of God.

In Exodus we see further gospel truth. The Exodus event became the great salvific moment in the Old Testament. It is recalled over and over again throughout the books of the Old Testament, reminding the people of God's power to save. It was not by accident that Jesus also traveled to Egypt as a child and came out as well. Nor did Luke accidently use the word *exodus* in his account of the transfiguration of Jesus. Luke tells us Jesus discussed with Moses and Elijah his *exodus* (Luke 9:31), referring to his death and resurrection that would allow us to pass, not through a sea, but from death to life.

The covenant at Sinai was where God told his people they were to be a "kingdom of priests" (Exod. 19:6). A priest was to point others to God, intercede on behalf of others, and teach the redemption of God to all people. The fact that Israel did not always fulfill this command did not take away their obligation to tell the nations about the only true God.

The Commandments (the Law) gave the standard of a holy God. Galatians tells us the law shows us how we need the gospel. Even as a person cannot be saved apart from recognizing his lost state, we cannot comprehend grace apart from the standard of the law of God. However, merely keeping the Ten Commandments cannot save. Even in the Old Testament, they were given to God's covenant people.

In Leviticus, the sacrificial system modeled the means of redemption. Hebrews tells us that without the shedding of blood there is no forgiveness. The sacrificial system paved the way for the ultimate sacrifice, Jesus the Son of God. The Day of Atonement, held once annually for forgiveness of sins, was replaced by the atoning work of Christ.

In Numbers, we see a picture of God's work of redemption in the bronze serpent (Num. 21). What a beautiful shadow of the work of Christ on the cross. The proud, stubborn people of Israel were bitten by poisonous snakes. The cure was simple: look upon the bronze serpent. Most did, but a few were too proud—and they died. In the same way, Jesus compared the bronze serpent to his work on Calvary, for as the people of Israel had only to look and live, today we need to believe on Jesus to live (John 3:16).

EVANGELISM AND THE HISTORY OF ISRAEL

As we move from the Pentateuch to the time of conquest, the promise-fulfillment motif becomes more apparent. Central to the Old Testament message was this idea of promise and fulfillment.

God promised Abraham a special land; it was ultimately fulfilled in Joshua's time. Joshua, the Hebrew equivalent of the Greek "Jesus," was the man who delivered the people *into* the land of promise; Jesus delivers us *out* of the kingdom of darkness.

The Book of Jonah demonstrates God's mercy to any nation that repents. Jeremiah spoke of a new covenant, the covenant provided by the death of Jesus (see Jer. 31). Ezekiel gives us a stern warning: "Nevertheless if you warn the wicked to turn from his way, and he does not turn from his way, he shall die in his iniquity; but you have delivered your soul" (Ezek. 33:9).

The prophetic records give ample witness to the importance of passion in proclaiming the word of the Lord in any generation.

Messianic passages abound with prophetic glimpses into the redemptive heart of God. Scores of passages give light, but only a few select passages can be offered here.

- Isaiah 7:14: "Behold, the virgin shall conceive and bear a son."

- Isaiah 9:6 speaks of the Wonderful Counselor, Mighty God, the Everlasting Father, the Prince of Peace.

- Isaiah 53 describes the Suffering Servant, giving a picture of a vicarious sacrifice.

The prophets spoke God's word in the face of tremendous opposition at times. Our zeal for God should move us to speak out for him.

Imagine for a moment that you have a small child, a little girl. She is playing in the road, unnoticed by you. Your neighbor Bill looks up from his yard work, only to see a tractor trailer bearing down on your daughter. Bill runs to the scene, pushing your child to safety just in time. She is scratched and scared but unhurt. But Bill was not so lucky. He awoke the next day in a hospital bed to the diagnosis that he would never walk again.

How would you feel about Bill? Would you not rush to the hospital to thank him, to ask him if there were anything you could do for him? Suppose you did visit him, and he said, "No, thanks, but I'm OK. My family is here. I will make out all right."

But then suppose he looked at you and said, "There is one thing you can do for me. Would you mind telling just five people over the next several years about my actions to save your daughter? It would mean a lot to my family."

You would probably respond to Bill, "I have already told everyone I have met about what you have done! I will speak of you for
the rest of my life!" The Old Testament showed us our need for a
Savior, and it pointed the way for him. Now that we know him—
and thinking of all he endured for us—can we truly be silent?

THE EVANGELISM OF JESUS

The incarnation was evangelistic in intent. Paul records the significance of the coming of Christ: "But when the fullness of the time
had come, God sent forth His Son, born of a woman, born under
the law, to redeem those who were under the law, that we might
receive the adoption as sons" (Gal. 4:4–5). The angel told Mary to
name her firstborn *Jesus,* for "he will save His people from their
sins" (Matt. 1:21). Jesus is the Greek form of the Hebrew name
Joshua, meaning "God is savior."

Jesus made it clear during his ministry why he became flesh:

- "Then the angel said to them, 'Do not be afraid, for behold, I
  bring you good tidings of great joy which will be to all people.
  For there is born to you this day in the city of David a Savior,
  who is Christ the Lord'" (Luke 2:10–11).

- "For even the Son of Man did not come to be served, but to
  serve, and to give His life a ransom for many" (Mark 10:45).

- "The next day John saw Jesus coming toward him, and said,
  'Behold! The Lamb of God who takes away the sin of the
  world!'" (John 1:29).

- "For the Son of man has come to seek and to save that which
  was lost" (Luke 19:10).

The coming of Christ demonstrated the evangelistic heart of God.

Rome had emerged as the dominant world power. No nation
could stand against its might. From the Atlantic eastward to the
Euphrates, from the Sahara to the Danube, the Roman Empire per-
sonified the word *dynasty.* Palestine existed as one tiny state under
the heavy boot of Rome. Augustus, the cynical Caesar who
demanded a census to determine a measurement to enlarge taxes,
was declared a god following his death. Who could have noticed a
couple making an eighty-mile trip south from Nazareth? What difference could a carpenter and a teenaged girl make compared to

Caesar's decisions in Rome? Who cared about this Jewish baby born in Bethlehem?

God cared. Unwittingly, mighty Augustus became an errand boy for the fulfillment of the words of the prophet Micah. He was a puppet in the hand of God, a piece of fuzz on the pages of prophecy. While Rome was busy making history, the One whose life split time—by whose birth we date our calendars—arrived. The world didn't notice. History had seen Alexander the Great, Herod the Great, and the great Augustus, but the world missed it when the One who flung the stars into the heavens was born. History missed the coming of its author. But now, we know, he is the one John called "the Lamb slain from the foundations of the world."[3]

Jesus' earthly ministry modeled evangelism. Our Lord demonstrated an *evangelistic passion*. He showed unusual compassion for people. The "people of the land," or ordinary Jews, were often disdained by the Pharisees. But Jesus looked at them with compassion. Following an intense time of ministry in which he visited all the cities in Galilee, he was moved with compassion for the people "because they were weary and scattered, like sheep having no shepherd. Then He said to his disciples, 'The harvest truly is plentiful, but the laborers are few. Therefore pray the Lord of the harvest to send out laborers into His harvest'" (Matt. 9:36–38).

The word translated "compassion" in this passage comes from the Greek term *splanchnon*. The word refers to the viscera, the intestines, meaning a deep hurt. When we are willing to feel the pain of lost people, to understand the depth of their sin and the gaping chasm of hell before them, we are close to sensing the compassion of Jesus.

Jesus also *practiced mass evangelism* or *evangelistic preaching*. He preached the gospel of the kingdom to the masses. The message of Jesus was succinct: Repent and believe the good news of the kingdom of God (see Mark 1:14–15).

The kingdom of God, the rule of God over all creation, has received little attention by evangelicals. This is due in large part to the emphasis earlier in this century by more liberal theologians who minimized the future hope of heaven. One example was the realized eschatology of C. H. Dodd. On a practical level, the preaching of the "victorious Christian life" in recent decades among evangelicals has received great attention. There is victory in Jesus, but the

focus on *believers* living victoriously rather than focusing on *God*—
as Jesus did in his preaching of the gospel of the kingdom—should
be balanced. The focus of our Lord's preaching was less on the benefit of the hearers than the honor of the One on whom the message
was centered.

Jesus taught the importance of evangelism. Jesus taught the *priority* of evangelism. He taught that salvation is the greatest thing in
the world. His parables of the pearl of great price and the treasure
in the field illustrate this (see Matt. 13:44–46).

Jesus taught the *love of the Father* for one lost soul. Luke 15
demonstrates the love of God as seen in the lost sheep, the lost
coin, and the lost son. In fact, the only time God is pictured in a
hurry is when Jesus describes the father hurrying to meet the returning prodigal son.

Jesus also trained others to evangelize. Before he gave the Great
Commission, Jesus sent out the Twelve and the seventy to preach.
Robert Coleman's book, *The Master Plan of Evangelism,* cites the
role of Jesus in training his followers to witness.

How Jesus Taught Evangelism

The eight characteristics of how Jesus taught evangelism
to his disciples, from Robert Coleman's *Master Plan of
Evangelism:*[4]

1. *Selection.* Men were his method: "His concern was not with
   programs to reach the multitudes, but with men whom the
   multitudes would follow."
2. *Association.* He stayed with them: "His disciples were distinguished, not by outward conformity to certain rituals, but by
   being with Him, and thereby participating in His doctrine."
3. *Consecration.* He required obedience: "[The disciples] were
   not required to be smart, but they had to be loyal. This
   became the distinguishing mark by which they were
   known."
4. *Impartation.* He gave himself away: "His was a life of giving—
   giving away what the Father had given Him."
5. *Demonstration.* He showed them how to live: "Surely it was
   no accident that Jesus often let His disciples see Him con-
   versing with the Father. . . . Jesus did not force that lesson

> on them, but rather He kept praying until at last the disciples got so hungry that they asked Him to teach them what He was doing."
> 6. *Delegation.* He assigned them work: "Jesus was always building His ministry for the time when His disciples would have to take over His work, and go out into the world with the redeeming Gospel."
> 7. *Supervision.* He kept check on them: "Jesus made it a point to meet with His disciples following their tours of service to hear their reports and to share with them the blessedness of His ministry in doing the same thing."
> 8. *Reproduction.* He expected them to reproduce: "Jesus intended for the disciples to produce His likeness in and through the church being gathered out of the world."

Jesus practiced *personal evangelism.* There are over forty accounts in the Gospels of Jesus' personal evangelism. Studying these accounts demonstrates several truths. Jesus could adapt his presentation to different audiences. He obviously knew people well. He was sensitive to his Father's leadership. He was urgent and persistent. And even our Lord did not reach everyone with whom he shared. The following illustrations help us to see how Jesus evangelized people.

Jesus *sought* people. In Luke 19, we read how Jesus sought Zacchaeus. He intentionally set out to meet him and even made an appointment to meet him at the tax collector's house. He met Zacchaeus where he was (v. 5) as he sat in a tree. He identified with a sinner, regardless of the consequences (v. 7). Jesus further convicted Zacchaeus of his sin. Finally, this account shows us Jesus did not just *meet* sinners, he sought to *save* them (vv. 9–10).

Jesus was *approachable.* In John 3, we read of Nicodemus approaching Jesus by night. Nicodemus was searching for truth (v. 2). The reply of Jesus was direct. He boldly confronted Nicodemus (v. 3). A dialogue ensued concerning the gospel, but no immediate change was indicated (vv. 4–21). However, there is evidence of Nicodemus's possible change (see John 7:50–52). He brought gifts to anoint the body of Jesus after his death (see John 19:39).

Jesus *made the most of every opportunity.* While every example of the witness of Jesus is critical, his encounter with the Samaritan woman in John 4 is especially enlightening. Observing the evangelism of Jesus reminds us that the reason many people are not saved is because no one has told them how to be saved!

His death and resurrection embody the message of evangelism. Our primary need is not education; thus, Jesus' ministry was not essentially about teaching. He came for one main purpose—to die for our sins. Some people speak of those he came to save—the lost—as "pre-Christians." Such a term smacks more of political correctness than biblical fidelity. It is a presumptuous term, considering the New Testament's emphasis on lostness.

However, the word *lost* implies value. People are worth the death of the Son of God! Recently, as I sorted through the mail, I saw a flyer with the picture of a missing child. The number to call caught my attention: 1-800-THE LOST. Certainly no one sees the word *lost* as negative in that setting. Should we not have the same urgency for people separated from their Creator? Without the death and resurrection of Jesus, the Good News we preach would merely be another story passing through history. But the death of Jesus makes the difference!

Jesus Christ did not come to give us a moral example of how to live. He did not come just to teach us how to live. He came to die and to live again so that we could die to sin and live—eternally.

Jesus' commission demands that we evangelize. Every Gospel narrative and the Acts has a Great Commission passage:

- "Go therefore and make disciples of all the nations, baptizing them in the name of the Father and of the Son and of the Holy Spirit, teaching them to observe all things that I have commanded you" (Matt. 28:19–20).

- "And He said to them, 'Go into all the world and preach the gospel to every creature'" (Mark 16:15).

- "That repentance and remission of sins should be preached in His name to all nations, beginning at Jerusalem. And you are witnesses of these things" (Luke 24:47–48).

- "So Jesus said to them again, 'Peace to you! As the Father has sent me, I also send you'" (John 20:21).

- "But you shall receive power when the Holy Spirit has come upon you; and you shall be witnesses to Me in Jerusalem, and in all Judea and Samaria, and to the end of the earth" (Acts 1:8).

How much more significant are the words of our Lord? Jesus Christ knew he was about to ascend to heaven. He was in control of the events. This reality only adds to the magnitude of his final directive to his followers. What did he tell us to do? Not to build buildings, or social ministries, or great worship services, or discipleship courses. All these are noble and vital. No, he told us to be witnesses—something every believer can do.

THE EVANGELISM OF PAUL

Paul was a prepared witness. Before he was converted, Saul of Tarsus was being prepared for his future ministry. Schooled in Judaism, he studied under the great rabbi, Gamaliel. Reared in Tarsus, he was born a Roman citizen. Bright, zealous, and knowledgeable in Greek thought, this man was destined to make an impact. His conversion also prepared Saul to become Paul the apostle.

Paul's radical conversion has been misunderstood. Some who have not come to Christ expect a "Damascus road" type of conversion. While salvation is life changing, few people have experienced such a powerful conversion. In Paul's case, it was expected and necessary. He certainly never got over it! He never forgot what it meant to be lost, calling himself the "chief of sinners."

Paul was prepared by the commission he received from the Lord: "But the Lord said to him, 'Go, for he is a chosen vessel of Mine to bear My name before Gentiles, kings, and the children of Israel'" (Acts 9:15). Paul set the pace for the spread of the gospel across the Mediterranean world. While Paul was the apostle to the Gentiles, he consistently preached to the Jews as well. The most overlooked feature of his commission is the admission by the Lord that Paul would suffer greatly for the sake of the gospel.

Evangelism for Paul flowed out of his passion for God. I have a hunch scholars have missed a central feature in Paul's effectiveness. Imagine for a moment that you are in heaven as God scans Palestine. He is looking for a man, not just any man, to lead the fledgling Christian movement. He passes over Peter, although this fiery fisherman was a key leader. He overlooks James and John, the best of the inner circle of the disciples. In fact, none of the Twelve are chosen. Neither are any of those who followed Jesus during his earthly ministry. The thousands of early converts are skipped as well. Even the seven deacons, though significant in their own way, fail to meet God's standard for *the* key leader.

Instead, the Father scans Palestine to find the most passionate, jealous, surrendered individual in the region. Never mind that the man is a stiff-necked Pharisee or even that he is currently engaged in persecuting God's children. *That* could be changed! There he is, Saul of Tarsus, relentless in his efforts to stop the church, acting in his mind in the name of God?

Suddenly, there is a bright light. The man falls to his knees, blinded. He hears a voice, and history is forever changed because of him. I have a hunch the passionate nature of Paul played a key role throughout his years of ministry. Paul's effectiveness as a leader cannot be understood apart from his zeal. His call guided his life.

What is your mission statement? I think Paul's could be summed up like this: "to know Christ and to make Him known." Paul was single-minded. He became arguably the greatest Christian and the greatest soul-winner (the two go hand in hand) in history. He could not be stopped. When faced with death, Paul did not blink. "To die is gain" (Phil. 1:21), he said. When allowed to live, he boasted, "I am not ashamed of the gospel of Christ" (Rom. 1:16). When made to suffer, he remembered, "That I may know Him [Christ] and the power of His resurrection, and the fellowship of His sufferings" (Phil. 3:10), and "I consider that the sufferings of this present time are not worthy to be compared with the glory which shall be revealed in us" (Rom. 8:18).

The evangelism of Paul cannot be understood apart from the man—his call, his zeal, his sacrificial obedience. Upon this strong foundation, several methods were built.

Personal evangelism. Paul consistently shared his faith with individuals. In Acts 13 we read of his witness to the proconsul. Acts 16 tells us of the witness of Paul to the jailer at Philippi. Later he shared personally with Agrippa (Acts 25:23–27). In Paul's life, as in any church or individual Christian, personal evangelism was the basis upon which all other methods were developed.

Mass evangelism. In the Book of Acts, we also find at least nine references to messages preached by Paul. In 1 Corinthians 1:23, Paul reminded the believers at Corinth of the centrality of preaching the cross.

Household evangelism. At Thessalonica, Paul used a house as a base to share Christ. In Philippi, Lydia's home became a doorway for the gospel.

Apologetic evangelism. In Acts 18:4, Paul "reasoned" in the synagogue at Corinth. Acts 17 records his defense of the gospel at Mars Hill. In later years, the work of the apologists and polemicists would not only strengthen the faithful in times of persecution but also lead to the conversion of many.

Power evangelism. In Acts 13, we read of a sorcerer who was blinded, followed by the salvation of the proconsul (see also Acts 19:11–12). Although the miraculous played a part in the evangelism of Paul and other early Christians, there are numerous occasions in which Paul preached Christ without miracles. In Antioch, Lystra, Derbe, Thessalonica, Berea, and Corinth, there is no mention of miracles. God can use the miraculous to reach some people, but we must be careful lest we make the miracle of conversion secondary to lesser miracles such as healing. Conversion is the most significant supernatural event anyone can experience.

Educational/teaching evangelism. One of C. H. Dodd's errors in *The Apostolic Faith and Its Development* was his sharp distinction between the *kerygma*, or evangelistic proclamation, and the *didache*, or the teaching ministry of the church. Teaching was also a part of evangelism. An obvious example of this approach came when Paul visited Ephesus, teaching at the lecture hall of Tyrannus.

Literary evangelism. One might think in our day that the practice of literary evangelism began with Bill Bright's *Four Spiritual Laws* or Billy Graham's *Steps to Peace with God.* Not so. Paul's treatise to the Romans gives a brilliant explanation of the gospel message. Beyond the ministry of Paul, the Gospel of John was written with an evangelistic intent (John 20:31). Mark's and Luke's accounts were written at least in part for evangelistic purposes as well. Paul also wrote letters that sought to evangelize as well as to encourage.

Church planting. Because Paul preached where the gospel had not been heard, he planted churches where he went.

Urban evangelism. Paul consistently went to the great urban centers. Asia was reached with the gospel message from the base established at Ephesus. We could learn much from Paul concerning the importance of reaching the cities.

Follow-up. Paul utilized a follow-up strategy we would do well to emulate. First, he typically visited those he had won to Christ. His missionary journeys normally retraced the steps of his preaching and evangelistic ministry. Second, Paul wrote letters to encourage young believers. Read 1 Thessalonians as one example. He also sent others, such as Epaphroditus to encourage the believers as well. Finally, he prayed consistently for those he had won to Christ.

Paul also gave instruction concerning evangelism. He told the Philippians that the gospel was so important that even those who preached out of impure motives were doing valuable work (Phil. 1:15–16). The most significant teaching of Paul on evangelism is the charge he gave to Timothy. Paul told Timothy, and thus all seeking to minister for Christ, to preach the Word "in season and out of season" (2 Tim. 4:2)—when you feel like it and when you don't! Further, he instructed Timothy to "do the work of an evangelist" (2 Tim. 4:5). In Paul's mind, under the inspiration of the Spirit, the evangelistic mandate was to be a central part of the ministry.

While teaching a required New Testament class at Houston Baptist University, I was conscious of the fact that some students in my class were not Christians. Without preaching at them, I tried to demonstrate the clear message of the New Testament throughout the course. I prayed that the course would be more than another academic exercise for the students. I became humbled by the comments written at the end of a final exam. One student, a married woman about thirty years old, had never said a word the entire class. On her exam, however, she wrote these words: "Because of this class, both my husband and I have been saved and baptized, and we now read the Bible together every night. Thank you for this class!"

There is power in the Word of God!

APPLICATION

Let me close with a challenge that you spend more time studying the Scriptures to learn about evangelism. We must give attention to study, memorization, and meditation upon God's Word.

Not too long ago I was in a conference with North American Mission Board President Robert Reccord. He asked the congregation where we spoke to raise their hands if they had been a Christian for at least five years. The majority raised their hands. Then he asked how many of them could quote, from memory, twenty-five verses of the Bible. Very few hands went up. Then Reccord said: "Do you realize that it would only take memorizing *five* verses a year to memorize 25 verses in five years?" He was not chastising the people; he was making a point. We must learn the Scriptures, until we are, as Spurgeon put it, "Bibline when we bleed." Then we can more effectively communicate the treasure of the gospel to a lost and hurting world.

BIBLIOGRAPHY

Coleman, Robert E. *The Master Plan of Evangelism.* Old Tappan, N.J.: Fleming H. Revell, 1972.

Dobbins, Gaines. *Evangelism According to Christ.* Nashville: Broadman, 1949.

Miles, Delos. *How Jesus Won Persons.* Nashville: Broadman, 1982.

3

A Singular Jesus for a Pluralistic Culture: Evangelism in the Early Church

The disciples commissioned by Jesus were noticeable in their lack of ability. Not well educated or influential, residents of a small province located far from mighty Rome, they were not good candidates for success. Yet succeed they did—not through their ability but by the power of God.

PREPARATION FOR THE GOSPEL

The early believers faced big obstacles. They had no New Testament canon, no established organization, and few clearly defined leaders. They faced hazardous persecution, and they were greatly misunderstood. Still, the spread of the gospel had its allies as well. As Paul aptly put it, Jesus came in the fullness of time—or at just the right time (Gal. 4:4). The sovereign God of the universe had ordered events to prepare the way for the Great Commission. What helped the gospel to spread?

For one, there was the universal peace provided by Rome, or the *Pax Romana*. Michael Green said it well, "The spread of Christianity would have been inconceivable had Jesus been born half a century earlier."[1] Rome controlled the entire known world at the dawn of the first millennium A.D. Beyond the peace, enforced by Caesar Augustus through his mighty army, the continuous expansion of roads aided the spread of the Good News. I have seen the remains of Roman roads as far north as England, and they can still be traversed after many centuries.

Before Rome's political peace, *Greek culture* paved the way as well. Alexander the Great's conquests and concomitant process of hellenization produced a culture that spoke the same language—Greek—across the Mediterranean region. One can hardly underestimate the impact of a common tongue on the preaching of Christ by early missionaries.

The *Jewish faith* gave the early believers a heritage upon which to build. The first Christians knew the Old Testament Scriptures as their Bible. Further, the Jewish diaspora in the centuries before the birth of Jesus resulted in the establishment of synagogues across the Roman Empire. The synagogue not only provided a place for Paul and others to begin presenting Christ on missionary excursions but provided a model for corporate worship in the early church as well.

A *spiritual vacuum* and *political unity* helped to set the stage for evangelization as well.

"Politically and religiously," states F. F. Bruce about the first century, "the world was ready for the gospel at that time as it had not been before."[2] I believe the world today is ready for the gospel as well! Bruce commented further on the significance of that period:

> The greater part of the civilized world was politically united, but the old classical religions were bankrupt. Many people had recourse to the popular mystery cults in their search for liberation from evil powers and assurance of well-being in the after-life. Others . . . were attracted to the Jewish religion, but it labored under the disadvantage of being too closely tied to one nation. When the Christian message began to be proclaimed among the peoples of the Roman Empire, it showed a capacity to satisfy both the craving for salvation which the mystery

cults professed to meet and the ethical ideas which, as many Gentiles believed, were realized in the Jewish way of life even more than in Stoicism.[3]

The coming of Jesus was central to the plan of God in history. To this day, we date our calendars based on his incarnation. The current excitement about the beginning of a new millennium is possible only because Jesus was born and died and rose from the grave.

A NEW TESTAMENT STRATEGY DEVELOPS

The New Testament plan for evangelism is one of *total* evangelism. In other words, the evangelistic imperative permeated the fabric of the early church. The strategy has been summarized under two headings.[4]

TOTAL PENETRATION

Total penetration means the goal of the church is to reach everyone for Christ. Jesus made this clear:

- Go into *all* the world and preach the gospel (Mark 16:15).

- *Make disciples* of *all* nations (Matt. 28:19–20).

- Repentance and remission of sin should be preached in his name to *all* nations (Luke 24:47). Applied specifically, it means each congregation seeks to reach its area with the gospel.

Three important groups during the first century were open to the gospel: (1) Jews; (2) Proselytes (non-Jews who kept the laws of Judaism); and (3) God-fearers (non-Jews attracted to monotheism of Judaism but who did not obey all its laws and were not circumcised).

Of the five to six billion people in the world today, approximately 50 percent have not heard of Jesus Christ. A popular soft drink made a commitment a few years ago that all the world would have a drink of their cola. Their goal was the total penetration of the world with their product. Worldwide, people recognize the golden arches of McDonald's restaurants more than the cross of Christianity.

TOTAL PARTICIPATION

Total participation means involving every believer in evangelism. Jesus expects all believers to be involved in evangelism. Everyone who receives the Holy Spirit is to witness (see Acts 1:8). Increasingly on a large scale, evangelicals are taking this mandate seriously. Emphasis by various mission groups on reaching the 10/40 window—referring to the section on the globe representing the most unchurched people groups—has raised awareness of the challenge to take the gospel to all peoples.

At this unusual time in history, various strategies are involved in a larger movement called "A.D. 2000," including Mission America 2000 in the United States. This is an attempt to take the New Testament strategy and apply it globally. It is a cooperative effort by different denominations and different organizations to share the gospel with every person in the world. Southern Baptists have had a similar emphasis called Bold Mission Thrust. Campus Crusade for Christ had a similar emphasis. All these emphases focus on total evangelism—total penetration through total participation.

While I affirm such lofty goals, the more critical issue on a practical level is to apply the same philosophy of reaching the world and getting every single church in the world committed to the strategy. It is much easier to put together a grandiose plan to communicate the gospel to the whole world than it is to get individual churches committed to win specific areas to Christ or to motivate individual believers to win their neighborhoods to Christ. The New Testament pattern of evangelism involves beginning with Jerusalem, where the believers were, and reaching out from there. We see this played out in the Acts of the Apostles.

EVANGELISM IN ACTS

Over the years I have read hundreds of books in the field of evangelism. Many have been helpful, a few have been wonderful, and others have been disappointing. When asked to name the greatest book I have ever read on evangelism, I immediately reply, "the Bible." More specifically, the Book of Acts gives more insight into the evangelistic work of the early church than any other source. How did the early church accomplish its task?

THE THEME OF ACTS

Acts 1:8 lays the foundation for the entire book. Luke's narrative describes how the early believers, through the Holy Spirit's power, witnessed in expanding areas. The *purpose* for each believer is stated like this: "You are my witnesses." The disciples asked about the signs of the times, but Jesus responded by telling them to be soul winners, not stargazers.

The *personnel* involved in witnessing is noted in Acts 1:8 and demonstrated for the next twenty-eight chapters—all believers. The apostles, laity, men, women—all kinds of people—took the Good News to others. William Carey faced a belief among fellow churchmen of his day that the Acts 1:8 mandate was only for the early church. The hyper-Calvinists of Carey's day said that if God wanted to save the heathen, God would do so. Thankfully, Carey's view won the day. Due to his influence, modern missions was born in the late eighteenth century. It grew into one of the greatest missions movements in church history.

The *power* needed to win the world is the Holy Spirit. Some modern believers live as though there is a form of spiritual entropy at work in which the power of God is waning in the face of cultural rot. Not so! God is still at work today as he was working in the lives of the early believers.

See what the Holy Spirit did in the early church. Take Peter, for example. What caused Peter to change from the cowardly, denying disciple we see in Luke 22 to the courageous preacher described in Acts 2? Peter got an old-fashioned dose of the Holy Spirit!

If the Book of Acts tells us anything about evangelism, it is that the Holy Spirit is central to the fulfillment of the Great Commission. The Book of Acts could rightly be called the "Acts of the Holy Spirit," because the key person in the book is the Holy Spirit. Jesus ascended, another Comforter came, and he empowered believers to do the work of the early church.

Note that the twenty-eighth chapter of Acts ends abruptly. Why? Because it's still being lived. You are the twenty-ninth chapter of Acts. I'm the twenty-ninth chapter of Acts. All believers are the twenty-ninth chapter of Acts. Give this vision to your church. We are still part of what God began two thousand years ago. The canon is closed, but the church still grows.

Several aspects of evangelism in the early church are worthy of close examination.

ALL BELIEVERS WERE INVOLVED IN PERSONAL EVANGELISM

The idea of a course or seminar on personal witnessing would have been foreign to the first believers. Witnessing was one of the defining marks of authentic Christianity. Even on the day of Pentecost, known for Peter's great sermon, personal witnessing permeated the city, as noted by Conant and Fish:

> It is widely imagined that those three thousand converts (Acts 12) were brought to Christ by Peter's sermon alone, but nothing could be farther from the truth. The private witnessing of all the disciples culminated in the public witnessing of one disciple and brought the results of that day. In other words, if the private witnessing had not preceded Peter's sermon, there is not the least likelihood that any such results would have followed.[5]

The apostles on the day of Pentecost spoke in all the different languages about the mighty acts of God. So all 120 people were sharing the gospel, and then the crowd got together and Peter preached to them. Another passage worth mentioning is Acts 11:19 and following. These were laypeople, men of Cyrene and Cyprus, who spread the gospel. The early deacon, Stephen, was a witness, and Philip was even called an evangelist. Virtually every time believers in Acts were involved in some kind of verbal activity, they were witnessing, praising God, and gaining favor among the people.

Examples of personal evangelism in the Book of Acts are numerous. Notice the witness of Philip to the eunuch (Acts 8); Peter to Cornelius (Acts 10); and Paul to the proconsul (Acts 13). Today, personal evangelism is the exception, not the rule; in Acts, the opposite was true. The Great Commission has experienced a great reversal. It is essential that we recapture a commitment to aggressive, winsome, unashamed personal evangelism!

"We cannot hesitate to believe," Harnack said, "that the great mission of Christianity was in reality accomplished by means of informal missionaries."[6] None of the first disciples of Jesus came from the clergy of their day, so we should not be surprised that the gospel spread primarily through "amateur" witnesses. Michael Green assesses the first-century church and in so doing gives an indictment of the American church:

In contrast to the present day, when Christianity is highly intellectualized and dispensed by professional clergy to a constituency increasingly confined to the middle class, in the early days the faith was spontaneously spread by informal evangelists, and had its greatest appeal among the working classes.[7]

History gives the same witness. In times of great awakening, personal evangelism receives renewed fervor. One of the more overlooked features of the leaders during past revivals is their commitment to personal soul-winning.

Mass Evangelism Was Conducted by Certain Believers Set Apart by the Spirit

One can argue that personal evangelism was conducted by all believers. But notice that public proclamation of the gospel was more limited. Peter, Stephen, Paul, and others preached—not all believers.

The public preaching of the gospel was undergirded by personal witnessing, as evidenced in Acts 2. Early Christian believers had no church buildings. Today we suffer from the "edifice complex," an overemphasis on buildings and budgets with little attention to people and passion. In the early church, preaching in the open air was the norm, not the exception. When George Whitefield and John Wesley began preaching in the fields with great effect in eighteenth-century England, they were criticized for using such a lowly approach. But they were only following the example of the early church!

They Shared the Gospel Message and the Testimony of their Changed Lives

There was no confusion in the early church about the message they preached. Consistently throughout Acts, the messages have a singular emphasis.

One of the most debated aspects of the Book of Acts centers on the question of whether there was a fixed pattern in the early church's gospel preaching. C. H. Dodd's work, *The Apostolic Preaching and Its Developments*, claimed there was a noticeable pattern. This pattern included: (1) Jesus inaugurated the fulfillment of messianic prophecy; (2) he went about doing good and performing miracles; (3) he was crucified according to God's plan; (4) he was raised and exalted to heaven; (5) he will return in judgment; and (6) therefore, repent, believe, and be baptized.[8]

Many scholars agreed with Dodd. These included Martin Dibelius, A. M. Hunter, and C. T. Craig. There is some disagreement among them on the basic points of early Christian preaching.

Scholars in recent years have increasingly disagreed with Dodd's findings. It is fair to say that the message was clear to all in the early church, but the application of the message varied. Perhaps Green, in his survey of early church evangelism, said it well when he stated that the proclamation of the early Christians was "united in its witness to Jesus, varied in its presentation of his relevance to the varied needs of the listeners, urgent in the demand for decision."[9]

What is abundantly clear in Acts is that a consistent message is proclaimed throughout. Note the comparison of key sermons in the comparative chart.

COMPARISON OF SERMONS IN ACTS

TEXT	ACTS 2	ACTS 3	ACTS 7	ACTS 13
Description	Peter at Pentecost	Peter after the Lame Man's Healing	Stephen	Paul
1. Jesus fulfilled messianic prophecy.	2:14–21	3:11–13a	7:2–53	13:16–27
2. Jesus did good deeds and performed miracles.	2:22	3:13–15 (implied)	7:52 "Just One"	13:23–25
3. Jesus was crucified.	2:23–24a	3:15	7:52	13:28–31
4. Jesus has been raised and exalted.	2:32a	3:21	7:54–56	13:32–35
5. Christ will return as Judge.	2:34–36	3:21–23	7:60 (implied)	
6. Repent, believe, be baptized.	2:38	3:19		13:38–39

The objective message of the cross and Jesus' resurrection permeated the witness of the early church. With this objective truth, they added the more subjective element of their personal testimonies. The message of the cross, when paired with a changed life, is still the most formidable weapon for storming the gates of hell.

One of the most moving verses on evangelism in the Bible is Acts 4:13. Peter and John had been arrested by the Sadducees for preaching the message of the cross and Jesus' resurrection. The religious leaders described Peter and John as *unlearned* and *ignorant.* But they could not explain the apostles' changed lives. "They marveled," we are told, and "they took knowledge, that [Peter and John] had been with Jesus." The testimony of these men gave evidence of the reality of their message. The question for us is, How long does a person have to speak with us before he or she recognizes that we have been with Jesus? When the authorities threatened Peter and John, Peter replied, "We cannot but speak the things which we have seen and heard" (Acts 4:20).

For these early believers, the objective message of the gospel was so dynamic in their lives that they would die for the Christ they preached. Their lives were so radically changed that they were willing to live for him as well.

Little Chad was a shy little boy. One afternoon in late January, Chad told his mother he wanted to make a valentine for each one of his classmates. *I wish he wouldn't do that!* she thought. She knew how the children ignored her son. Her Chad was always behind them when they walked home from school. Chad was never included. Nevertheless, she decided she would help. She bought construction paper, glue, and crayons. For three whole weeks, night after night, Chad made thirty-five valentines by hand.

When Valentine's Day arrived, Chad was excited. His mom, fearing his disappointment if he received no valentines, told Chad she would have his favorite cookies baked and ready when he came home from school. *Maybe that will ease the pain a little*, she thought.

That afternoon the kids were later than usual. Chad's mom had the cookies and milk on the table. Finally she heard them coming, laughing and talking with one another. And, as usual, Chad was in the rear. She feared he would burst into tears as soon as he got home. His arms were empty, she noticed, and when the door opened, she choked back the tears.

"Mommy has some warm cookies and milk for you."

Chad just marched right on by, and all he said was, "Not a one . . . not a one."

Her heart sank.

And then he added, "I didn't forget a one, not a single one!"[10]

Chad was so focused on giving that he had given no thought to receiving. He had something to share, and so do we!

THEY SHARED CHRIST IN SPITE OF OBSTACLES

The greatest outpouring of the Spirit in history came on the Day of Pentecost. When great revival comes, everything goes well, right? Well, if that is your view of revival, you had better stop asking God for it! No, when God works, Satan rears his ugly head. The early church faced an array of internal and external obstacles, but they turned these obstacles into opportunities for God to work. Nothing could stop their passion for soul-winning.

Notice three of the *inward* obstacles.

1. *Hypocrisy.* Hypocrisy is not a twentieth-century phenomenon. Ananias and Sapphira (see Acts 5) lied about the circumstances surrounding their material gifts. Peter confronted the obvious sin; an evangelistic church must be unafraid to confront known sin. The Book of Acts is the story of the greatest evangelistic spiritual awakening in history. But consider the difficulty the early Christians faced. The problem with Ananias and Sapphira was hypocrisy. Have you ever had hypocrisy at your church?

A pastor friend faced a crisis in his church. He discovered a staff member was involved in immorality. While being sensitive to the man's family and being as gentle as possible, he and the church confronted the sin, dealt with it, and the staff member was removed. The church later experienced a deep and powerful revival. If the church had failed to confront sin, it would have been robbed of some of the power of God.

2. *Ministry needs.* Acts 6 tells us of the neglected hellenistic widows. Notice the complaint of the widows was about a real need. Not everyone who brings up an issue is a complainer; a growing church must deal with legitimate needs. The apostles were hindered from doing their ministry, so the church dealt with the issue by enlarging the organization. However, it was not simply changing the structure by setting apart the first deacons that solved the problem. The selection of Spirit-filled leaders made the difference.

The hellenistic widows were saying, "We're being neglected." Peter didn't say, "Would you be quiet?" He said, "You know, there's a problem here. Let's appoint some deacons so we can serve the

Lord in the ministry of the Word and prayer, and you can serve the tables and take care of these ministry needs."

3. *Theological convictions.* Theological matters also played a key role in the evangelism of the early church. The Jerusalem conference described in Acts 15 dealt with a theological issue directly tied to evangelism: Did Gentiles have to become Jews to be Christians? From that day onward, the evangelistic effectiveness of the church has often depended on how it deals with matters of theology. Evangelism is more than methodology. We must deal with theological concerns in order to be effective in evangelism.

Beyond the *inward* obstacles, the church also grappled with *outward* persecution. Note these three examples.

1. *Threats.* The Sadducees arrested Peter and John, ordering them not to preach any more. How did the apostles respond? First, they courageously *preached* the gospel (Acts 4:8–12). Then they *testified* concerning their unwillingness to be silent (Acts 4:20). Finally, upon their release, they *prayed* with other believers (Acts 4:23–31).

In their prayers, they began by acknowledging God's sovereignty (Acts 4:24). They also acknowledged God as Lord of creation and history. When the early believers prayed, they prayed for *boldness* (Acts 4:29). Notice the answer: "And when they had prayed, the place where they were assembled together was shaken; and they were all filled with the Holy Spirit, and they spoke the word of God with boldness." Now *that's* praying!

2. *Physical beating.* Acts 5 tells us that persecution moved from threats to actual physical abuse. But notice the response: They rejoiced "that they were counted worthy to suffer" (Acts 5:41). Joseph Tson, who was persecuted greatly in Romania before the collapse of Communism, said most American Christians have not faced enough persecution to be counted worthy of suffering.

3. *Martyrdom and a general persecution.* Stephen paid the ultimate sacrifice for his conviction about the gospel (see Acts 7 and 8).

George Whitefield, the great preacher of the first Great Awakening, said that a man cracked a whip at his feet while he preached on one occasion. That night he wrote, "I was blessed of God this day to have rocks and stones and pieces of dead cat thrown at me." He preached for two or three hours that day, and hundreds of people were moved to Christ. When John Wesley preached one time, his opponents ran an ox through the crowd. He wrote in his journals about having his mouth bloodied, and still he kept on preaching. We must understand that the gospel is worth any cost.

Paul Brand and Philip Yancey wrote a stirring book entitled *Pain: The Gift Nobody Wants*. It's about leprosy and pain in general. Brand describes a leper colony in India and the main leper colony in the United States, in Louisiana. The main problem with leprosy is that it causes you to lose your feeling. Some people in these leper colonies kept losing fingers and ears, and they didn't know why. They put a camera in their dormitories. They discovered that while these people were sleeping, rats would chew on their fingers. The lepers didn't even know it. They couldn't feel.

The point of the book is that there is something worse than pain—the inability to feel pain. Those lepers would give anything to feel pain. The three most prescribed drugs in America today are classified as antidepressants or pain relievers. We try to blot out our pain, even in the church! We must understand that there is no service to God without pain. His desire is not to give us comfort but to build the character of Christ in us.

HISTORY IMMEDIATELY FOLLOWING THE FIRST CENTURY

EVANGELISM LEADERS IN THE SECOND AND THIRD CENTURIES A.D.

The pace set by the early church to reach out with the gospel continued into the next century. Polycarp, bishop of Smyrna, is best remembered for his courageous martyrdom. This second-century church father found himself before the proconsul, standing in the arena. The proconsul ordered the elderly saint to recant his faith in Christ. Polycarp replied, "Eighty and six years have I served Him, and He never did me any injury: how then can I blaspheme my King and my Savior?"[11] When threatened with wild beasts, Polycarp remained undaunted. When threatened with fire, he answered: "Thou threatenest me with fire which burneth for an hour, and after a little is extinguished, but art ignorant of the fire of the coming judgment and of eternal punishment."[12]

Polycarp was sentenced to be burned at the stake. But the fire didn't burn him. Finally, he was pierced with a dagger. He was praised not primarily for his courage but because his death was "altogether consistent with the Gospel of Christ."[13] Polycarp also led in the advancement of the gospel to new lands. Irenaeus recorded Polycarp's role in sending Pothinus to Celtic Gaul as an evangelist. Ignatius, bishop of Antioch, wrote an epistle to Polycarp, identifying himself as a witness for Jesus Christ. These early church fathers saw evangelism as central to the Christian faith.

Irenaeus was a disciple of Polycarp. His work *Against Heresies* refuted the Gnostic heresy, which threatened to sap the evangelistic fervor of the early church. While in Rome, Irenaeus heard of the horrible persecution in Lyons, in which the famous martyr Blandina was killed. Wild animals, beatings, molten copper, and other atrocities caused Blandina's martyrdom. Many believers in Lyons were revealed as worthy of the martyr's crown.

Irenaeus came to the city to be bishop, and eventually the city was declared to be Christian. Tertullian's famous statement written a few years later that "the blood of the martyrs is the seed of the Christians" was apparent in Lyons. Irenaeus eventually dispatched missionaries to other areas in Gaul and beyond.

The apologist Justin Martyr, another second-century saint, is known for his martyrdom and his writings that defended Christianity. This Christian philosopher also saw evangelism as a priority:

> At last [Justin] became acquainted with Christianity, being at once impressed with the extraordinary fearlessness which the Christians displayed in the presence of death, and with the grandeur, stability, and truth of the teachings of the Old Testament. *From this time he acted as an evangelist, taking every opportunity to proclaim the Gospel as the only safe and certain philosophy, the only way to salvation.*[14]

Born about 205, Gregory Thaumaturgos evangelized the city of Neo-Caesarea. The saying was that when Gregory came there, only seventeen Christians could be found; when he died, there were only seventeen pagans. His name means "miracle worker," referring to the miracles attributed to his ministry.

Michael Green offers an apt summary of evangelism immediately following the New Testament era:

> One of the most striking features of evangelism in the early days was the people who engaged in it. Communicating the faith was not regarded as the preserve of the very zealous or of the officially

designated evangelist. Evangelism was the preroga-
tive and the duty of every church member. We've
seen apostles and wandering prophets, nobles and
paupers, intellectuals and fishermen all taking part
enthusiastically in this primary task committed by
Christ to His church. The ordinary people of the
church saw it as their job: Christianity was supremely
a lay movement, spread by informal missionaries.
The clergy of the church saw it as their responsibility, too: bishops and presbyters, together with doctors of the church like Origin and Clement, and
philosophers like Justin and Tatian, saw the propagation of the gospel as their prime concern. They
seem not to have allowed the tasks of teaching, caring and administering to make them too busy to
bring individuals and groups from unbelief to faith.
The spontaneous outreach of the total Christian community gave immense impetus to the movement
from the very outset.[15]

As the years passed, the church followed the pattern of Old Testament Israel, gradually substituting passion for God with ritual. In
the centuries after the New Testament era, the sacramental system
developed. It focused more on the practice of certain forms in the
church rather than a relationship with Christ lived in the world.
Evangelism particularly suffered as the sacraments of baptism and
the Eucharist replaced the message of the gospel.

Montanism emerged in the late second century in response to the
growing formalism in the church. The movement was named for
Montanus of Asia Minor, who was characterized by a mystical
demeanor and a focus on the Holy Spirit and the imminent return
of Christ. The most notable adherent of Montanism was Tertullian.
Montanists denounced the growing distinction between clergy and
laity in the church.

Novatianism arose from the influence of Novatian, leader of a
spiritual reform movement in Rome in the third century. Taylor
declared, "His zeal for the gospel brought him many honors."[16]
Novatianism was a reform movement against the growing worldliness in the church.

Donatists, named for Donatus, arose after the persecution of the Roman emperor Diocletian (284–305). Donatists opposed those who recanted the faith when faced with persecution. Donatists emphasized godly living and disciplined Christianity.

The fight to keep evangelism as a priority in the face of ritualism is with us still. Green writes:

> Unless there is a transformation of contemporary church life so that once again the task of evangelism is something which is seen as incumbent on every baptized Christian, and is backed up by a quality of living which outshines the best that unbelief can muster, we are unlikely to make much headway through techniques of evangelism. Men will not believe that Christians have good news to share until they find that bishops and bakers, university professors and housewives, bus drivers and street corner preachers are all alike keen to pass along, however different their methods may be. And then will continue to believe that the church is an introverted society composed of 'respectable' people and bent on its own preservation until they see in church groupings and individual Christians the caring, the joy, the fellowship, the self sacrifice, and the openness which mark the early church at its best.[17]

APPLICATION

Take a few minutes to consider how the New Testament strategy for evangelism applies to your church field. If churches could just get this concept—total penetration and total participation—what an impact we could make across America.

When I was a pastor or a church staff member, I believed the churches that I served were accountable to God for reaching their communities for Christ. Church leaders must get their people to understand the need to reach their field for Christ.

Imagine this scene (Figure 3.1). The New Life Baptist Church, in Lotsapeople, North Carolina, is your church field. Following the New Testament pattern, what can you do to reach this church field with the gospel?

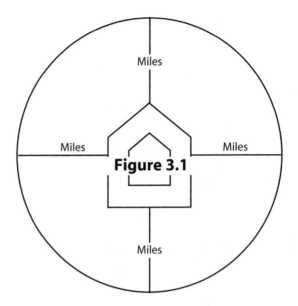

Figure 3.1

BIBLIOGRAPHY

Autrey, C. E. *Evangelism in the Acts*. Grand Rapids: Zondervan, 1964.
Coleman, Robert E. *The Master Plan of Discipleship*. New York: Revell, 1987.
Bruce, F. F. *The Spreading Flame*. Grand Rapids: Eerdmans, 1958.
Green, Michael. *Evangelism in the Early Church*. Grand Rapids: Eerdmans, 1970.

4

Living by Fate or by Faith? Evangelism in Christian History

As a university professor, I heard many stories about college students struggling with two major concerns: money and grades. That's why I love this story of a college coed told by Chuck Swindoll. After a long struggle, she finally wrote an ingenious letter to break the news to her parents:

> Dear Mom and Dad,
>
> Just thought I'd drop you a note to clue you in on my plans. I've fallen in love with a guy named Jim. He quit high school after grade eleven to get married. About a year ago he got a divorce.
>
> We've been going steady for two months and plan to get married in the fall. Until then, I've decided to move into his apartment (I think I might be pregnant).
>
> At any rate, I dropped out of school last week, although I'd like to finish college sometime in the future.

On the next page she continued:

Mom and Dad, I just want you to know that everything I've written so far in this letter is false. NONE
of it is true.

But Mom and Dad, it IS true that I got a C in
French and flunked Math. It IS true that I'm going to
need some more money for my tuition payments.[1]

Creative, huh! Poor grades and an empty pocketbook fare better
with Mom and Dad than illegitimacy and a bad marriage.

Perspective is exactly why studying history is so important.
History helps provide a foundation and a perspective for contemporary ministry. Santyana's dictum that those who do not learn from
history are doomed to relive it is sage advice.

From about Augustine's time (354–430) until the Reformation,
evangelism suffered. However, there were faint stars that lit the distant skyline of the West. The Reformation paved the way for the
remarkable evangelistic expansion across the globe. In the modern
era, several great awakenings and global missions expansion ushered untold multitudes into the kingdom of God.

EVANGELISM IN THE MIDDLE AGES

One can trace the health of the church throughout history by its
commitment to evangelism. The Dark Ages were so named for
many reasons. But from a spiritual vantage point, one can see the
twilight of evangelistic conviction and work throughout much of the
established church during this era. The rising dominance of the
Roman Catholic Church brought a theological shift from biblical
authority alone and a rise in ritualism. The shift in focus from the
New Testament gospel to the sacraments in the church blunted the
spread of the true message of salvation.

Still, God always has a people, a righteous remnant of the faithful. Certain individuals are worthy of a passing mention as we survey history.

Ulfilas (318–388) reached his own people, the Goths, in the
fourth century A.D. Barbarians along the Roman Empire's northern
border captured many Romans and enslaved them. Ulfilas was won
to Christ by the witness of Roman Christians who had become

slaves. Ulfilas in turn won many of his own people to Christ, translating much of the New Testament into the Gothic language.

Patrick of Ireland evangelized parts of Britain in the fifth century. He was taken captive from his native Scotland to Northern Ireland by marauding pirates. After his capture, he recalled the teachings and prayers of his godly mother and was converted at age sixteen. His six years in prison bred a desire to see his captors converted, along with all the Irish. Patrick established over 365 churches and reached well over 120,000 people for Christ.[2] He is now honored as the patron saint of Ireland.

The person responsible for evangelizing much of Scotland in the sixth century was Columba (521–597). Converted at age twenty-one, he and twelve priests left Ireland for Scotland in 563. Columba ministered chiefly on the island of Iona, laboring here for the Lord for thirty-four years. Others would come to Iona to be equipped, then would go forth bearing the good news.

Near the end of the sixth century Augustine of Canterbury (545–605) evangelized Britain. This Augustine, not to be confused with the more famous Augustine of Hippo, nevertheless had a significant ministry for Christ. Traveling to the British Isles in 597, Augustine and his companions won Ethelbert, the area ruler, to Christ. The king told Augustine his people would not "hinder your preaching and winning any you can as converts to your faith."[3] The king gathered the people daily at one point to hear the gospel preached. Augustine established a ministry center named Canterbury, where he eventually became the first archbishop. Many Angles and Saxons came to Christ through the outreach of Augustine. His ministry established Christianity in southern England.

Boniface preached the gospel first in Germany and Belgium. He earned the title "apostle of Germany" and became the first archbishop of Mainz. So successful were his efforts that he was questioned by the Pope in Rome. His ministry experienced what modern missiologists call "people movements"—a movement of entire communities to Christ at once. He chopped down a sacred tree for the pagan god Thor. When nothing happened to him, he reached many people with the gospel. Boniface died as a martyr at the hands of pagans in 754. Historian Latourette said of him, "Humble, a man of prayer, self-sacrificing, courageous, steeped in Scriptures . . . he was at once a great Christian, a great missionary, and a great bishop."[4]

EVANGELISM ON THE EVE OF THE REFORMATION

In the face of the ritualism and worldliness so common in the Catholic church at this time, several movements that emphasized biblical evangelism emerged before the Reformation.

Peter Waldo ministered in the twelfth century. A wealthy merchant in the city of Lyons, France, Waldo became disheartened with money, and experienced renewal and conversion. He took a vow of poverty and eventually begged alms for the necessities of life. His followers were called the "Poor Men of Lyons," and eventually "the Waldenses." His movement challenged the formalism and authoritarianism of the established church. His followers were looking for a return of the vibrancy of the apostolic era.

Many Waldenses were martyred at the hands of the Catholic church, often because of their conviction concerning the believer's baptism following conversion. They promoted an aggressive evangelism, and their goal was to recapture the dynamic, Bible-centered program of the first-century church. The Waldenses proclaimed the gospel and opposed the established church, as did other groups such as the Henricians, the Arnoldists, the Cathari, the Lollards, and the Petrobrusians. Such groups were the forerunners of the Reformation of the sixteenth century.

Francis of Assisi (1181–1226) was a minister of the gospel to Italy in the thirteenth century. His early days of licentiousness and folly ended when he came to Christ. He went from riches to rags to Christ, rejecting any inheritance from his family and devoting his life to the preaching of Christ. Francis's abounding love and joy had a great influence on the people. He organized followers into twos and sent them out to evangelize the multitudes. These followers eventually were called "Franciscans." The Franciscans were particularly effective in preaching to the common people.

Jerome Savonarola (1452–1498), a giant of prayer and preaching, sought to propagate the gospel in fifteenth-century Italy. His mental capabilities were great even in his early years, and he faced a promising career in academia. But God had other plans for this brilliant young Italian. In 1475 he enrolled in a monastery in Bologna, where he offered himself as a living sacrifice of service. For the next seven years, he devoted himself to Bible study and prayer.

Savonarola soon was transferred to St. Mark's monastery in Florence, where he began to fail in his preaching effectiveness. He spent much time praying and fasting over the Scriptures. The Lord eventually led him to Revelation and the message of the apocalypse. This proved to be God's message for the people of that day. Savonarola's preaching from the Revelation brought a powerful awakening and reformation to Florence.

Biographer Misciattelli quoted a contemporary of Savonarola who described his preaching: "Savonarola introduced what might be called a new way of preaching the Word of God; an apostolic way; not dividing his sermons into parts, or embellishing them with high sounding words of elegance, but having as his sole aim the explaining of Scripture, and the return to the simplicity of the primitive church."[5]

Savonarola was eventually promoted to spiritual and political leader in Florence. He declared Florence a theocracy and led a city-wide revival. This lasted for about two years until the corrupt leaders began to get a following. Savonarola was eventually martyred for his stand against the immoral practices of the papacy.

Other notable Christian leaders during the years leading up to the Reformation could be cited: Bernard of Clairvaux (1091–1153); John Tauler (1290–1361), the mystic of Germany; John Wycliffe; and Jan Hus—to name only a few. Others who will never be known except in eternity also contributed to the spread of the gospel over these centuries. Still, the ominous influence of the established Catholic church, along with its political might, hindered the followers of Christ from spreading the Good News. But a light was dawning on the horizon—the light of the Protestant Reformation.

EVANGELISM DURING THE REFORMATION

The sixteenth century stands as a watershed in human history. The influence of the Renaissance, with the rebirth of classical learning, and the Reformation, which paved the way for later spiritual awakenings, can still be felt today. While the Reformation was not primarily an evangelistic movement, it provided the theological basis for the spread of the gospel.

Martin Luther (1486–1546) became convinced of the doctrine of justification by faith. Luther was called the "Apostle of Faith." His emphasis on salvation by faith pointed people to the error of the Catholic church's salvation-by-works system of merit. His contributions to the field of evangelism and church growth are fourfold.

First, Luther helped to bring about a clear and concise gospel. He clarified for the church the message of salvation—salvation by faith, not by works.

Second, he emphasized the preaching and teaching of the Word of God. Preaching was central to the public worship service, and the Word of God was to be central to preaching. The Reformation was a call back to the Word of God.

Third, Luther emphasized the priesthood of believers, which helped to abolish the spiritual caste system. This also led to an emphasis on personal responsibility for believers to be servants of Christ.

Fourth, Luther considered evangelism to be of great importance. He considered himself an evangelist and preached evangelistically.[6]

John Calvin (1509–64) also made a fourfold contribution to the Reformation and the discipline of evangelism.

First, he highlighted the work of God's grace in a person's salvation. Out of this came a focus on the doctrine of salvation based on the principle of divine grace as the only factor in salvation. With his basic premises (sovereignty of God, hopelessness of man, adequacy of Christ, salvation through grace, and grace bestowed through divine election), Calvin renounced salvation by works.

Second, he emphasized hymn-singing, insisting on Bible-centered songs. Thus, he linked truths of God to worship.

Third, Calvin practiced extemporaneous preaching, emphasizing eloquent speech coupled with an evangelistic accent.

Fourth, he practiced personal evangelism through personal appeal and correspondence. He desired that all classes come to Christ.

The most effective group in emphasizing biblical revival during the Reformation was the *Anabaptists*. This group desired to bring the church back to its New Testament roots. Following the baptism of a group at Felix Manz's home on January 21, 1525, the Anabaptists (rebaptizers) grew. They emphasized the New Testament concept of believer's baptism following conversion. Balthasar Hubmaier (1481–1528) was an Anabaptist theologian and evangelist. He baptized six thousand people in one year and was burned at the stake in 1528 for his beliefs.[7]

MODERN SPIRITUAL AWAKENINGS AND EVANGELISM

In the modern era in the West, effective evangelism was almost always related to spiritual awakening. The greatest evangelistic results, methods, and leaders were born out of revival. In fact, much modern church history in the West may be traced along two central themes: the impact of the Enlightenment and a succession of mighty spiritual awakenings.

In recent centuries, spiritual awakenings have led to virtually all advances in evangelism, both in the numbers of converts and in new methods. There were certainly evangelistic emphases and contributions apart from times of great revival. However, the most significant evangelistic impact in the modern period is related to awakenings. Evangelism does not always lead to revival, but revival always brings the church back to a renewed evangelistic passion. A general overview of evangelism in modern history must emphasize a survey of historical revival movements.

Spiritual awakening or revival is a divine intervention into the church that causes a serious reflection on personal sin and open confession of sin. This results in a renewed awareness of God's presence and fresh power for ministry.[8]

There is much confusion in our day over the terms *revival, awakening*, and *spiritual awakening*. Some people use *revival* to refer to the work of God among believers, and *awakening* to speak of the conversion of masses to Christ. This is a valid use, seen in the writings of Jonathan Edwards in the eighteenth century and such recent books as Henry Blackaby and Claude King's *Fresh Encounter*. However, I choose to use these terms as synonyms for the following reasons.

First, too many evangelicals think "revival" refers to a four-day meeting with an evangelist, aimed at reaching the lost. This is actually mass evangelism. Such meetings are important, but they are not revival. Today, many churches hold such meetings aimed at revival of the saints and conversion of the lost, but it is still a *meeting* unless God moves in a mighty way. Such protracted services might be called "revival meetings" but not *revival*. Occasionally, God does send revival in the midst of a meeting! So I use *awakening* and *revival* as synonyms because the word *revival* has lost its true meaning for many people.

A second reason I use these two terms as synonyms is the biblical terminology associated with them. Several terms in Scripture relate to spiritual awakening. In the Old Testament, key terms include *chayah*, "to live or make alive again," found in Psalm 85:6: "Will you not *revive* us again, that your people may rejoice in You?" The term is also seen in Habakkuk 3:2 and Hosea 6:2. *Chadash* means "to repair or make new," as seen in Psalm 51:10: *"Renew* a steadfast spirit within me."* David's prayer of repentance following his sin with Bathsheba demonstrates the cry of a saint seeking personal revival. *Chalaph*, "to alter or change," is found in Isaiah 40:31.

New Testament terms include *anakaino*, translated as "to make new again." The word is found in Romans 12:2: "Be transformed by the *renewing* of your mind." It can also be seen in 2 Corinthians 4:16; Colossians 3:10; and Titus 3:5. *Eknepho*, "To be sober, to come to one's senses," is seen in 1 Corinthians 15:34. Finally, the word *egeiro*, meaning "to awaken from sleep," is the closest biblical expression for "spiritual awakening." Romans 13:11–13, one of the most important texts in the New Testament on genuine revival, uses this term in verse 11: "It is high time to *awake* out of sleep."

So, while some people use the word *revival* to refer to God's activity among his people and *awakening* to refer to the result of revival on culture, the terms will be used interchangeably in the following overview.

Spiritual awakening is the supernatural work of God. It is divinely initiated. It is the story of God's involvement in history. It is not primarily for our benefit, but for God's glory. Spiritual awakening normally comes after a time of spiritual decline in the church and moral decay in the culture. Too many people seek revival simply to help their church grow, or to solve problems, or to curb a moral slide. These may result from revival, but we should seek revival simply because we want to know and honor God!

An awakening brings the church to a renewed sense of wonder toward God. Our house is nestled at the end of a cul-de-sac in a wooded area, and for some time, my wife has been feeding deer. During the summer, about eight o'clock at night, a doe has been coming to eat behind our house. The kids love to watch the deer! Having lived in urbanized Houston, it's interesting to see animals like that.

One night I was walking through the bedroom and glanced out our bedroom window. There was the doe, eating away. We came into the bedroom and watched. Then two young bucks walked up to lick at the salt block and then eat grain. Hannah, our four-year-old, said, "W . . o . . w" and just stood there against the window. She wanted to crawl through the window to get as close as possible to the deer. To a four-year-old, to look out the window of your bedroom and see such beautiful animals is an awesome thing. This childlike wonder and awe is a picture of what we need as Christians—a sense of wonder before God.

While God acts in his way and in his time, he has chosen to use his children as facilitators for his activity. In 2 Chronicles 7:14 we read: "If *my* people . . ." The pattern of this Bible verse is seen in historical revivals. When God is at work, his people do the following:

Humble themselves. The greatest hindrance to revival in our day is self. "The world has yet to see what God can do through one man totally committed to Him," Henry Varley said to D. L. Moody.

Pray. Every great awakening has been preceded by united, concerted prayer. While a student in a spiritual awakening class in seminary, I heard a guest speaker quoting Leonard Ravenhill: "In revival praying, God doesn't answer prayer—he answers *desperate* prayer." I have never forgotten that. In revival, people are given to extraordinary prayer.

Seek God's face. Romans 13:14 puts it this way, "Put [on or dress up] like the Lord Jesus Christ." "God does not have favorites," Charles Stanley said, "He has intimates." It is God's *face* and not his hand we are to seek. Spiritual awakening is not primarily a remedy for church problems. It is not a church growth plan or a moral renewal plan. *It is the drawing closer of believers to God himself.* All other needs are met as a result of experiencing God. The greatest evangelistic church growth in history has come as a result of spiritual awakening.

Turn from their wicked ways. Romans 13:12 tells believers to cast off iniquity like removing a dirty garment. Revelation 2:5 is more direct: "Repent." Without exception, all awakenings in the Bible and in history have been characterized by brokenness over sin. God will use a vessel of any size, big or small, but only if it is clean. When true revival comes, both the church and society benefit. When awakening comes, believers are affected; and all of society is touched as well.

Historians are not in agreement as to the number of awakenings in recent centuries. The first great awakening is an obvious movement of God's Spirit; beyond that, anywhere from one to five more awakenings have been designated. Awakenings differ in depth and extent, but I am convinced at least four awakenings can be seen in the last four centuries. The most significant were the first two, but the latter two made their own mark.

Awakening in the eighteenth century occurred on three fronts: Pietism in Europe, the Evangelical Awakening in Britain, and the First Great Awakening in the American colonies.

Pietism

In response to a cold formalism, the movement known as Pietism began in Europe in the late 1600s. [9] One of the early leaders of this awakening was Philip Spener, who wrote the book *Pia Desideria* (Pious Desires), an appeal to spiritual reform.

Pietism's origin is typically associated with the publication of *Pia Desideria* in 1675.[10] Spener, called the father of Pietism by many, emphasized the personal nature of the Christian experience. He secured the appointment of A. H. Francke at the University of Halle in 1692. Under Francke's leadership, Halle became "a pietistic center of higher education and revivalism."[11]

Nicholaus Ludwig Von Zinzendorf (1700–1760) studied at Halle. Zinzendorf organized prayer groups among the students while at the university.[12] Zinzendorf eventually went to the University of Wittenberg, where he formed the Order of the Grain of Mustard Seed in 1718. In 1722 he acquired an estate that became a safe haven for persecuted members of the Hussite Church. It was from this group that the "Unitas Fratrum" (Unity of the Brethren) or Moravians were born. A particularly powerful movement of the Spirit came at a communion service on August 12, 1727. Following this, a continuous prayer structure developed, and a missionary enterprise began, resulting in one missionary for every sixty Moravians.

Zinzendorf's impact can be traced to his early years at Halle. Key emphases of this awakening included an obvious conversion experience, experimental faith, small-group discipleship, and foreign missions. Pietism ultimately emphasized experiences to the neglect of theology, however—a move that hindered its impact.

THE FIRST GREAT AWAKENING

The First Great Awakening generally includes the period from the 1720s to the 1740s, although revival embers were lit in later years in the South. Revival fires blazed as early as 1726 through the ministry of Theodore Freylinghuysen in the Dutch Reformed Church in New Jersey. He emphasized four things:

1. *evangelistic* preaching;

2. *zealous* visitation;

3. *church* discipline; and

4. *lay* preachers.

The Tennent family witnessed awakening in the Presbyterian Church in Pennsylvania. William, the father, began the "log college," a place to train his sons and other young men. This was a prototype for seminaries. Many evangelists, church planters, and revival leaders came from William's influence. Gilbert Tennent was an outspoken leader. He preached a famous sermon, "The Dangers of an Unconverted Ministry," denouncing the unregenerate clergy of his day.

Jonathan Edwards was a catalyst in New England. Edwards was a brilliant student, graduating from Yale as valedictorian at age sixteen. He read Latin by age six. He pastored a significant Congregationalist church in Northampton, Massachusetts. He witnessed two primary revival movements during the First Great Awakening, including the valley revival of 1734–35. Edwards recorded this revival in his *Narrative of Surprising Conversions.* Keys to the outpouring of God's Spirit, which caught Edwards and his church by surprise, included:

• biblical preaching;

• personal tragedies; and

• youth involvement.

Edwards, one of the greatest theologians, practitioners, and writers in the history of spiritual awakening, wrote his *Narrative* to give an account of the powerful revival that began in 1734–35 in and around Northampton, Massachusetts, where he was pastor. He prefaced this account by noting five powerful revivals during the long tenure of his predecessor and grandfather, Solomon Stoddard. The revival surfaced following a series of messages on justification by faith, and it spread quickly to neighboring towns. Edwards describes the effects of the revival:

> Presently upon this, a great and earnest concern about the great things of religion, and the eternal world, became *universal* in all parts of the town, and among persons of all degrees, and all ages . . . all other talk but about spiritual and eternal things, was soon thrown by; all the conversation, in all companies and upon all occasions, was upon these things only, unless so much as was necessary for people carrying on their ordinary secular business.[13]

In 1740–42 came the most powerful season of revival during the First Great Awakening. During this time, Edwards preached his famous sermon, "Sinners in the Hands of an Angry God." In the same period, Edwards wrote a treatise entitled *Some Thoughts Concerning the Present Revival of Religion in New England.*

In 1741 Edwards published *The Distinguishing Marks of a Work of the Spirit of God,* a collection of sermons that included five "marks" that illustrated the Spirit's true activity in revival (see "The Five Marks").

The Five Marks

1. When the operation is such to raise their esteem of Jesus.
2. When the spirit that is at work operates against the interests of Satan's kingdom, which lies in encouraging and establishing sin, and cherishing men's worldly lusts; this is a sure sign that it is a true, and not a false spirit.
3. Men show a greater regard to the Holy Scriptures.
4. If it leads persons to truth, convincing them of those things that are true, we may safely determine that it is a right and true spirit.
5. If the spirit that is at work among a people operates as a spirit of love to God and man, it is a sure sign that is the Spirit of God.

Edwards contributed greatly to the field of spiritual awakening with his writings.

George Whitefield, also involved in the Evangelical Awakening in England with John and Charles Wesley, came to the colonies several times. He preached from north to south, uniting the various movements.

In the southern colonies, revival spread mainly through Methodists and Baptists. The leaders among Baptists were Shubal Stearns and Daniel Marshall. Most Southern Baptist historians trace our roots to this movement, particularly the ministry of Stearns and the Sandy Creek Church in North Carolina. In seventeen years the Sandy Creek Church birthed forty-two churches, which in turn produced 125 ministers.[14] In the late 1700s Methodism spread rapidly in the South.

Several truths can be gleaned from the First Great Awakening.

God used different types of people and different denominational perspectives—Gilbert Tennent, Jonathan Edwards, George Whitefield, Theodore Freylinghuysen, and many others.

There was a greater emphasis on joy and enthusiasm. A conversion experience was emphasized, which was to be followed by a committed life. Effective ministry training developed. The log college and the birth of many colleges are examples. Laity were involved in ministry. Biblical theology was emphasized. Genuine revival is more than an experience; it includes a deepened understanding of the truths of God's Word.

THE EVANGELICAL AWAKENING IN ENGLAND

John Wesley (1703–91) and George Whitefield (1714–70) were two key leaders of the Evangelical Awakening in England during the eighteenth century. Some historians have stated that this awakening prevented England from going through an ordeal like the French Revolution. Wesley's experience as a college student at Oxford is probably best remembered by the "Holy Club" that involved both John and his brother Charles, George Whitefield, and a handful of others. Whitefield was converted during those days.[15]

The fact that Wesley was not actually converted until years after his Oxford days does not minimize the impact made on his subsequent ministry by the Holy Club.[16] The Holy Club at Oxford is significant because this experience forged relationships between the men who figured prominently in the awakening in England and the American colonies.

Wesley's oft-noted conversion came in 1738. On May 24, 1738, John Wesley attended a society meeting on Aldersgate Street in London. While someone read the prologue to Martin Luther's commentary on Romans, Wesley was converted. Here is the account from his *Journal:* "About a quarter to nine, while he was describing the change which God works in the heart through faith in Christ, I felt my heart strangely warmed. I felt that I did trust in Christ, Christ alone, for salvation."[17] His remarkable ministry that, along with Whitefield's influence and Charles Wesley's hymn-writing, affected the spiritual life of the entire nation. Wesley never desired to sever ties with the Church of England, but the Evangelical Awakening resulted in the formation of the Methodist Church.

Under the influence of the Wesleys, the Methodist Church was born. By John Wesley's death in 1791, there were 79,000 Methodists in England and 119,000 around the world.

The "methods" (hence the name "Methodist") that the Wesleys and Whitefield developed included

- societies;

- field preaching;

- hymn-singing;

- disciplined living; and

- publications.

Howell Harris, Daniel Rowland, and others were instrumental in the revival in Wales. Beyond his impact in England, Whitefield made seven trips to the New World. His itinerant ministry spread the gospel across the colonies. What makes this more impressive is that Whitefield was only twenty-six years old in 1741 when the First Great Awakening was at its peak!

THE SECOND GREAT AWAKENING

Following the multiple movements in the great revival of the eighteenth century, the next great season of awakening came at the turn of the nineteenth century with the Second Great Awakening. This revival instilled a fresh passion for God in the emerging American nation.

This came soon after the Revolutionary War. Various ideologies affected the church (Deism, skepticism, etc.). In addition, moral deficiencies were rampant in society. Revival touched both the established states on the Atlantic coast and the western frontier beyond the Appalachian Mountains.

Concerts of prayer were called by a group of New England ministers. This appeal was well received across the country.

Circular Letter of 23 New England Ministers Calling for Concerts of Prayer for Revival

To the ministers and churches of every Christian denomination in the United States, to unite in their endeavors to carry into execution the *humble attempt to promote explicit agreement and visible union of God's people in extraordinary prayer for the revival of religion and the advancement of Christ's Kingdom on earth.*

In execution of this plan, it is proposed that the ministers and churches of every Christian denomination should be invited to maintain public prayer and praise, accompanied with such instruction from God's Word, as might be judged proper, on every first Tuesday, of the four quarters of the year, beginning with the first Tuesday of January, 1795, at two o'clock in the afternoon, if the plan of concert should then be ripe for a beginning, and so continuing from quarter to quarter, and from year to year, until the good Providence of God prospering our endeavors, we shall obtain the blessing for which we pray.

A major precipitating factor in this movement was the outbreak of revival on college campuses. Skepticism and infidelity characterized the colleges. During this period immediately following the birth of the United States, the colleges in the East were often greatly influenced by European thinkers of the Enlightenment.[18]

The campus of Hampden-Sydney College in Virginia became the first in a series of college revivals. The fertile field of young students played a pivotal role. Four young men—William Hill, Carey Allen, James Blythe, and Clement Read—were instrumental in the beginnings of revival at Hampden-Sydney in 1787 and the years following. Because they feared severe antagonism from the other students, the four young men began meeting secretly in the forest to pray and study. When they were discovered, they were greatly ridiculed by fellow students.

President John Blair Smith heard of the situation and was convicted by the infidelity on the campus. He invited the four students and others to pray with him in his parlor. Before long, "half of the students were deeply impressed and under conviction, and the revival spread rapidly through the college and to surrounding counties."[19] Hill later chronicled the revival's impact:

> Persons of all ranks in society, of all ages . . . became subjects of this work, so that there was scarcely a Magistrate on the bench, or a lawyer at the bar but became members of the church. . . . It was now as rare a thing to find one who was not religious, as it was formerly to find one that was. The frivolities and amusements once so prevalent were all abandoned, and gave place to singing, serious conversations, and prayer meetings.[20]

In addition, subsequent revival movements came to the school in 1802, 1814–15, 1822, 1827–28, 1831, 1833, and 1837.[21]

The Yale College revival began under the leadership of President Timothy Dwight, the grandson of Jonathan Edwards. Dwight came to the school when it was filled with infidelity. He began to preach against unbelief in the college chapel. By 1797 a group of students formed to improve moral conditions and pray for revival. A powerful spiritual movement swept through the school in the spring of 1802. A third of the student body was converted. Goodrich wrote of the change in attitude on campus:

> The salvation of the soul was the great subject of thought, of conversation, of absorbing interest; the convictions of many were pungent and overwhelming; and "the peace of believing" which succeeded, was not less strongly marked.[22]

The movement spread to Dartmouth and Princeton. At Princeton three fourths of the students made professions, and one fourth entered the ministry.[23]

A group of students at Williams College in Massachusetts made a tremendous impact on missions. Samuel Mills entered the college during a time of awakening there between 1804 and 1806. He and four others began to pray regularly for missions. In 1806 at one particular meeting they had to seek refuge from the rain in a haystack. During this "haystack meeting," Mills proposed a mission to Asia. This event was a precipitating factor leading to a major foreign missions enterprise. The first missionaries included Adoniram Judson and Luther Rice.[24] Beyond the colleges, revival began in Northington, Connecticut, with meetings initiated by young people.[25]

After a series of gatherings in 1799, the first real camp meeting was held in June of 1800 at the Red River Church in Kentucky. Crowds gathered in a given community for several days of worship and the observance of communion. Then, in August 1801 at Cain Ridge, Kentucky, 25,000 came together. Leaders included James McGready and Barton Stone, who were Presbyterians. Unusual phenomena were associated with some of the camp meetings. Many leaders, including Methodist circuit rider Peter Cartwright, discouraged such practices.[26]

Charles Finney has been called the "father of American revivalism." A lawyer by training, Finney was powerfully converted in 1821 and embarked on a ministry of revival and evangelism. Finney is perhaps best known for his "new measures," innovative approaches that he incorporated into his ministry. These included protracted meetings and "anxious benches." The "anxious seats" were a forerunner to the modern public invitation, as described by Finney:

> It was at Rochester that I first introduced this measure. . . . I made a call for the first time for persons who were willing to renounce their sins and give themselves to God to come forward to certain seats which I requested to be vacated, and offer themselves up to God while we made them subjects of prayer. A much larger number came forward than I expected.[27]

Finney on Revivals

"Revival is the renewal of the first love of Christians, resulting in the awakening and conversion of sinners to God. A revival of true Christianity arouses, quickens, and reclaims the backslidden church and awakens all classes, insuring attention to the claims of God. Revival presupposes that the church is mired in a backslidden state" (Charles G. Finney, *Lectures on Revivals of Religion* [Minneapolis: Bethany, 1988], 15). Here is a samling of Finney's views:

What Happens in a Revival?
- Christians are convicted of their sins.
- Backslidden Christians repent.
- The faith of Christians is renewed.
- The power of sin in believers' lives is broken.
- Effective evangelism results.

When Can We Expect Revival?
- When the Providence of God—His ordering of events— signals an awakening is at hand (by unusually effective tools, events, etc.)
- When the sinfulness of sinners grieves Christians. The prevalence of sin is not necessarily a sign revival is far away; in fact, revival often comes in times of great sin.
- When there is a spirit of prayer for revival—that is, "They pray as if they want it."
- When pastors make revival and the awakening of sinners their goal.
- When Christians begin to confess their sins to one another.
- When Christians are willing to sacrifice to carry it on.

The Second Great Awakening stirred a powerful evangelistic movement, with multitudes converted. Further, it introduced significant new methods: the camp meeting and Charles Finney's "new measures," among others. One of the greatest results of this revival came in missions. In 1810 Adoniram Judson and Luther Rice were two of the first missionaries sent overseas by the American Board of Commissioners for Foreign Missions. The missions movement followed a similar time of revival that touched the lives of men such as William Carey in Great Britain.

Many societies were birthed as well. The American Bible Society began in 1816; the American Tract Society in 1825. Educational impact was seen in the formation of the first seminaries in the United States, including Andover in 1808, Princeton in 1812, and Yale Divinity in 1818. Further, the American Sunday School Union was founded in 1824. Finally, society was changed. The Second Great Awakening began what some have called the "golden age of Christianity."

THE LAYMAN'S PRAYER REVIVAL OF 1857–59

By the mid–nineteenth century the effects of the Second Great Awakening subsided, due in part to growing prosperity, political turmoil over slavery, and religious extremism (such as the Millerites, who wrongly predicted the return of Jesus in 1843–44).

Several simultaneous events occurred at the beginning of this movement, known as the Layman's Prayer Revival. Union prayer meetings, led by Jeremiah Lanphier, began in 1857; they spread quickly to involve over 50,000 within six months across the eastern part of the United States.

Unusual church revivals were reported in Canada, Massachusetts, South Carolina, and other places in 1856–57.

Evangelism conferences held by the Presbyterian Church erupted in revival in 1857.

Sunday school outreach efforts in the East were also a factor.

In New York and Philadelphia, many businesses closed daily to pray.

Multitudes were converted. Seventy-five people were converted in a Brooklyn church revival meeting. A Catskill church saw 115 professions of faith in a few days. In Newark 3,000 people were converted in two months. In Philadelphia a man began a prayer meeting like those in New York. Soon 6,000 people met daily, and a tent revival was held. It continued for more than four months, with 150,000 attending. Over 10,000 were converted in one year.

God was exalted in this revival. This was the only awakening without a single well-known leader. Also, it came unexpectedly. Further, there was great cooperation among believers. It was part of a worldwide movement, including the revival in Wales in 1859 and the revival in the ministry of Andrew Murray in South Africa. It strongly influenced D. L. Moody during his youth. The Layman's Prayer Revival of 1857–59 was characterized by its wide appeal. Several colleges experienced revival during this time. J. Edwin Orr documented revival movements at Oberlin, Yale, Dartmouth, Middlebury, Williams, Amherst, Princeton, and Baylor.[28]

THE GLOBAL AWAKENING OF 1900–10

At the turn of the twentieth century, fresh winds of the Spirit again touched many people. The most visible example of the period was the revival of 1904–08. This included the Welsh Revival and other occurrences as well in the United States and abroad. Some features of the period were controversial, including the birth of modern-day Pentecostalism in 1901 and the subsequent Asuza Street Revival.[29]

The Welsh Revival concerns specifically the movement that began in 1904 in the tiny country of Wales. During one period, one hundred thousand people were converted in less than six months. A key leader was Evan Roberts. Roberts had four principles for revival:

1. Confess every known sin.

2. Put away every doubtful habit.

3. Obey the Holy Spirit promptly.

4. Confess Jesus publicly.

In the United States many denominations reported record growth. During this time the Home Mission Board of the Southern Baptist Convention began its department of evangelism, and Southwestern Seminary was founded.

Also, during the last part of the nineteenth century and the early years of the twentieth century, many prominent evangelists began to minister. Following in the line of D. L. Moody, these evangelists saw multitudes converted and many instances of genuine revival. These evangelists included R. A. Torrey, Billy Sunday, Sam Jones, Mordecai Ham, and Wilbur Chapman.

This period also witnessed the rise of music evangelists. Ira Sankey worked with D. L. Moody. Others included Homer Rhodeheaver and Charles Alexander.

RECENT REVIVAL MOVEMENTS

While there has been no revival that one could call a "great awakening" in America since the 1904–08 awakening, several localized or more specialized revivals have occurred since then. The late 1940s and the 1950s was a time of unparalleled church growth and evangelism. The Southern Baptist Convention's greatest years of growth came during this period. J. Edwin Orr, in his final message delivered before his death, noted that "about 1949 there was a wave of revival in colleges throughout the United States."[30]

In the middle of the youth protests surrounding the Vietnam War, the Jesus Movement served to call youths to a radical commitment to Jesus. The closest thing to spiritual awakening that affected youth specifically was the Jesus Movement of the late 1960s and early 1970s. This movement, which did not rival earlier awakenings in impact, generally paralleled the unrest among America's youth during this era. Only a brief summary can be offered here.[31]

Many people familiar with the Jesus Movement tend to emphasize the countercultural Jesus People (or Jesus "Freaks"), but the renewal among youth was actually much broader. It included powerful church revivals and campus awakenings as well as the more colorful phenomena such as underground newspapers, coffeehouses and communes, and the new music. It was expressed in youth choir tours, youth evangelism conferences, and music festivals. Contemporary Christian music and the rise of praise and worship songs flowed from the stream of this youth revival.

The Southern Baptist Convention (SBC) reported records in baptisms in the early 1970s, propelled mainly by a remarkable increase in youth baptisms. For example, the SBC record for baptisms occurred in 1972 with 445,725. Of that number, 137,667 were youth—the largest number and the highest percentage of youth baptisms during any year in SBC history. The second highest number of youth baptisms was in 1971. Even more significant than the total baptism figure was the more substantial youth baptism figures. The Jesus Movement reached its peak in 1970–71.

A Fifteen-Year Survey of Youth Baptisms in the Southern Baptist Convention 1971–88[32]

Year	Youth Baptized	Total Baptized	Percent Youth	U.S. Youth Population	Percent of Youth Pop. Baptized
1971	126,127	409,659	30.7	N/A	N/A
1972	137,667	445,725	30.8	24,997,000	0.550
1973	119,844	413,990	28.9	25,287,000	0.473
1974	115,345	410,482	28.1	25,454,000	0.453
1975	116,419	421,809	27.6	25,420,000	0.457
1976	103,981	384,496	27.0	25,305,000	0.410
1977	88,838	345,690	25.6	25,014,000	0.355
1978	97,118	336,050	28.9	24,549,000	0.395
1979	93,142	368,738	25.2	23,919,000	0.389
1980	108,633	429,742	25.2	23,409,576	0.464
1981	101,076	405,608	24.9	23,409,576	0.444
1982	102,259	411,554	24.8	22,358,000	0.457
1983	97,984	394,606	24.8	22,199,000	0.441
1984	91,431	372,028	24.6	21,958,000	0.416
1985	86,499	351,071	24.6	21,632,000	0.399
1986	86,387	363,124	23.8	21,300,000	0.405

In addition, record enrollments and continuous increases characterized all six Southern Baptist seminaries during the decade following the Jesus Movement.

Campus Crusade for Christ, the college parachurch ministry, held Explo '72 in Dallas. It resulted in "the most massive gathering of students and Christian laymen to ever descend on one city."[33] Its purpose was to equip and inspire young people in evangelism. Over 80,000 registered for the event, with some 150,000 attending a Saturday music festival concluding the meeting.[34] Evangelist Billy Graham was very favorable toward what he called the "Jesus revolution." He even wrote a book about the movement.[35] Graham noted that during the period an unusually high number of youth attended and professed faith in Christ at his crusades.

A famous revival occurred at Asbury College in 1970,[36] beginning spontaneously during a chapel service. The dean of the college was scheduled to speak, but he felt impressed to have a testimony service. Students began to flood toward the altar to pray. For 185 hours they continuously prayed, sang, and testified. Henry James of the college reported on what happened next: "Before long, appeals began coming from other campuses for Asbury students to come and tell the story. This intensified the burden of prayer even as it heightened anticipation of what God was going to do. . . . The revival began to take on the dimensions of a national movement. By the summer of 1970 at least 130 colleges, seminaries and Bible schools had been touched by the revival outreach."[37]

Many other recent instances of revival could be named. A stirring example in a local church is Houston's First Baptist. John Bisagno came to First Baptist in 1970, when the church was a declining downtown church. Bisagno watched the Jesus Movement. Unlike many in Southern Baptist circles, Bisagno affirmed the youth of the day, arguing that he would rather see youth yelling for Jesus than sitting barefoot on a park slope taking drugs.

Bisagno led the church to get involved in an effort called SPIRENO (Spiritual Revolution Now), led by evangelist Richard Hogue. As a result the church baptized 1,669 during 1970–71, with the vast majority coming from young people.[38] One reporter stated: "By taking the initiative, they gave their church and hundreds of others in Houston a chance to jump into the flow of this Jesus movement."[39]

Coffeehouse ministries, ocean baptisms, new music, personal evangelism, and many other phenomena characterized the period. There were controversial elements, including the overemphasis on a simplistic approach to the gospel and emotional experiences, the charismatic movement, and the appearance of many of the counter-cultural converts. The benefits certainly outweighed the liabilities, however. Beyond the evangelistic results cited above, the Jesus Movement helped many traditional churches to focus again on the work of the Holy Spirit. Many leaders in evangelism today were converted during the Jesus Movement or radically touched by its impact.[40]

EVANGELISTIC INNOVATIONS IN THE TWENTIETH CENTURY

Citywide, interdenominational crusades began in the nineteenth century and blossomed in the twentieth. D. L. Moody (1837–1899) began the march of an army of urban evangelists. Moody teamed with musician Ira Sankey to form the first successful evangelistic team. Their meetings drew thousands in cities from the United

States to England. Evangelistic results always occurred; and, at times, deep revival also arose.

Moody developed the practice of organizing a steering committee to guide preparations for his crusades. Many have followed his lead, including Billy Graham.

Other evangelists ministering in the cities during the nineteenth and twentieth centuries include:

- Sam Jones (1847–1906), Methodist evangelist who was particularly effective in the southern United States;

- Wilbur Chapman (1859–1918), a Presbyterian evangelist influenced by Moody and who helped Billy Sunday get started;

- Rodney "Gypsy" Smith (1860–1947), a British evangelist who also preached in America; and

- Billy Sunday (1862–1935), the flamboyant former baseball player. He built tabernacles whose floors were covered in sawdust; hence the expression "hitting the sawdust trail."

Of course, the best-known evangelist in history is William Franklin "Billy" Graham. Graham was converted in Charlotte, North Carolina, under the preaching of another prominent evangelist, Mordecai Ham. Graham has preached to more people than any other preacher in history. He has served as a model of a man of integrity and has remained single-minded in his call to be an evangelist.

OTHER TWENTIETH-CENTURY INNOVATIONS

A final summary of key evangelistic developments in the twentieth century must conclude our brief overview.

Denominational evangelism rose to prominence during the 1900s. At the outset J. Wilbur Chapman, famous for his worldwide crusades, served as evangelism director briefly for Presbyterians in America.

In the first decade the Southern Baptist Convention began a division of evangelism for the Board of Domestic Missions (now the evangelization group of the North American Mission Board). At first this consisted of a team of evangelists who preached meetings. The organization developed into a strategy and program-producing arm of the denomination. The Southern Baptist program of evangelism in the 1950s was one of the most successful campaigns.

In more recent years, simultaneous mass evangelism efforts and evangelistic outreaches in conjunction with the annual Southern Baptist Convention (known as Crossover) serve as examples of the evangelistic leadership of the denomination.

Parachurch evangelism also came into prominence during this century. The best-known example of this is Campus Crusade for Christ, International, now the largest parachurch organization in the world. Significant contributions include the "Four Spiritual Laws" witnessing booklet, the "Here's Life" campaign and "Explo '72" in the early 1970s, and the use of the *Jesus* video around the world.

Other parachurch organizations that give some focus to evangelism include Youth for Christ, Youth with a Mission, the Navigators, Young Life, and more recently, Promise Keepers. In the 1990s parachurch groups and denominations have joined hands as a part of A.D. 2000, a cooperative effort involving scores of evangelical denominations and parachurch ministries, with a goal of sharing Christ with every person on earth by the year 2000.

Methodological evangelism is a catchphrase for other key emphases. D. James Kennedy launched his Evangelism Explosion approach to personal evangelism at the Coral Ridge Presbyterian Church in 1970. Churches from various denominations have been trained by this approach. The Church Growth Movement's impact can hardly be underestimated in the latter part of this century; however, it will be considered in a later chapter.

APPLICATION

In our time, a great interest in awakening has grown. There have been exciting instances of genuine revival, such as a season of awakening in Brownwood, Texas, in 1995.[41] More than a few movements have emphasized other phenomena rather than a focus on God's Word.[42] What if God should send revival? What if a mighty awakening should ignite?

Picture for a moment two angels standing in heaven gazing at a church below. "Do you think God will send revival to that church?" the first asks. "Well," says the second, "I believe God desires to send revival there—but do you think God can *trust* that church enough to send revival?"

BIBLIOGRAPHY

Hanegraff, Hank. *Counterfeit Revival.* Dallas: Word Books, 1997.
McDow, Malcolm and Alvin L. Reid. *Firefall: How God Shaped History through Revivals.* Nashville: Broadman & Holman, 1997.
Taylor, Mendell. *Exploring Evangelism.* Kansas City: Beacon Hill, 1964.
Terry, John Mark. *Evangelism: A Concise History.* Nashville: Broadman & Holman, 1994.

5

Truth Matters:
The Theology of Evangelism

One of the legends surrounding the Taj Mahal concerns the death of the favorite wife of the Emperor Shah Jahan. Devastated at losing her, the king determined to honor her by constructing a temple as her tomb. The coffin was placed in the middle of the construction site. An expensive, elaborate edifice began to rise around the coffin. As the weeks became months, the Shah's passion for the project surpassed his grief.

One day during the construction, a wooden box was discovered. The emperor ordered the workers to throw the box out; after all, it was only in the way. Shah Jahan had no idea that he had ordered the disposal of his wife's casket, hidden beneath layers of dust and time. The very person for whose honor the temple was built was forgotten.[1] Tragic? Yes. But the same thing can happen to us. Without maintaining a focus on theology, founded on the Word of God, we can forget why we evangelize in the first place.

Christianity is founded on the conviction that the God of creation has revealed himself to humanity. The record of God's self-revelation is found in the Bible; most specifically and finally, God has revealed himself through his Son, Jesus. This chapter seeks not to prove this reality but to demonstrate how such a conviction relates to the task of evangelism.[2] The tendency today is to discover a method that works, then find a Bible verse to prove the method is OK. We need evangelism which is grounded in scripture.

THE RELATIONSHIP BETWEEN EVANGELISM AND THEOLOGY

One cannot adequately practice evangelism apart from a firm biblical base that is rooted in history and founded on a clear theology. At the same time, theology is incomplete without a view toward evangelism. Thus, *there is a need to keep evangelism and theology together.* This is true for several reasons.

1. *Evangelism and theology must be kept together to avoid extremism.* Wrongly interpreted and applied, some have used the Bible to lead many people into cults and other heresies. Evangelism keeps theology tied closely to Scripture. Linking evangelism and theology avoids certain aberrations.

Evangelism divorced from theology leads to superficial Christianity. It produces Christians who are ten miles wide and one-half inch deep. B. H. Carroll, the first president of Southwestern Baptist Theological Seminary, told his successor, L. R. Scarborough, that he must keep the seminary lashed to the cross. Theology keeps evangelism lashed to biblical truth, safe from error. Without a doctrinal base, we may eventually forget the very purpose for which we preach!

Truth matters more than our technique or our ability. Essentially, the truth that we share permeates and transcends everything else we do. I heard a story about the Little Frisky Dog Food Company. Sales were falling, so the sales manager brought in all the salesmen to encourage them. "You know, we have some of the finest salesmen in the world," he declared. "We have some of the best ad campaigns. We have some of the best slogans."

They replied, "That's right; we sure do." And he said, "We've got some of the best approaches to marketing this product. We're on the cutting edge." The salesmen began to get encouraged, to get excited. They began to say, "Yeah, that's right, that's right. Boss, we can do it!" He said, "You know the bag looks great, and you know that we've gone into all the major markets, and you know that we have the best sales team." Everyone was getting excited, working themselves into a lather. Finally, one man in the back raised his hand.

"Yes?"

"There's only one problem."

"What's that?"

"The problem is the dog food. The dogs *hate* it!"

We need to present *truth,* not some watered-down, cheap imitation of the real thing. We need to give people the life-changing, God-inspired gospel without corrupting the message.

Theology without evangelism leads to dead orthodoxy. Vance Havner said you can be straight as a gun barrel and just as empty. There are conservative churches across America that are ineffective and spiritually dead. They have the right doctrine, but their practice is far from the biblical standard. In fact, theology without an evangelistic priority means we haven't really understood theology.

2. *Theology and evangelism must remain linked because the Bible always weds theology with practical matters like evangelism.* In the Book of Acts, we read sermons filled with doctrinal content. At the same time, the testimony of the believers, their faith in action, played a vital role in their mission. Paul's letters often emphasized doctrine and practice, and we recognize Paul was both a theologian and an evangelist.

3. *People who have been used of God have generally kept theology and evangelism in unity.* Not every great leader in church history was a noted theologian. But at key points in history, when God raised up individuals to play strategic roles in the furtherance of the Christian faith, almost without exception those leaders were adept theologians and active evangelists. Martin Luther, although he was a theologian, called himself an evangelist. John Wesley, so pivotal in British history, was an Oxford man whose sermons were filled with doctrinal content and evangelistic themes. Jonathan Edwards was one of the brightest minds ever produced in America. His writings contain some heady doctrine, but he also played a critical role in the conversion of multitudes in the First Great Awakening.

EVANGELISM AND THE GREAT DOCTRINES

While all doctrines relate to evangelism, this chapter will examine crucial subjects related to the evangelistic task. Entire volumes are dedicated specifically to the theology of evangelism.[3] Central issues are considered below.

THE SCRIPTURES

Jurassic Park is my all-time favorite movie—but not because of the special effects, as realistic as they are. The same goes for the dinosaurs, although as a boy I wanted to be a paleontologist. I loved the movie because of its underlying message that science has gotten too high and mighty and has put itself in the place of God. This message is needed in our culture. An emphasis on the genius of man encourages a disdain toward Scripture. *Nothing* cuts the cord of evangelism faster than a lack of respect for the teaching of the Word of God.[4]

I will not argue for the uniqueness and authority of Scripture here; other writings have done that well.[5] I simply note that the uniqueness of Christianity begins with its Holy Book. The Bible makes the bold assertion, without giving any significant defense of its position, that it is the one-of-a-kind self-disclosure of the only true God—the Lord of history. Most significantly, it reveals to us what we must know about Jesus, the Son of God, our Savior. There are enough extrabiblical accounts of the life of Christ to demonstrate that he lived, but a person must come to the Scriptures to find any significant information about God's final self-revelation.

The Bible gives us objective, verifiable information about God and our relationship to him; however, it is fundamentally a book of faith. The Bible does not tell us everything we *want* to know about reality, but it does tell us what we *need* to know! I do not mean to imply that the Bible's historical or other factual information is irrelevant or inaccurate. But a person must do more than read the Bible and admire its majesty. One must encounter its primary Author to truly understand the words of life. One must *live* the Bible.

I believe the Bible is the infallible, inspired, inerrant word of God. It is wholly trustworthy and accurate, and it is the unique words of God as well as the Word of God.[6] Of course, one can hold to a high view of Scripture and not be evangelistic. But a person is hard pressed to come to the Bible with a heart of faith and not see the obvious implications and commands of God to proclaim the gospel message.

However, a more insidious affront to scriptural authority has sapped the life of the modern church. This is the invasion of liberalism, which questions the uniqueness of Scripture. Those who have followed this path in modern history have been anything but evangelistic. The findings of modern scholarship, including higher criticism, has to some degree helped our understanding of Scripture. The key is found in the presuppositions one takes to Scripture. In other words, the interpretation of the Bible is as critical as the view of the Bible's authority, but the two are not easily separated.

Drummond succinctly concludes his chapter on the authority of Scripture with these words:

> So there it stands: in the Holy Scriptures God has delivered an authoritative, trustworthy, true, propositional revelation of Himself that stands the epistemological test of comprehensiveness, coherence, correspondence, noncontradiction, and experience. Therefore, we build our theological structures on that sound theological base. So we construct our theology of evangelism on scriptural propositions, led by the indwelling Holy Spirit.[7]

GOD

Any discussion of theology must center on the doctrine of God. Drummond said it well when he noted that "evangelism begins in theology, not anthropology."[8] Unfortunately, most modern books on evangelism begin with the need of people—not the sovereignty of God. Most errors related to evangelism are made at this point. While we must understand contemporary culture to communicate the gospel effectively, we must not begin at that point to develop our theology. Starting with the doctrine of man emphasizes *relevance,* which is important; but more critical is starting with the doctrine of God, which emphasizes *significance.*

God is Creator. God the Creator implies God the Redeemer. God took the initiative to create, to make man in his image, to redeem fallen humanity.

God is One—in three persons. The God we serve is uniquely one God who has manifested himself in three persons. The Trinity is the granite from which the monument of evangelism is carved. In God's plan "the Father was to send His Son into the world to redeem it,

God the Son was voluntarily to come into the world in order to merit salvation by His obedience unto death, God the Holy Spirit was to apply salvation to sinners by the instilling of renewing grace within them."9

God is holy. The attributes of God relate to evangelism; the urgency of evangelism is tied to the character of God! He is holy, and we are not, so we stand condemned.

If we could see God face-to-face, our immediate impression would be to stand in awe of the holiness of God. That attribute would transcend all others. Think of Moses' encounter with God in Exodus. He did not jump a pew; he removed his shoes. Think of Isaiah and the cry of the seraphim, "Holy, holy, holy" (see Isa. 6). Move to the New Testament and John's vision of God in Revelation where the heavenly chorus responded with "holy, holy, holy" (Rev. 4:8).

The biblical words for *holy,* both the Hebrew word *qodesh* and the Greek *hagios,* have essentially the same meaning: "to be separate, distinct." God is not the same as us. In fact, there are more references in Scripture to the anger, fury, and wrath of God than to the love of God. Yet God is not only holy, just, and wrathful; he is also love.

God is love. While God is holy, he offers us a personal relationship with him which we don't deserve. Drummond is right in noting that *agape* love is the central motif of the New Testament. However, the *love* of God and the *holiness* of God must be held in balance.

We cannot evangelize biblically without both—his holiness and his love. Without God's love, we become mean-spirited. A pastor friend was eating at McDonald's while he watched his six-year-old son play in the playland. He was shocked to see his son putting another little boy in a headlock! He rushed outside to rescue the frightened little lad and sternly reprimanded his son.

The son looked at his Dad with a confused expression. "But Dad," he replied, "I was trying to tell him about Jesus, but *he just wouldn't listen!*"

In contrast, without a view of God's holiness, we refuse to confront people with their need for him. We become soft, even sentimental, toward others. We must keep a balance between conviction and compassion in our evangelism. This balance is essential to evangelism.[10]

CHRIST AND SALVATION

We can think of Christ in terms of the *person* of Christ—who he is—and the *work* of Christ—what he has done. He is the God-man, the unique, only begotten Son of God. Historically, two extremes have hindered the understanding of who Jesus is. On one hand, the Docetics emphasized the deity of Jesus, denying he ever became man. He only appeared to be human. On the other hand, the Ebionites said Jesus was *just* a man, denying his deity. Historically, liberalism has typically fallen on the side of the Ebionites, while conservatives at times have minimized the humanity of Christ.

The work of Christ includes his virgin birth (more properly, virginal conception), sinless life, death and resurrection, reign in heaven, return, and eternal reign. Most specifically, it concerns the work of Christ on the cross for our salvation. This relates specifically to soteriology.

The atonement of Christ is the centerpiece of Christianity. Throughout history, a variety of views of the atonement have been debated. While some of these are unbiblical, many theories of the atonement have truth in them. They are like different facets of a jewel.[11]

While these views help to explain the wonder of the cross, the key word in understanding the atonement is *substitution*. Drummond says it best: "If all the other theories are facets of the jewel of atonement, *substitution* is the core stone from which all the facets are cut."[12] This term is held in contempt by modern liberal scholarship, but the idea of a sin substitute is evident throughout Scripture.

The key question in Christianity is, Why the cross? Why did Jesus die? Erickson offers these five implications of the substitutionary death of Christ:

1. It confirms the biblical teaching of the total depravity of humans.

2. It demonstrates both the love and the justice of God in a perfect unity.

3. Salvation comes from the pure, sovereign grace of God.

4. The believer can be secure in the grace of God.

5. We are motivated not to neglect so great a salvation that came at such a great cost.[13]

While many terms in the New Testament emphasize the work of Christ to save us, Paul gave a clear view of the work of the cross in Romans 3:21–26. He used three terms in this passage that reflect the work of Christ. *Redemption* bears the idea of one who is a slave and whose freedom is purchased. *Justification* is a forensic term, used in the courts. Jesus' death declares us "not guilty." The expression *sacrifice of atonement* looks back to the Old Testament temple service and the idea of shedding blood. Jesus purchased our freedom from the slavery of sin, declares us not guilty, and has washed us clean—glory to his name!

The conditions of salvation are very clear in Scripture. These are repentance and faith.

If there is a missing word in evangelism today, it is *repent*. One of my students told me he served with a pastor who said he never preached repentance because it made people nervous. Such preaching makes *sinners* nervous! That's like the preacher who said he never preached about tithing because it made people nervous. Yes, it makes *thieves* nervous.

A noble desire to be seeker sensitive may cause some to shy away from repentance. But to minimize repentance is to preach a crossless gospel. Notice the following:

- In Matthew's Gospel, the first word of Jesus' preaching was *repent* (Matt. 4:17).

- Our Lord's herald, John the Baptist, preached a message of repentance (Matt. 3:2).

- Jesus declared that unless a person repented, he would perish (Luke 13:3).

- At Pentecost, Peter urged the people to repent (Acts 2:38; 3:19; 8:22).

- Paul consistently said a person must repent (Acts 17:30; 20:21; 26:20).

The Greek word *metanoia* translates as "repentance." It means to change the mind but in a deep manner—to change one's heart, mind, or purpose. This word is often confused with two other New

Testament terms, *metamellomai,* which means to have regret or remorse, and *elupesa,* which means to have sorrow.

We have misunderstood the difference between sorrow and repentance. My little girl Hannah says "I'm sorry, Daddy" every time I catch her doing something wrong. If I say, "Hannah, why did you take that crayon and write on the wall?" she looks up at me with her sad, big blue eyes and says, "I'm sorry, Daddy, I didn't mean to!" Baloney! Of course she meant to. It was not an accident—at least not the fifth or sixth time she did it! What do people think of when they think of repentance? Being sorry? Grieving? Regretting? That's not what the New Testament word means.

Look at 2 Corinthians 7:8–10. In verse 10, all three of these words are used in the same passage. Verse 8 says, "Even if I made you sorry with my letter, I do not regret it. Though I did regret it—I see that my letter hurt you, but only for a little while—yet now I am happy, not because you were made sorry, but because your sorrow led you to repentance. For you became sorrowful as God intended and so were not harmed in any way by us." Paul was talking about a time, described in 1 Corinthians, when he had to rebuke the church.

But he went on to remind them about salvation in verse 10: "Godly sorrow produces repentance leading to salvation, not to be regretted." Notice that godly sorrow *leads* to repentance. Godly sorrow is the conviction of the Holy Spirit that leads to repentance unto salvation.

At Houston Baptist University, some of the baseball players wore a *"No Fear"* shirt that said, "Bottom of the ninth, down by three, bases loaded, you're at the plate, two strikes, three balls—no fear." I love that shirt. The Christian shirt, however, is not "no fear." The Christian shirt is "no regrets."

Godly sorrow works repentance unto salvation not to be regretted, but the sorrow of the world brings death. You can be sorry about your sin before God and still spend eternity in hell. You can die in your sin if you don't get beyond "I'm sorry I did wrong." There has to be a desire in our lives that results in this message: "God, I want to change, I want to repent."

What we believe about salvation is crucial because our soteriology will determine our evangelism! For example, the hyper-Calvinist believes God has chosen who is saved and damned, so evangelism doesn't matter. On the other extreme, some emphasize an "easy believism" that stresses human work to the neglect of God's work to save. Many people suffer from a weak soteriology that underestimates the sinfulness of sin and, therefore, minimizes the majesty of God's grace.

We must constantly remind ourselves that God *owes* us one thing—hell. Yet he has lavished his love on us through Christ! Jesus' work on the cross sets us free from the power of sin and death. He did not die just to make *bad* people *good* but to make *dead* people *live* (see Eph. 2). A conviction about a great salvation leads to a passion for evangelism.

ANTHROPOLOGY AND HARMARTIOLOGY

The doctrine of man, *anthropology*, and the doctrine of sin, *harmartiology*, are closely linked. God created man to bring him glory and pleasure. But it is impossible for a lost person to bring pleasure to God. When Adam and Eve disobeyed, sin entered the human race (see Gen. 3; Rom. 5:12–15). We are at enmity with God.

We are born with a sinful nature. Augustine said that it is impossible not to sin. Sometimes this nature is referred to as "the old man" or "the flesh." When we are saved, the old nature, our sinful nature, is not eradicated. Instead, God came into us with his own nature. We were born with a sinful nature; we are born again with the nature of God. The Bible calls this a "new man." Second Peter talks about being partakers of the divine nature. What happened to the old nature? Romans 6:2 tells us that it is dead. Romans 6:6 says our old nature was crucified with Christ, and yet we still struggle with sin. Positionally the sinful nature is dead, but experientially, we still wrestle.

The doctrine of sin, or harmartiology, is greatly neglected in our day. In the Old Testament, the most common word for sin is *chata,* meaning "to miss the mark." The main New Testament term, *hamartia,* has essentially the same meaning. This idea of missing the mark reminds us that the central issue is not the *quantity* of sin but the *reality* of sin. If a person hangs over a great abyss by a chain, only one link must break to bring his death. One need rob a bank only once to be called a bank robber, commit adultery once to be an adulterer, and murder once to be a murderer. All people have sinned. The central issue is not, Have I sinned less than others?

Instead, we need to ask, "Is sin existent in my life?" The key is sin, not individual sins.

We must also remember that it is not simply individual sins that we commit that separated us from God. Rather, it is the sin nature within us—our rebellion that has caused the breach between us and God. Individual sins are symptomatic of a deeper problem.

There are other terms for sin. *Pasha* carries the idea of rebellion (Isa. 1:28). *Awah,* "twisting," means intentional perversion. *Rasha* means to act wickedly. In the New Testament, *paraptoma* signifies trespass, *parabasis* means transgression (Rom. 4:15), and *asebeia* refers to ungodliness (Rom. 1:18). The root of sin is unbelief. Unbelief is a volitional act (see John 3:19).

ECCLESIOLOGY

Evangelism is essential to the church because the church will cease to exist without evangelism. Further, God's plan to reach the world is through local congregations. The New Testament word for church is *ekklesia,* meaning the "called out ones." In the Greek world, it usually described an assembly of people. This word occurs 115 times in the New Testament. It refers to a local congregation ninety-five times; the other references are to the general church.

The church is a congregation of baptized believers who join together to honor God and to fulfill his mission in the world. In a larger sense, the church includes all believers of all time. Implications for the doctrine of ecclesiology on evangelism are many. Some emphases today hinder evangelism because they grow out of a faulty view of the church.

First, some people have forgotten that the local church is God's plan to reach the world. I have a great love for parachurch organizations. I led the first person to Christ in my own personal evangelism through the *Four Spiritual Laws* booklet produced by Campus Crusade for Christ. I was discipled in college with materials produced by the Navigators. I have participated in rallies with such organizations as Young Life and Promise Keepers. Such groups have played a wonderful and significant role in the furtherance of the gospel. But the base for reaching the world, according to the New Testament, is the local church.

The apostle Paul planted churches wherever he went. His letters are to churches or leaders of churches. In Revelation, Jesus addressed churches. There is much in the New Testament to give guidance to those leading local churches.

Second, some people see the church as irrelevant. Many today are down on the church. And it is true that some churches are irrelevant. I have seen some whose favorite hymns must be "I Shall Not Be Moved," because they won't do anything for God! But the church is God's idea, and we dare not run ahead of him! When a local church is the church as God intended—not perfect, but functioning as the body of Christ—nothing is more powerful for reaching a community for Christ. Even as I am finishing this chapter, I am on a plane returning from a strong, vibrant, evangelistic church. There is nothing on earth that can substitute for it! What an awesome tool it is in the hand of God!

Jesus is the head of the church. The pastor is not; the deacons are not; the charter members are not. The church is the visible manifestation of the kingdom of God in this age. A person cannot love Jesus and despise his church.

Third, some people today are victims of the "edifice complex." They see the church as a building—not people. The church is *not* at Fourth and Vine or on Main Street. The *building* is there. On Sunday morning, the church is *gathered* in that geographical location where the church facilities are. On Monday, the same church is *scattered*—on the job, at the store, at school, in the neighborhood. We must recapture this biblical ideal. It is hypocritical to sing praises to God with all our hearts on Sunday as the church gathered and say nothing about his goodness throughout the week as the church scattered. If the body of Christ acted throughout the week as we do in Sunday worship, what a difference it would make!

Fourth, some people make a sharp clergy-laity distinction that is not scriptural. Yes, God has set apart ministers to lead churches, but they are to *lead* the work—not *do* all the work. Ministers are to equip the saints to do the work of the ministry (see Eph. 4:11–12). Now, ministers are also saints, so we are to do the work also. Many ministers never share Christ with others. We must lead by example. I share my faith because I am a Christian; I preach and teach because I am a minister.

Fifth, there is sometimes an unhealthy and unbiblical emphasis on fellowship. This is particularly true in rural Baptist churches in the South where the most significant time in the church year is homecoming with dinner on the grounds! My aunt, a member of a rural Alabama Baptist church, once quipped that Baptists won't get to heaven without a paper plate in their hands! The New Testament does speak of fellowship meals, but these meals were held around the observance of the Lord's Supper—not in honor of Granny Smith's banana pudding.

Fellowship, as in biblical *koinonia,* is crucial. But fellowship is not built on food or by avoiding conflict, as in the sentiment, "Let's not hurt anybody's feelings." How do you build a great team? I grew up in Alabama, where Bear Bryant's football coaching was legendary. Alabama's teams never seemed to have the number of all-Americans that Notre Dame or Southern Cal did. Bryant's genius was in convincing good players to play like all-Americans. He could build a team with a clear focus. Their focus was on winning, and they were single-minded.

Do you want to build fellowship in your church? Then get a single-minded focus in the church—a focus on reaching people for Christ. The early church shared Christ in one accord at Pentecost. When they faced persecution, they united in prayer for boldness to speak the Word of God (see Acts 4:29–31).

ESCHATOLOGY

If you were involved in a church in the 1970s, you probably remember the eschatological fever associated with the Jesus Movement. The most popular saying at that time was "one way!" The second biggest saying was "Jesus is coming soon—are you ready?" The eschatological chorus, "I Wish We'd All Been Ready" was the signature song of this movement. I know many people who came to Christ during those days out of concern that they would not be ready when the Lord returned.

This was also the conviction of the early church. The imminent return of Christ was one of the motives for their evangelism, and it should be for us as well. Jesus declared that the gospel must be preached all around the world, and then the end will come (see Matt. 24:14). The Lord Jesus tied evangelism to the end of the world and the coming of Christ.

The Doctrine of Eternal Punishment
in Contemporary Evangelicalism

The most deceptive and destructive shift in the evangelical church in our day is a reinterpretation of the biblical doctrine of divine retribution. Such a shift is the result of a radical move in the modern era from a conviction about absolute truth to moral and theological relativism. "Lying between the middle of the nineteenth century," says David Wells, "to the middle of our own century is a historical divide."[14] This divide came as a result of the Enlightenment. "The real outcome of the Enlightenment, however, has not been the preservation of noble values but their collapse into complete relativism."[15] Add to this the effects of Darwinism and Einstein's theory of relativity, along with the whole revelation caused by quantum physics, and the result is a lack of conviction about certainty.

While we are currently shifting in culture from modernity to postmodernity (see chapter 14), the legacy of the Enlightenment looms large. According to Wells, this is obvious with regard to theology.

> It is not that the elements of the evangelical creeds have vanished, they have not. The fact that they are professed, however, does not necessarily mean that the structure of the historic Protestant faith is still intact. The reason, quite simply, is that while these items of belief are professed, they are increasingly being removed from the center of evangelical life where they defined what life was, and they are now being relegated to the periphery where their power to define what evangelical life should be is lost. . . . It is evangelical *practice* rather than evangelical profession that reveals the change.[16]

As a result, other views beyond the historic Christian understanding of divine judgment and hell have been offered as more suitable for the modern day. Universalism is the belief that ultimately no human being will be lost. Some people are universalists because they believe all humanity is intrinsically good and thus will be "redeemed." Others argue that Christ's death was necessary but that his death was for all humanity—period. What then is the historical, biblical position? *Explicit faith in Christ in this life is necessary for salvation*. Karl Marx once said, "He who controls the definitions controls the movement." American culture is decidedly favorable toward universalism.

Why is this view becoming so popular? Beougher notes several reasons:

- human nature
- pluralistic culture
- lack of biblical authority
- the vastness of the missionary task[17]

Earlier forms of universalism emphasized the goodness of man and held that he is too good for God to damn; more recent forms affirm that God is too good to damn man. Some people don't espouse these views explicitly but wish they were true. Some universalists actually make their argument from Scripture, emphasizing

- God's desire to save all people (1 Tim. 2:4; 2 Pet. 3:9);
- Jesus' death for all people (John 12:32); and
- God's promise to save all people (Eph. 1:10).

Of course, a plethora of texts illustrate the uniqueness of the gospel and the reality of eternal judgment.

More dangerous for evangelism is a practical universalism in churches. We live as if all people are saved. On the other hand, it is just as bad to live as if we don't care whether people are lost.

Pluralism is the view that salvation can come through a variety of religious traditions.[18] That is, devout people, whether Hindus, Buddhists, or Christians, will be saved. John Hick says there is a Copernican revolution in theology, in which we must move from Christocentrism to Theocentrism. Therefore, Hick says, Christian distinctives must end.

The problem with pluralism is that even pluralists, though emphasizing tolerance, are not willing to accept *any* religious system. Some systems, such as the Peoples' Temple of Jim Jones, fail to be good enough. Ronald Nash notes that "pluralists have not identified a criterion to mark the line between authentic and inauthentic 'responses to the Transcendent' clearly enough to make it work on a broad scale."[19]

Further, pluralism fails to note the obvious contradictions in any serious examination of religious systems. Compare the eightfold path of Buddhism, the five pillars of Islam, and the Book of Romans, for example.[20] The most pressing problem for pluralism from the Christian perspective is the obvious and clear declaration that Jesus Christ is the only way to God (John 14:6, Acts 4:12).

The problem with these philosophies is that they ignore the claims of Scripture, and they reduce all religions to meaningless-ness—all have exclusivistic tendencies.

We live in a day when hell is generally nothing more than another curse word. Woody Allen said, "Hell is Manhattan at rush hour." The *Western Report* had an article entitled "Soft-Selling Hell: Don't Worry, It's Really No Worse Than a Three-Star Hotel."

What does the New Testament say about hell? The Greek term *Gehenna* is used twelve times to refer to hell. The term *eternal* is used sixty-four times with heaven and seven times with hell. It takes no hermeneutical genius to understand that both are considered eternal. Part of our problem today is that we make God after our personality.

Another view that undermines the biblical conviction of divine retribution is *annihilationism*. All people are resurrected, according to this view, but the impenitent will ultimately cease to exist. John Stott holds this view tentatively, while Clark Pinnock and Michael Green hold it tenaciously. Stott, in *Evangelical Pathbreaking,* argued, "Would there not, then, be a serious disproportion between sins consciously committed in time and torment consciously experienced throughout eternity."[21]

The fallacy of this view is that Stott sees sins as crimes, and the punishment should fit the crime. In contrast, Jonathan Edwards, in his sermon "The Justice of God in the Damnation of Sinners," taught that sin is infinite because it is against an infinite God; therefore, we cannot argue that the punishment must meet the crime in an earthly manner.

Let me offer this counsel on this difficult issue.

- Get your view of eternal punishment from the Bible. Jesus knew more about the love of God than anyone, yet he spoke more on hell than heaven.

- Preach the subject of hell—to the church! Teach sin from the perspective of God. Renew your passion for the lost. Never forget God's grace in redeeming us.

Why is this critical? Because that which is neglected by this generation is rejected by the next.

Perhaps the greatest theological threat to the church today is *inclusivism,* or the belief in a wider hope for those who have not heard of Christ. Evangelicals are increasingly adopting such views. J. D. Hunter in *Evangelicalism: The Coming Generation,* found one of three evangelicals held to a wider-hope view of soteriology—that people who have not heard the gospel can be saved apart from its message.[22]

"Inclusivists agree with pluralists that God's salvation is not restricted to the relatively few people who hear the gospel and believe in Jesus Christ," Nash writes. "Inclusivists agree with exclusivists that God's universally accessible salvation is nonetheless grounded on the person of Jesus Christ and his redemptive work."[23] Clark Pinnock is the foremost advocate of this position among evangelicals.

I would argue that the adoption of inclusivism by Pinnock, John Sanders, and others qualifies them as *former* evangelicals. One of my colleagues refers to such individuals as "post-evangelicals."[24] Pinnock argues, "What God really cares about is faith and not theology."[25] The argument that he and Sanders makes is that the death of Jesus for sins is ontologically necessary; it need not be revealed to individuals epistemologically. Others argue from philosophy that Jesus Christ is the only Savior, but many more people will be saved than exclusivists think.

This so-called "optimistic hermeneutic" makes a distinction between Christ's *ontological* work (what he did, necessity of the atonement) and *epistemological* work (what we need to know about the cross). It gives a salvation role to general revelation.

Consider the following story to illustrate this problem. Two young women from southern California spent the day Christmas shopping in Tijuana, a Mexican border town several miles below San Diego. After a successful day of bargain-hunting, they returned to their car. One of the ladies glanced in the gutter and noticed something moving as if in pain. As they bent down and looked closer, the two women saw what appeared to be a dog—a tiny Chihuahua—struggling for its life. Their hearts went out to the pathetic little animal. Their compassion wouldn't let them leave it there to die.

They decided to take it home with them and do their best to nurse it back to health. Afraid of being stopped and having the dog detected by border patrol officers, they placed it on some papers among their packages in the trunk of their car. Within minutes they were back in California and only a couple of hours from home. One of the women held the sick little Chihuahua the rest of the way home.

As they pulled up in front of the first woman's home, they decided she would be the one to keep and tend the little orphan through the night. She tried feeding it some of her food, but it wouldn't eat. She patted it, talked to it, cuddled it, and finally wrapped it in a blanket and placed it beneath the covers on her bed to sleep beside her through the night. She kept feeling the dog to make sure it was OK.

The next morning the woman decided to take it to an emergency animal clinic nearby. As she handed the weakened animal to the doctor on duty, he quickly interrupted her and asked, "Where did you *get* this animal?"

"We were shopping in Tijuana and found this little Chihuahua in the gutter near our car."

"This is no Chihuahua, young lady. What you brought home is a rabid Mexican river rat!"

What appeared to be harmless to these two young women proved to be extremely dangerous.[26] The *ontological* reality that they were endangered by a rabid Mexican rat made a difference only when they had it shown to them *epistemologically!*

We must never allow culture to dictate to us the character of God.

APPLICATION

In the kinder, gentler culture in which we live, conviction is touted as a vice, while tolerance is seen as a virtue. God has become so sentimentalized that he has lost his sovereign nature, even in the church. Many scholars, even from within the evangelical camp, are espousing views of the judgment of God that would have been considered heretical in previous generations. We are too easily swayed by our own humanness; we too quickly underestimate the greatness of God.

Consider those people whom you lead, even as you examine yourself. Does theology have a proper place in your Christianity? In your evangelism? We must always return to the foundational question: What does the Bible say about this?

BIBLIOGRAPHY

Brown, Harold O. J. *Heresies.* Garden City, N.J.: Doubleday, 1984.

Carson, D. A. *The Gagging of God.* Grand Rapids: Zondervan, 1996.

Drummond, Lewis A. *The Word of the Cross: A Contemporary Theology of Evangelism.* Nashville: Broadman & Holman, 1993.

Packer, J. I. *Evangelism and the Sovereignty of God.* Chicago: InterVarsity Press, 1961.

Poe, Harry L. *The Gospel and Its Meaning.* Grand Rapids: Zondervan, 1996.

Part 2

HOW WE MUST LIVE:
THE SPIRITUAL BASIS OF EVANGELISM

D avid Livingstone sat at his father's knee and heard stories of great people of faith.[1] As a teenager in Scotland, David began to pray this prayer: "God, send me anywhere, only go with me. Lay any burden on me, only sustain me. And sever any tie in my heart except the tie that binds my heart to yours." He met Mary Moffat, told her of his passion, and together they went to Africa.

Soon after they arrived in Africa, Mary Moffat grew very ill. Having had two children and unable to handle the rigors of life in Africa, she said, "Oh, David, I must go back to England. What are you going to do?"

Livingstone replied, "The smoke of the fires of a thousand villages in the African morning sun haunts my soul." And she said, "Then, David, you've got to stay." He said, "I'll join you back in England in a few months." But those few months turned into a year, and that year to two, and then to three and four.

When Livingstone returned to England, the queen of England said when he walked into the royal throne room of Great Britain, it was as though the presence of God had been ushered in. A lion had mauled his arm, and he had lost one eye to the jungle brush. After he had been home only a few months, his wife Mary asked, "David, where are you?" And again he said, "The haunting smoke of a thousand villages in the African morning sun haunts the soul within me." And she said, "Then let's go back." Not long after they returned, Mary Moffat Livingstone died.

David also died deep in the heart of Africa. The Africans carried his body through the jungles to a ship for its return to England where it now resides. But before they sent the body, they cut out his heart, and it was buried in Africa. The African people said, "His body may go, but his heart must stay, for he brought the heart of the gospel to the heart of our nation."

Our beliefs must be biblically grounded, and our evangelism methods must be effective. But our hearts must be filled with a passion for God.

Part 2 deals with the spiritual resources related to evangelism. A spiritual passion for evangelism is essential, as noted by Wesley Duewel: "All other passions build upon . . . your passion for Jesus. A passion for souls grows out of a passion for Christ."[2] John Wesley recognized this and shook a nation. He said, "Give me one hundred preachers who fear nothing but sin and desire nothing but God, and I care not a straw whether they be clergymen or laymen, such alone will shake the gates of hell and set up the kingdom of heaven on earth."[3]

6

Modeling the Gospel: The Character of the Witness

T he transformed character of Christian men and women is the key to world evangelization at the end of the twentieth century and beyond."[1] I heartily agree with these words of Leighton Ford. In the first century, the changed lives of believers played a vital role in their witness. Their fearlessness in the face of persecution, conviction before skeptics, integrity in a culture of ungodliness, and boldness to proclaim the gospel stands in sharp contrast to the mediocre lives of so many American Christians.

One striking characteristic of the first Christians was their reflection of Christ. When the Jewish religious leaders realized that Peter and John were unlearned and ignorant, "they marveled; and they realized that *they had been with Jesus*" (Acts 4:13, italics added). The character of Christ shined through the prism of their witness for him. Character apart from biblical truth lacks the heart of the Christian faith; but the truth of the gospel devoid of character is the epitome of hypocrisy.

While in Houston, we lived only thirty minutes from Six Flags. So when my son Joshua turned six, I took him to the theme park.

Our zeal clouded our judgment. I took Joshua up the Skyscreamer, a ride that lifts you up several stories and then drops you like a rock. About one millisecond into the drop, I knew it was a mistake. I was scared out of my wits, and Joshua was screaming and crying, scared to death. I promised him we would never take that ride again. He still reminds me of that promise at times!

Adventure is great, but we can push our limits. Christianity is the greatest adventure we will ever face. But it is an adventure fraught with challenges. Only the most disciplined person can traverse the path to godliness and be all that God has called him or her to be. We dare not follow Christ frivolously as if the choices we make have no consequence for our faith and our witness.

What are the marks of those who live the Christian life to the fullest? This chapter examines the very practical matters that make a big difference in evangelism. Skills, methods, and experience in evangelism are good; doctrine is essential. But the gospel presented by a believer whose life exemplifies the character of Christ is best.

The apostle Paul is the perfect model. You cannot separate the preaching of Paul from the character of his life. Paul addressed the leaders of the church at Ephesus (see Acts 20). This passage offers a glimpse into the role of the relationship between a person's lifestyle and his or her witness.

If there is one word that summarizes how we must reach this culture—from the Millennials, to the Generation Xers, to the aging Boomers, to the retiring Builders, it is this word: *real*. Be real. Believers must be real. Our culture is sick of phonies. The world is not looking for Christians who are perfect; they are looking for Christians who are real, who demonstrate a changed life, whose lives give honor to Christ.

Some believers fail to witness because they know there are issues in their lives that bring reproach to the name of Christ. While some mistakenly think they have to be on some higher spiritual plane before they can witness, there are issues of obedience we must face to be effective in personal evangelism.

In a post-Christian world, people need a demonstration of the gospel that accompanies an explanation of its truth. Some people don't attend our churches because they are afraid they may become like us! They are still without excuse, but we are also accountable for our behavior. I agree with those who say the chief mark of character is self-control. Great saints in history have been marked by an awareness of the role of Christian character.

The Life of the Witness

- Robert Murray McCheyne: "Lord, make me as holy as a saved sinner can be."[2]
- R. A. Torrey: "Power is lost through self-indulgence. The one who would have God's power must lead a life of self-denial."[3]
- Spurgeon: "Whatever 'call' a man may pretend to have, if he has not been called to holiness, he certainly has not been called to the ministry."[4]

What are the building blocks of Christian character? Paul's counsel in Acts 20 guides us.

INTEGRITY

Paul told the Ephesian Christians: *"You know* how I served the Lord" (Acts 20:19). He was not bragging; he was stating reality. They had watched him three years. Paul went on to say, "I have coveted no one's silver or gold or apparel" (Acts 20:33). One of my best friends in the ministry, Steve Gaines, made this statement to one of my classes: "You will spend half your life in ministry just staying out of trouble." Now that seems so obvious, but I had never thought of it like that. A significant part of serving God is avoiding those things that pull us away from him.

This is especially true of evangelism. The first thing an individual, a church, or a denomination loses is commitment to evangelism. Only a life demonstrating the character of Christ will keep evangelism as a priority. D. L. Moody, the great evangelist, knew this. He once said that character is what you are in the dark. If our motives are impure, they will eventually be discovered. Paul's evangelism was consistent with his life.

Let me give two historical vignettes to demonstrate this point.

G. Campbell Morgan told of that great English actor Macready. An eminent preacher once said to the actor: "What is the reason for the difference between you and me? You are appearing before crowds night after night with fiction, and the crowds come wherever you go. I am preaching the essential and unchangeable truth, and I am not getting any crowd at all."

Macready replied: "This is quite simple. I present my *fiction* as though it were *truth;* you present your *truth* as though it were *fiction.*"[5]

A more positive picture of the impact of integrity is told by Duewel:

> A British nobleman was passing through a village in Cornwall, England, and after searching in vain for a place to purchase alcoholic beverages, asked a villager, "How is it that I cannot get a glass of liquor in this wretched village of yours?" The old man, recognizing the rank of the stranger, respectfully took off his cap and bowed. . . . "My lord, something over a hundred years ago a man named John Wesley came to these parts." The peasant then turned and walked away.[6]

John Wesley was a man of small stature but great character.

HUMILITY

Paul said to the Ephesian elders, "I served the Lord with great humility" (Acts 20:19 NIV). In ministry, the greatest temptation is the desire for status. That is one of the major hindrances to evangelism in the church. Many churches today are hindered in their evangelism because key laypersons as well as ministry staff are more concerned with their personal standing than the evangelistic growth of the Lord's church. Pride hinders evangelism.

Early in ministry, we typically say, "Why me, Lord?" surprised that God would save and use people like us. But as we become experienced, educated, and inflated, we are more tempted to say, "Why *not* me, Lord?" wondering why we were overlooked for this or that position.

I was brought to tears by a student in my spiritual awakening course. A big, strong, handsome guy who had been radically saved for only three years, Brad was a bona fide "Jesus freak." In our prayer time, Brad shared with the class that the church he attended had called him to be a youth intern. Most in that class were pastors or were serving the Lord in a variety of staff positions beyond "intern." But this was Brad's first position. With a gleam in his eye, and childlike wonder, he told the class: "I feel like a lottery pick in the NBA draft. I can't believe a church would ask me to serve on its staff." Brad's humility and awe at the call of God is a glowing example of a humble life.

My heroes are men like Roy Fish, my major professor at Southwestern Seminary, a man of God; Robert Coleman, who wrote *The Master Plan of Evangelism;* Bill Bright of Campus Crusade for Christ; and Billy Graham. You know why these men in their sixties and seventies are in their greatest years? Because they have humility. Humility helps us finish well.

PASSION

Paul said to the Ephesians, "I served the Lord with great humility *and with tears*" (Acts 20:19 NIV). "So be on your guard, and remember that for three years I never stopped warning each of you night and day with tears" (Acts 20:31 NIV). See the passion of Paul: "And see, now I go bound in the spirit to Jerusalem, not knowing the things that will happen to me there" (v. 22). For what are you passionate? What drives you? What causes you great joy? Is it a passion for God? You will never overcome the rejection that comes with evangelism apart from a passion for God.

People who have been used of God, particularly in times of great revival, came from different backgrounds, traditions, and educational experiences. Yet they had in common a deep passion for God. One thing I try to do at least once a year is read a biography of a great saint: someone like Jonathan Edwards, Whitefield, or Moody. I look for the reason God used them so effectively.

One thing I've discovered about these people is that they all had a passion for God. They were very zealous toward their heavenly Father. Consider what George Whitefield, that great preacher in the First Great Awakening, wrote in his journal: "I was honored today with having a few stones, dirt, rotten eggs, and pieces of dead cats thrown at me."[7]

What about Paul? He had a passion for evangelism: "You know that I have not hesitated to preach anything that would be helpful to you" (Acts 20:20, NIV). "I have declared that they must turn to God in repentance and have faith" (Acts 20:21 NIV). Can I get a witness? Again, let's go to Whitefield. Whitefield said, "God forbid that I should travel with anyone a quarter of an hour without speaking to them about Christ."[8] What about passion for the gospel? Paul said, "I have declared . . . that they must turn to God in repentance and have faith in our Lord Jesus" (Acts 20:21 NIV).

Consider that monk, Martin Luther. See Luther standing before the Diet of Worms and listen to what he said: "My conscience is captive to the word of God. I cannot and will not recant anything, for to go against conscience is neither right nor safe. Here I stand. I cannot do otherwise. God help me. Amen."[9]

I'm convinced that the main reason Christians never witness is that we have *gotten over Jesus.* It's just that simple.

Consider what Jonathan Edwards, that fiery, brilliant Puritan, said: "Two things exceedingly needful in ministers as they would go about any great matters to advance the kingdom of Christ are zeal and resolution. . . . A man of but ordinary capacity will do more with zeal and resolution than one of ten times the parts in learning without them. More may be done in a few days or at least weeks than can be done without them in many years. Those fewer possessed of them carry the day in almost all affairs."[10]

People may listen to the preacher's preaching, but they will follow his passion. Puritan pastor Richard Baxter wrote: "That will be most in their ears, which is most in your hearts."[11] A colleague was preaching a revival meeting in a church in the Midwest. The church had no pastor, so the song leader led in the service. During the announcements, he exhorted the people to bring someone on Tuesday night. He enthusiastically called all the members to go into the highway and hedges and compel them to come.

A little girl about six years old spoke up, not realizing she was talking so loudly everyone could hear her. "Well, who are you going to bring, Brother Joe?" she innocently asked, referring to the song leader. He paused, his face turning red. He looked down, then announced the next hymn and went on with the service.

On Tuesday night, only two people brought a guest, and one was brought by the guest evangelist! People may hear our words, but they will follow our passion. Our passion is more important than our technique.

Duewel writes, in his book *Ablaze for God*: "A passionless Christianity will not put out the fires of hell. The best way to fight a raging forest fire is with fire."[12] He continues:

> There is no greater need in our churches and schools today. It is not enough to be evangelical in

faith and heart; we must be totally possessed by Christ, utterly impassioned by His love and grace, utterly ablaze with His power and glory.

We do not need wildfire; wildfire does not glorify our holy Christ. It is holy fire, the fire with which the Holy Spirit baptizes us. We need the fire and zeal of the early church when almost every Christian was ready. . . . to be a martyr for Christ.[13]

Duewel also declares:

When William Booth . . . was asked by the king of England what the ruling force of his life was, he replied, "Sir, some men's passion is for gold, other men's passion is for fame, but my passion is for souls."

A notorious British murderer was sentenced to die. The morning of his execution the prison chaplain walked beside him to the gallows and routinely read some Bible verses. The prisoner was shocked that the chaplain was so perfunctory, unmoved, and uncompassionate in the shadow of the scaffold. He said to the preacher, "Sir, if I believed what you and the church say you believe, even if England was covered with glass from coast to coast, . . . I would walk over it—if need be on my hands and knees—and think it worthwhile, just to save one soul from an eternal hell like that."[14]

PURITY

Paul's testimony to the Ephesian elders (see Acts 20) is a model of purity. A life of personal holiness and purity is essential for effective soul-winning.

In an interview in *Christianity Today* (July 10, 1987), a church leader discussed those issues that contributed to his failure in this area:

It was a number of things. From about 1982 on I was desperately weary in spirit and body. I was working harder and enjoying it less. Satan's ability to

distort the heart and the mind is beyond belief. I
assume the responsibility for what I did; I made
those decisions out of a distorted heart. In addition,
*I now realize I was lacking in mutual accountability
through personal relationships. We need friendships
where one man regularly looks another man in the
eye and asks hard questions about our moral life, our
ambitions, our ego.*

Ecclesiastes 4:9–10 offers helpful advice: "Two are better than
one, because they have a good reward for their labor. For if they
fall, one will lift up his companion. But woe to him who is alone
when he falls, for he has no one to lift him up."

We must keep ourselves in an environment where we are open
to correction. Years ago I heard of a preacher who acted holier than
he was. You know the type—he was a legend in his own mind. He
insisted on being called "Reverend," and he talked with that eccle-
siastical twang even *outside* the pulpit.

One day the "Reverend" was taking a walk. He came upon a
group of boys standing around a dog. "What are you lads doing?"
asked the preacher in the most pious tone. "We are telling lies,
preacher," one little boy said. "We all want the dog, so the biggest
liar gets to keep it." The minister was shocked. "I can't believe this!"
he said. "You boys must know that I have never done something so
terrible as to tell a lie—never!"

The boys looked at each other and nodded their heads. "OK,
preacher, you can have the dog."

I had the privilege of hosting a Paul-Timothy conference in
Houston during 1995. Thirty pastors sat at the feet of three effective
ministers: John Morgan of Sagemont Church in Houston, John
Bisagno of Houston's First Baptist, and Fenton Moorhead of the
Sugar Creek Baptist Church in Sugar Land, Texas. Heed the words
of John Bisagno: "My father-in-law, with three earned doctorates, a
Baptist preacher, said only 1 out of 10 men who started in ministry
at 21 is in it at 65. I didn't believe it. I wrote the names of 25 men
I knew in college. Today only 5 survived, and we're not 65 yet."
Bisagno added the four pitfalls believers should diligently avoid:

- Sex

- Money

- Discouragement

- Ambition

I have an evangelist friend with a great burden for an awakening in our day. Years ago he studied in Edinburgh, Scotland. He visited the tiny principality of Wales, which has been visited with mighty revival several times in the modern era. He discovered a lady who had been converted in the Welsh Revival of 1904–05 as a little girl, and who knew Evan Roberts personally. Roberts was a principal human agent in the Welsh Revival.

My friend sat in the little cottage of the elderly woman. "What was the secret of Evan Robert's power?" he asked. She simply looked into her fireplace, and in her thick Welsh accent, replied, "Mr. Roberts was a very godly man."

"Yes, I know that, but tell me more. Why did God use him?"

The lady continued to look into the fire. "God used Mr. Roberts because he was a godly man," she said.

My friend was frustrated. Pressing further, he said, "Yes, I know, but tell me specifics. How did he pray? What did he do?"

The elderly lady turned and faced my friend. "Young man," she said sternly, "the reason God used Mr. Evan Roberts was that he was a very, very godly man." Finally he got the point. You can be gifted as a preacher, an organizer, a leader, but there is no substitute for godliness.

CONVICTION

Paul told the Ephesian elders he held back nothing from them. He made his convictions clear. When I was a teenager, my high school class was the first in Alabama to begin mandatory driver's education. One of our assignments was watching a gruesome film that consisted of photographs of automobile accidents involving young people who were drinking and driving. It showed tremendous carnage, burned bodies, decapitations. It was horrible.

When we left that film, we were convinced we would never drive that way and end up like that. But, in the months to come, we got our licenses, and not everyone drove the way we said we would.

This is a familiar scenario—repeated in many settings. Some people live by conviction, while others live by intention.

How do we live a life of conviction? Here are three simple principles.

1. *Live by principle, not by feelings.* We pray because it is important, not because we feel "spiritual" all the time. We should witness out of obedience—not because we are comfortable doing it. Our character must grow out of convictions hammered on the anvil of the Word of God.

2. *Listen to God, not to popular opinion.* Even in the church, popular opinion can be wrong. We live in a culture driven by popular opinion polls. Our political leaders make decisions by these polls. Further, with the proliferation of talk shows on television, call-in shows, radio talk shows, and Internet chat rooms, individual opinions have displaced the Word of God for many people. But it doesn't matter in the final analysis what Oprah Winfrey, or Rush Limbaugh, or even the President of the United States believes. What really matters is what God says.

3. *Prioritize sacrifice rather than comfort.* Again, our culture leads us astray at this point. The path of least resistance is the rule, not the exception. The typical approach is, "How much do I have to do to get by at the job?" "Just let me pass the course; I don't care how much I learn."

A man and his wife went to the doctor. The man had a serious illness. Finally, the doctor found the problem, diagnosed it as very serious, and brought the wife in first to talk to her. "Your husband has a rare condition," he said, "and he will die unless you do certain things. First of all, you have to sterilize everything in your home, and you'll have to do that on a regular basis. Second, you will have to prepare special meals. These meals are not easy to prepare, and it's going to take some time. Third, you must wash everything in the house every week in a special solution that's very expensive. Finally, you're going to have to wait on his every need and take care of him in every way. If you don't do this, he has only a few weeks to live."

While they were driving home the husband asked, "What did the doctor say?" "Honey," she replied, "he said you only have a few weeks to live." Human nature takes the easiest path.

4. *Consider the long-term consequence of your decisions.* Compromise is birthed in the maternity ward of immediacy. I tell my students that it is not where they are but where they are headed that matters. We must keep our eyes on the long haul of ministry.

If evangelism is important to you, your conviction will stand in the face of anything that seeks to lead you astray. Billy Graham passed through a serious time of spiritual testing shortly before his Los Angeles crusade. His friend Charles Templeton had rejected the authority of Scripture and ridiculed Graham's convictions. After a time of struggle, Graham experienced personal revival and a deep time of consecration to the Word of God. Following a talk with a Christian leader, Graham placed his Bible on a stump, declaring, "I accept this book by faith as the Word of God."[15] From that point on Graham was ready for God to use him in an uncommon manner. His convictions have guided his life.

PRIORITIES

Paul indicated his priority in his address to the Ephesian elders: "So that I may finish my race with joy, and the ministry which I received from the Lord Jesus" (Acts 20:24). We have almost made busyness a spiritual gift. Calendar planners are like the Bible to most people in our culture. The truth is that if you don't control your time, someone else will. And if you don't live by your priorities, you will die at the hand of circumstances.

John Morgan of Sagemont Church in Houston illustrated the many forces tugging at our time. "I remember a personnel committee meeting. One person said, 'Be careful about overextending yourself.' Another said, 'Your ministry comes first.' Another said, 'Your family is your ministry.'"

Morgan's dad, a pastor, took him deer hunting the day the season began every season since he was six years old. He spent time with his son. After decades of pastoring, John determined one of the greatest things his church did was to set aside each Thursday for family night. "We have designed our churches to destroy our families," he told a group of young ministers. "I went eighteen years before I took a vacation. It was the most foolish thing I ever did."

How do you know if your family is the priority it should be? Can you write what your wife is looking forward to? Your children? "I give my wife my day off," says Fenton Moorhead. "It's not for me; it's for her." He adds,

> In the seventies, in student ministry, I was gone every night of the week, speaking in schools, winning awards. One night Mary said, "You know everyone's kids better than your own." I left mad, came back in fifteen minutes, and we talked. We moved to North Carolina and began a retreat center. That probably saved our marriage. My family is first. My kids are serving the Lord. The 2959 plan by Peter Lord taught me to pray daily for my kids. God has answered scores of requests.[16]

Those of us in ministry must avoid the temptation of seeing ourselves as more significant than our spouses due to our calling. In our driven culture, failing to live by our priorities can sap our evangelistic effectiveness.

If you are biblical and godly in the way you treat your family, you will treat the things of God, especially the gospel, in a godly manner as well. John Bisagno once told me that his sons recalled the greatest day of their lives was when he bought a new boat and took them out of school two hours early to go fishing. Howard Hendricks once asked his adult children to name the most significant memory of him from their childhood. Their reply was not some deep theological truth he taught them; it was those times he got on the floor and wrestled with them!

Bisagno advises: "Every day, do something in your spouse's world. Wash dishes, go buy gas, something that touches her world." Paige Patterson gave me excellent counsel about time with my kids. He said to find out what they really like, then do it with them. So I am a soccer coach for my son—bad hip and all—and I play lots of games with Hannah!

If your life is not guided by priorities, you will never keep evangelism in its rightful place in your life.

ATTITUDE

Notice Paul's attitude regardless of what he faced. Knowing persecution awaited him, he said his desire was to "finish my race with joy" (Acts 20:24). The greatest hindrance to our personal evangelism is our attitude. On the other hand, the greatest aid to our witness is an attitude that honors Christ. Further, sour attitudes do much to disrupt the fellowship of the body of Christ. We are responsible for our attitudes.

We should never ignore significant hardships or times of pain. There is a time to hurt, to have sorrow, to be provoked because of ungodliness. But how many times do things of little consequence fuel our disposition and cause negative reactions?

A homeless tramp wandered into a quaint old English village. He stopped by a pub called the Inn of St. George and the Dragon.

"Please, ma'am, could you spare me a bite to eat?" he asked the lady who answered his knock at the kitchen door.

"For a sorry, no-good bum—a foul-smelling beggar? No!" she snapped as she almost slammed the door on his hand.

Halfway down the lane the tramp stopped, turned around, and eyed the words, "St. George and the Dragon." He went back and knocked on the kitchen door again.

"Now what do you want?" the woman growled.

"Well, ma'am, if St. George is in, may I speak with *him* this time?"

Here are some principles concerning our attitude.

1. *I am responsible for my attitude.* Our culture teaches us to blame others for our mistakes. I cannot always control my circumstances, but I can control my attitude.

2. *My attitude is either my friend or my enemy.* A man moved with his family to a new town. He asked a resident, "What are people around here like?"

   "What are they like where you come from?"

   "Really nice."

   "That's the way they are here."

   Another man moved in the next week and spoke to the same resident.

   "What are people like here?" the new citizen asked.

   "What are they like where you come from?"

   "Not friendly at all."

"That's the way they are here." The resident knew attitude makes the difference.

3. *I must constantly correct my attitude.* Paul faced times of discouragement. Your commitment to evangelism must overcome seasons of lean harvests and disappointments. Otherwise, despair and even bitterness can sap the life from us. Bitterness can ruin the witness of any Christian.

4. *My attitude is contagious.* While teaching at Houston Baptist University, I was privileged to have a young lady from Africa attend my required classes in Old Testament, New Testament, and Christian doctrine. She was a devout Muslim when we met. I shared Christ with her. While she seemed uninterested, I sought to live a contagious Christian life before her.

On the bottom of her final exam in Christian doctrine, she left me a note that thrills me to this day. "Dr. Reid, thank you for how you have spoken to me in your life. I now know that Jesus Christ is God's Son, and have given my life to Him. I have never been so happy!"

The key to reaching this young lady, more than my arguments, was a contagious Christian attitude.

5. *My attitude reflects my walk with God.* A person's relationship with God is not determined by church attendance or position, as important as they are. What really matters is the attitude we convey toward the things that matter to God, toward circumstances, toward the gospel. Therefore, our attitude affects our witness.

APPLICATION

Mike Landry was evangelism director for the Ohio Baptist Convention for many years. Mike was an atheist in the early seventies and late sixties, but he came to Christ through the Jesus Movement. Mike told me that the only difference between his life and those Christians he went to high school with was that he didn't have to get up early on Sunday morning. He got to sleep in—that was the only difference. But then after going off to college a year, he came back and he saw a change in some students' lives. The Jesus Movement had occurred, and some of the young people he knew had been radically changed. This led to a series of events that ultimately resulted in his conversion.

Mike's story demonstrates how a person's lifestyle can affect his or her witness among lost people.

Here is a practical exercise that can help you analyze your current lifestyle. Perhaps this will lead you to measure whether the character of Christ transcends your own agenda. Using the following grid, record how you spend your time during the next three weeks.

	SUN.	MON.	TUES.	WED.	THUR.	FRI.	SAT.
6:00 A.M.							
7:00 A.M.							
8:00 A.M.							
9:00 A.M.							
10:00 A.M.							
11:00 A.M.							
12:00 P.M.							
1:00 P.M.							
2:00 P.M.							
3:00 P.M.							
4:00 P.M.							
5:00 P.M.							
6:00 P.M.							
7:00 P.M							
8:00 P.M.							
9:00 P.M.							
10:00 P.M.							
11:00 P.M.							

Bibliography

One of the best ways to keep a focus on our character and its effect on evangelism is to study the life and writings of great Christians, including these:

Dallimore, Arnold. *George Whitefield.* 2 volumes. Edinburgh: Banner of Truth, 1980.

Pollock, John. *Moody.* Chicago: Moody Press, 1963.

Whitefield, George. *George Whitefield's Journals.* Edinburgh: Banner of Truth, 1960.

7

The Great Commission or the Great Suggestion? Evangelism as a Spiritual Discipline

Christianity has not so much been tried and found wanting, as it has been found difficult and left untried."[1] These words of G. K. Chesterton relate to the Christian life in general and to evangelism in particular. But Dallas Willard is right in noting that "we would do far better to lay a clear, constant emphasis on the cost of *non*-discipleship as well."[2] The subject of spiritual disciplines has become one of the topics of great interest in recent years. Richard Foster's *Celebration of Discipline* and Dallas Willard's *The Spirit of the Disciplines* have helped to bring a renewed interest in disciplined Christian living in an undisciplined culture. Don Whitney's *Spiritual Disciplines for the Christian Life,* which includes evangelism as a discipline, is this author's favorite.

Related studies such as *Experiencing God* by Henry Blackaby and Claude King, which focus on developing an intimacy with God, have been popular in the last few years. Such emphases have helped to shift the focus for many believers away from a "what's-in-it-for-me" attitude to a more biblical concept of living focused on honoring the will of God.

Spiritual disciplines refer to the New Testament reality that, while we are saved by God's grace, we are called to live lives worthy of our calling. Discipline in our day is considered a vice more than a virtue. Many people think of discipline in negative terms—with images of monks cloistered in seclusion, stern-jawed Olympic hopefuls who have given up a "normal" life for their goals, and so on. We may admire such people to some extent; we just don't want to pay the price to be *like* them. Give us an infomercial-style holiness—five minutes a day to become like Jesus—that is the Christianity too many of us crave.

Foster notes that the key to the disciplines is not sternness but joy: "The purpose of the Disciplines is *liberation* from the stifling slavery to self-interest and fear. . . . Singing, dancing, even shouting characterize the disciplines of the spiritual life."[3] Disciplines give focus and structure to the heart of what Christianity is: a personal, intimate relationship with our Creator. The disciplines give focus to the larger view of Christianity. Rather than focusing on specific details that look "Christian," such as turning the other cheek or going the second mile, the disciplines produce that "sort of life from which behavior such as loving one's enemy will seem like the only sensible and happy thing to do."[4] As Whitney puts it, "Discipline without direction is drudgery."[5]

Discipline for the sake of discipline leads to bondage and legalism. However, a lack of discipline leads to an unproductive life at best and a shipwrecked life at worst. Discipline is never an end in itself; it is a means to a greater good. An athlete is disciplined to win the race; a student is disciplined to learn important truths; a couple is disciplined to enjoy a long and joyful life together. And a Christian is disciplined because such a life leads to true intimacy with God.

Our Lord Jesus knew something of a disciplined life. Read the Gospel of Matthew, and see how Jesus responded to people. He had great compassion for the multitudes, always making himself available to them. He had little positive to say to the Pharisees and other religious hypocrites; note his scathing attack of them in Matthew 23. But there is another group: those who are committed to follow Jesus. Read the Sermon on the Mount and see the standard he expected of his disciples. Read his words in Luke 9:23

(NIV): "If anyone come after me, he must follow me, deny himself and take up his cross and daily follow me." There is a cost, to quote Deitrich Bonhoeffer, to discipleship.

The examples of great believers in Scripture also give witness to the importance of discipline. Behold Joseph, who was victimized over and over again, yet he never saw himself as a victim. How could this be? Joseph had great faith coupled with a disciplined life. Look at Moses, Daniel, and Paul. As you read about Whitefield, Edwards, Bunyan, and others, you find people who lived lives of great sacrifice.

Disciplines include the following, although the lists are not exhaustive. Note the slight differences among these three authors:

FOSTER:	WHITNEY:	WILLARD:
INWARD DISCIPLINES:	Bible Intake	DISCIPLINES
Meditation	Prayer	OF
Prayer	Worship	ABSTINENCE
Fasting	Evangelism	Solitude
Study	Serving	Silence
OUTWARD DISCIPLINES:	Stewardship	Fasting
Simplicity	Fasting	Frugality
Solitude	Silence and Solitude	Chastity
Submission	Journaling	Secrecy
Service	Learning	Sacrifice
CORPORATE DISCIPLINES:		DISCIPLINES
Confession		OF
Worship		ENGAGEMENT
Guidance		Study
Celebration		Worship
		Celebration
		Service
		Prayer
		Fellowship
		Confession
		Submission

Notice the disciplines are the same in some categories and quite different in others. Whitney, for example, includes evangelism as a discipline. I agree with him, and I will say more of this later. Disciplines have to do with those areas of spiritual growth in which we are to grow, through God's grace, into mature children of God.

Disciplines can be abused and become legalistic, binding, and even addictive. This is where corporate fellowship and worship with the body of Christ help us to maintain a balance. The disciplines are best attained in the context of personal accountability to a small group or a fellow believer. Legalism tears us down, emphasizing the times we miss our goal of godliness; accountability builds us up, focusing on our successes more than our failures.

Discipline composes an important part of all facets of life. What is true in education and in relationships is even more true in our walk with Christ. Paul told Timothy to discipline himself for the purpose of godliness (1 Tim. 4:7). The word for discipline in this verse is the Greek word translated as "gymnasium." The same discipline required for a healthy body is that necessary for a healthy Christian life. But, as important as a healthy body is, our spiritual health matters more, for it relates to eternal issues.

Second, we are not alone in our discipline. At our house, we have two exercise bikes, a treadmill, dumbbells, and ankle weights. They do little good. Why? Because we must be disciplined to use them. Don't you hate those infomercials with people like Chuck Norris and Christy Brinkley telling you to buy their product, when you *know* they are in such fabulous shape because they have a personal trainer? The greatest exercise help is another person to encourage us, to push us, to believe in us. I was in great shape in high school because my coach pushed me. Time in the weight room was not optional!

You may not have a personal trainer for your physical life, but you *do* have one for your spiritual life—the Holy Spirit! What did Jesus say? "When He comes, he will guide you into all truth." Solomon exhorted: "Apply your heart to instruction" (Prov. 23:12). The Holy Spirit of God will guide the serious believer who truly desires to "discipline himself for the purpose of godliness."

The greatest privilege we will experience is knowing Christ, being a child of God, having eternity in our hearts. And the greatest joy we can experience beyond conversion is seeing another person come to Christ. As evangelist J. Harold Smith said in our seminary chapel, leading someone to Christ is almost like getting saved all over again!

Still, the motivation of gratitude and the sense of privilege for being a herald of our great God are not the only reasons we share

Christ with others. Evangelism should be a disciplined part of our Christian life. When we are in school, we are held accountable. We take tests! We are required to be disciplined. I love to study, so I have stayed disciplined as a reader since finishing school. But it is easier to be disciplined when you have a teacher holding you accountable.

It is the same way in relationships. Many couples are disciplined in the way they treat one another while they are dating. But let them be married a few years, and see how they take each other for granted. Lack of discipline is the problem.

In this chapter we will examine several disciplines that play a significant role in personal evangelism.

THE DISCIPLINE OF STUDY

"The purpose of the Spiritual Disciplines is the total transformation of the person," writes Foster. "They aim at replacing old destructive habits of thought with new life-giving habits. Nowhere is this purpose more clearly seen than in the discipline of study."[6] The believer is to be transformed (see Rom. 12:2). How? By the renewing of the mind (see Phil. 4:8). In my own experience, the reading and study of the New Testament played a key role in my early commitment to evangelism. Too many believers are involved in the *trappings* of faith (church attendance, etc.) but live *defeated* lives. The battle is lost with the mind.

The foundation of study for the Christian is the Word of God. Studying alone is not the issue. What you study is crucial. Some people are "Gideon Christians," those who are always looking for signs. Others are "Mystical Christians," who live by "instinct" or feeling. Then there are "Guru Christians," who find a preacher they like, treat him like a spiritual guru, following him in print, sermons, and so on, as if his words are gospel. The need of the hour is for "Biblical Christians," who use Scripture as their guide.

I heard Paige Patterson, president of Southeastern Seminary, illustrate in a fascinating way how we have neglected the worth of the Bible. He told the congregation that he recently inherited a large sum of money unexpectedly. He offered $500,000 to any individual in the service that night who would do one thing—give up the Bible (he was talking to believers). "Is there anyone willing to give up reading the Bible, which means you can't read it, you can't quote it, you can't go hear it preached, you can't have any association with the Bible the rest of your life?" he asked. "Is there anyone here who's a believer who would be willing to do that? How many of you would be willing to do that?" No one volunteered to give up the Bible. Then he admitted:

> Well now, I've been living in Texas for a while, and one of the things you learn how to do in Texas is you learn how to lie. Now I really didn't inherit a lot of money, and I really don't have $500,000, but I wondered how many of you thought about the possibility of half a million dollars to give up the Bible. I think most of you would say there's no way you would spend the rest of your life apart from Scripture, the preaching of God's word. But if we wouldn't give it up for half a million dollars, *why don't we cherish it?* Why don't we read it? Why don't we take the opportunities we have to study the word of God?

At times I have students complain about taking tests. They grow weary of studying. This is what I tell them: Imagine you have a child with a brain tumor. You take him to see a brain surgeon. The doctor says, "Yeah, I can fix this. I've been to class. I've studied it. I've never been tested as to whether I can do brain surgery. But I am sure I can do it." You wouldn't want that person to perform brain surgery on your child, would you? Our faith will be tested and our growth challenged; we must give attention to study.

Foster cites four steps for study: repetition, concentration, comprehension, and reflection.[7]

1. REPETITION

We see the negative effect of repetition through the number of violent acts performed around us every day. Be repetitious in studying God's Word. Here are examples.

Read the Bible through annually. As a seminarian, I taught a group of retired persons a Bible study weekly for one year. One lady, a godly woman in her eighties, told me she had read the Bible through more than twenty times. I became ashamed. I could name books I had read several times, and I had read parts of the Bible over and over, but I had read the Bible through only once in my life, and I was a minister!

Since that time, I have read the Bible through every year, with one exception. Many years I used the *One Year Bible* (Tyndale). I cannot overestimate the treasure of wisdom I have gained from an annual, panoramic view of God's Word.

Read the same Bible book seven times (one time daily for a week), or thirty-one times (one time daily for a month).

Memorize Scripture. Memorizing Scripture can play a vital role in witnessing. We partner with the indwelling Spirit of God as we share. The Spirit helps us to know what to say, but we can certainly help by giving him material with which to work! Scripture memory certainly allows the Spirit more freedom to work.

Don't exhaust yourself in this memory work. If memorizing comes easily, then memorize portions: Psalm 1, Romans 8, etc. If you are a mere mortal like most of us, work on certain key verses consistently. My son had learned more Bible verses by memory by the first grade than I had learned by the time I finished high school. Why? Our church used the AWANAS program, which emphasizes Scripture memory.

While I was in high school, our minister of music had everyone who planned to go on choir tour memorize certain Bible verses. I still remember the first verse we learned: "Call to me, and I will answer you, and show you great and mighty things which you do not know" (Jer. 33:3). The verse still guides my life in a meaningful way. In college I was in a small accountability group. Each week we learned a new verse, using material from the Navigators. Become accountable to someone; hide God's Word in your heart. It will aid your witnessing by causing you to think more on the Lord, which will give you a spiritual sensitivity to lost people.

2. CONCENTRATION

Find time daily or at least weekly to study, to concentrate on what you have been reading. Let's be honest: laziness is a great sin in the contemporary church. R. C. Sproul puts it like this: "Here then, is the real problem of our negligence. We fail in our duty to study God's Word not so much because it is difficult to understand, not because it is dull and boring, but because it is work. . . . Our problem is that we are lazy."[8]

3. COMPREHENSION

Comprehension focuses on *knowing* the truth we study. This leads to "Aha!" moments of fresh discovery. George Whitefield read many books before and after his conversion. But he said he gained more from studying the Bible than all other books combined.

4. REFLECTION

"Reflection defines the *significance* of what we are studying." One of my professors once gave this formula: Knowledge - application = frustration. Reflection makes the truths we learn become personal. Use God's teachings to change your life and the lives of others. Hide the Word of God in your heart, and see how it helps your witness.

THE DISCIPLINE OF FASTING

Whitney gives an excellent definition of *fasting:* "A biblical definition of fasting is a Christian's voluntary abstinence from food for spiritual purposes. It is *Christian,* for fasting by a non-Christian obtains no eternal value because the Discipline's motives and purposes are to be God-centered. It is *voluntary* in that fasting is not to be coerced. Fasting is more than just the ultimate crash diet for the body; it is abstinence from food for *spiritual* purposes."[9] Fasting in a broader sense deals with more than food. It is the denial of any normal activity for the purpose of serious spiritual activity.

I almost never heard anyone speak of fasting in my younger days. Through the influence of leaders such as Bill Bright, fasting is being practiced by more and more believers. I often preach in churches where believers are involved in fasting and prayer for revival. This can only help the cause of evangelism!

The Bible is filled with examples of people who fasted: Moses, David, Elijah, Esther, Daniel, our Lord Jesus, and Paul. Corporate fasts are recorded as well, both in the Old Testament (Judah, 2 Chron. 20) and the New Testament (early church, Acts 13). Jesus spoke of the importance of fasting (see Matt. 9:15).

In the second century, Polycarp, bishop of Smyrna, exhorted the Philippians to "return to the word which was handed down to us from the beginning, 'watching unto prayer,' and persevering in fasting."[10] Obviously, fasting was still a significant practice in the church beyond the New Testament era.

Scripture indicates different types of fasts:[11]

- normal fast (abstaining from food) (Matt. 4:2; Luke 4:2);

- partial fast (Dan. 1:12);

- absolute fast (no food or drink) (Ezra 10:6);

- supernatural fast (Deut. 9:9);

- private fast (Matt. 6:16–18);

- congregational fast (Joel 2:15–16);

- national fast (2 Chron. 20:3); and

- regular fast (Lev. 16:29–31).

The purpose of fasting is to move our attention from our appetites to God himself. John Wesley, who led the Methodists to fast two days each week, said: "First, let [fasting] be done unto the Lord with our eye singly fixed on Him. Let our attention be this, and this alone, to glorify our Father which is in heaven."[12] Such a focus will give us insight into the heart of God for a lost world.

The Discipline of Meditation

The disciplines of meditation, silence, and solitude are not the same, but they are similar in that all involve quietness and disengagement from the busyness of our lives. Meditation in the Christian sense emphasizes obedience. As we meditate, we fill up our minds. This is different from emptying them, as in Eastern thought.

"Christian meditation is the ability to hear God's voice and obey His word."[13] How can we know God in an intimate way unless we learn to listen to him? The psalmist declared, "My eyes are awake through the night watches, that I may meditate on Your word" (Ps. 119:148). This is no syrupy sort of buddy-buddy relationship that dishonors the transcendence of God; on the contrary, we meditate upon him and his words in awe of the fact that he has condescended to us and desires intimacy with us.

In America we have a mountain called Rushmore! Consider the microwave, the Internet, fast food, E-mail, VCR, HOV lanes, books on tape, fax machines. All of these things encourage us to speed up the pace. I love music, but music is beautiful only when it has rests

to help you appreciate the melody. At times we need replenishment—physical, spiritual, emotional replenishment.

Christian meditation involves focusing on God—specifically on
obedience and faithfulness. Our culture's frenzied pace has infected
the church. I confess this is one of my greatest struggles. I am a
hyperactive, type A, driven person. Meditation is not the easiest
thing for me. I often succumb to the theory that the person who is
busiest is most important and, therefore, most spiritual. In our fast-
paced culture, an emphasis on meditation is needed.

Charles Spurgeon was a busy man, but he understood the importance of stepping aside regularly for times of meditation:

> Yet the best flame in the world needs renewing. I
> know not whether immortal spirits, like the angels,
> drink on the wing, and feed on some superior
> manna prepared in heaven for them; but the proba-
> bility is that no created being, though immortal, is
> quite free from the necessity to receive from without
> sustenance for its strength. Certainly the flame of
> zeal in the renewed heart, however divine, must be
> continually fed with fresh fuel. Even the lamps of the
> sanctuary needed oil. *Feed the flame, my brother.
> feed it frequently;* feed it with holy thought and con-
> templation, especially with thought about your
> work, your motives in pursuing it, the design of it,
> the helps that are waiting for you, and the grand
> results of it if the Lord be with you. Dwell much
> upon the love of God to sinners, and the death of
> Christ on their behalf, and the work of the Spirit
> upon men's hearts. Meditate with deep solemnity
> upon the fate of the lost sinner, and, like Abraham,
> when you get up early to go to the place where you
> commune with God, cast an eye towards Sodom and
> see the smoke thereof going up like the smoke of a
> furnace. . . . Think much also of the bliss of the sin-
> ner saved, and like holy Baxter derive rich argu-
> ments for earnestness from "the saints' everlasting
> rest." Go to the heavenly hills and gather fuel there;
> pile on the glorious logs of the wood of Lebanon,
> and the fire will burn freely and yield a sweet

perfume as each piece of choice cedar glows in the flame. There will be no fear of your being lethargic if you are continually familiar with eternal realities.

Above all, feed the flame with intimate fellowship with Christ. No man was ever cold in heart who lived with Jesus on such terms as John and Mary did of old, for *he* makes men's hearts burn within them. I never met with a half-hearted preacher who was much in communion with the Lord Jesus.[14]

THE DISCIPLINE OF SERVICE

About a year following the fall of Communism in Romania, I was privileged to travel there to teach and preach. I had never seen such poverty—people standing in line half a day for a tiny can of ham— and yet such a spirit of servanthood. The believers in Romania were so grateful to be free to worship and so happy that Christians from America came to help them learn the Word of God that they would literally give me anything.

One woman in her eighties wore a pair of men's boots, one with a hole in it—probably the only shoes she had. Yet she cooked us the best red peppers from her tiny garden. I don't like red peppers, but these peppers tasted like honey because I was overwhelmed by her servant heart.

Jesus said, "For even the Son of Man did not come to be served, but to serve, and to give His life a ransom for many" (Mark 10:45). We must discipline ourselves to serve. Such a focus makes evangelism more practical, for we are serving people with the greatest news imaginable. Servanthood evangelism, one of the most exciting approaches to sharing Christ in our day, will be considered in chapter 12.

How do we discipline ourselves to serve God? Whitney offers these motivations.[15]

- We are motivated by *obedience* (see Deut 13:4).

- *Gratitude* motivates us (see 1 Sam. 12:24). Recognition of the great salvation God has given us makes us cry with the psalmist, "I would rather be a doorkeeper in the house of my God than dwell in the tents of wickedness" (Ps. 84:10).

- *Gladness* spurs us to service: "serve the Lord with gladness" (Ps. 100:2).

- God's *forgiveness* is another encouragement.

- *Humility* and *love* provide two final reasons we can discipline ourselves to serve the Lord.

THE DISCIPLINE OF EVANGELISM

One of my most fulfilling experiences as a professor is taking a group of students or laypeople to share Christ with others. There is something exhilarating about setting aside time to share Christ. Evangelism is not easy work; it requires discipline.

It is true that evangelism is a natural result of a passionate life transformed by the gospel. But we must not witness only when opportunities jump into our laps. We must look for times and places to share the gospel. The average church member can fill his calendar with religious activities and push evangelism to the periphery. This is easy to do, because evangelism is so intimidating. Pastors can stay busy visiting the sick, counseling, preparing sermons, and going to meetings and never get around to evangelism. It takes discipline to do evangelism.

Whitney writes that witnessing is comparable to the postal service. Our success is not gauged by the response of the person to whom we deliver the message. Instead, "success is measured by the careful and accurate delivery of the message."[16] We can *discipline* ourselves to faithfulness, and such faithfulness leads to godliness.

This could mean establishing scheduled times to witness. When I served as evangelism director in Indiana, most of my time was spent with pastors and church leaders. I dealt with my need to witness in three primary ways. Whenever I was in town on the night our church had weekly visitation, I went. I taught witness training a great deal and took those I taught out to share our faith. I also joined a local health spa to be around people who needed a Christian witness. It was the only way I could consistently meet lost people.

In Houston it was much easier for me to witness. Houston Baptist University, though a Baptist school, drew many unchurched people, particularly to its pre-med and nursing programs. I set aside time weekly to talk to students specifically about Christ. Many met the

Lord; years later some still write me. Now I travel so much I have ample opportunities to share Christ in airplanes and restaurants. Each semester I take my classes out to witness, and I still witness when in town through our local church's ministry.

Obviously, my schedule is not typical. I share it to show that I have to make a constant, disciplined effort to share Christ regularly. And I don't do this because I teach evangelism; I do it because of my love for Christ.

When I was eleven years old I was a skinny kid. In fact, I had to run around in the shower to get wet! I had the physique of Olive Oyl. My Mom had to take up my pants, and when she did, I only had one back pocket! Maybe it wasn't *that* bad, but I was extremely thin and insecure. During my eleventh summer, I met Jesus in a life-changing way. I have never gotten over it! I was so grateful that God would save a skinny little hick like me. But I soon learned that my relationship with Christ required discipline.

In fact, that is the way God made us in every aspect of our lives. We need discipline. Children beg for discipline because they need limits; it gives them security. Our bodies need discipline in our eating and exercise. Unfortunately, the older and more "successful" we become, the less disciplined we tend to be.

Although I was thin as a youngster, I started playing football in the ninth grade and began lifting weights. By the end of my junior year, I could bench press three hundred pounds and was the strongest guy on my team—except for a teammate who played for Bear Bryant's national championship teams in 1978 and 1979. I can't lift that much now. I was much more disciplined as an athlete then. One reason I was disciplined was that I had a coach who encouraged me. What if all believers had a group of believers who held them to a high standard in the arena of personal evangelism?

APPLICATION

If you were to describe your discipline spiritually, would you be comparable to an Olympic athlete in training, a weekly gym rat, or a couch potato?

I heard of a man who was in serious need of exercise. He loved to watch golf on TV. His doctor told him he had to get more exercise, so he switched to watching tennis! Is evangelism a disciplined part of your regular schedule? How often do you consciously think about sharing your faith?

You cannot win until you begin. So start where you are, disciplined for the glory of God. And remember, you have the Spirit of God within!

BIBLIOGRAPHY

Foster, Richard. *Celebration of Discipline.* San Francisco: Harper San Francisco, 1988.

Whitney, Donald S. *Spiritual Disciplines for the Christian Life.* Colorado Springs: NavPress, 1991.

Willard, Dallas. *The Spirit of the Disciplines: Understanding How God Changes Lives.* San Francisco: Harper and Row, 1988.

8

Praying Your Friends to Christ: Linking Prayer and Evangelism

A young pastor of a rural congregation stood to preach. Unknown to him, his son had made a paper airplane during Sunday school. The preacher had no sooner given his first point than the little boy swung the plane through the air with a loud "vrooom!" A few people chuckled, but his dad was embarrassed. "Son," the pastor exclaimed, "don't do that again."

The young preacher returned to his message, while his son returned to his imagination. Sure enough, the boy let his thoughts get away from him and went "vroom!" even louder. A second time his father corrected him, obviously flustered. After regaining his composure, he began to preach again. Then the boy did the same thing again, this time letting the plane go. It made a perfect circle, landing in Sister Hazel's hair! All the people laughed, except the pastor and Sister Hazel. The preacher snatched up his son and headed out the back door. The entire congregation saw the little boy's face peering over his dad's shoulders screaming, "Pray! Pray! It's gonna be *bad!* It's gonna be *bad!*" This little boy learned the urgency of prayer.

135

THE IMPORTANCE OF PRAYER

Consider what these famous Christians have said about prayer:

- *Charles Spurgeon:* "Of course the preacher is above all distinguished as a man of prayer. He prays as an ordinary Christian, else he were a hypocrite. He prays more than ordinary Christians, else he were disqualified for the office he has undertaken."[1]
- *William Carey:* "Prayer—secret, fervent, believing prayer—lies at the root of all personal godliness."[2]
- *Martin Luther:* "I have so much business I cannot get on without spending three hours daily in prayer." "He that has prayed well has studied well."[3]
- *William Penn,* describing George Fox: "Above all he excelled in prayer. . . . The most awful, living, reverent frame I ever felt or beheld, I must say was in his prayer."[4]

THE NECESSITY OF PRAYER

What is prayer? The most common word for prayer in the Old Testament is *palal,* which means "to fall" or "to prostrate before" someone. It often signifies intercessory prayer. In the New Testament, the most common words are *euchomai* and *deomai. Euchomai* and its cognate *proseuchomai* are more general terms for prayer, while *deomai* has a more specific idea of seeking for a particular need.

Prayer is more than talking to God. It is *intimacy* with God. It is a reflection of our desire to know God. Prayer draws us closer to God, and it leads us away from the world, the flesh, and the devil. I like the definition of prayer used by my first doctoral student, Chris Schofield, who now serves in the area of prayer and evangelism at the North American Mission Board. Schofield defines prayer as "communion and dialogue with the triune God through a personal, love relationship with Jesus Christ."[5] This definition emphasizes both the *love* relationship and the *doctrinal* aspect of prayer by emphasizing the Trinity. I use this definition of prayer: intimacy with God that leads to the fulfillment of his purposes.

A few years ago, a survey showed that over 90 percent of Americans pray. If 90 percent of Americans *really* prayed, our country would be different morally! In the 1980s a survey of over 17,000 members of a major evangelical denomination who attended seminars on prayer for spiritual awakening gave frightening results. These believers, obviously interested in prayer, communicated that the laity spent less than five minutes a day in prayer; worse still, the pastors said they prayed no more than seven minutes a day on average![6]

Let me take this one step further. While at Houston Baptist University, I had the privilege of meeting several members of the Houston Rockets, in the period when they won back-to-back NBA titles. One was a devout Muslim. After winning their second championship, this player delayed a victory parade because it was his time of prayer. He fasts during the daylight hours for the entire month of Ramadan, one of the pillars of Islam.

A devout Muslim will wash his hands and face three times, kneel toward Mecca, and say his prayers five times each day. Imagine such devotion—talking to a god who does not exist! Part of the reason for the devotion is the salvation-by-works system in Islam. Still, should we as believers not be ashamed when we fail to spend time talking to the God of the universe?

Prayerlessness is one of the greatest sins of American Christians. One of the greatest hindrances to evangelism in our day is a lack of biblical prayer for evangelistic purposes. Consider the average church, and notice how much time is spent praying for physical needs. This is biblical and right (see James 5). But too many prayer meetings are like organ recitals: we pray for hearts, livers, and other organs. Very little praying is done for spiritual needs. How much times does your church spend praying specifically for lost people, for laborers, and for God to honor your evangelistic efforts?

WHY IS PRAYER SO IMPORTANT?

Prayer is vital because it is at the heart of Christianity. Prayer is intimate communication with God and is possible only because Jesus' death on the cross provided the means for our relationship with God. R. A. Torrey summarized the significance of prayer:

> Our whole life should be a life of prayer. We should walk in constant communion with God. There should be a constant looking upward to God.

> We should walk so habitually in His presence that
> even when we awake in the night it would be the
> most rational thing for us to speak to Him in thanks-
> giving or petition.[7]

There are other reasons to pray. Jesus set the example (Mark 1:35). God commands that we pray (Luke 18:1). Through prayer we receive from God: "Seek and you will find, knock and it will be opened to you. Ask and it will be given to you" (Matt. 7:7). This verse carries the idea of a child looking for a parent.

Our house was one of many in our area to be affected by hurricane Fran in September 1996. We had a hole in our roof from a huge limb, my car was crushed, Michelle's car was dented, we lost many trees, and the storm frightened our kids. When the hurricane came, we spent an entire night in the hall listening to our house being bombarded by missiles created from falling tree limbs.

One night some time later a thunderstorm came. Our daughter Hannah began to cry out to us. We didn't immediately answer, since we were asleep. Then she got up and began to look for us. We didn't tell her to go back to her bed. We didn't tell her she was being disobedient. We saw a frightened child in need of a dad and a mom. We let her crawl up in the bed with us, and we gave her comfort.

In the same way, God expects us to serve him out of obedience and to fulfill daily acts of obedience. But there are times when we need him in a desperate way, and we cry out to him, and we don't give up until we find him. During those times, God is more than willing to meet our needs like a good parent.

Prayer also brings relief from anxiety. Paul exhorted believers to replace worry with prayer (see Phil. 4:6–7). Prayer provides deep joy to the Christian as well: "Until now you have asked nothing in My name. Ask, and you will receive, that your joy may be full" (John 16:24). Through prayer, we have power in overcoming Satan (see Eph. 6).

Prayer is essential to a growing relationship with God. Above all else, Christianity is a *relationship* with God. Intimacy in prayer builds this relationship. Read the prayers of Abraham, Moses, David, and Paul, and see the intimacy they experienced. Finally, prayer is effective in the work of evangelism. We should pray for harvesters for evangelism work (see Matt. 9:36–38).

It is one thing to say we believe in prayer; it is another to pray in faith. S. D. Gordon said, "You can do more than pray after you have prayed, but you cannot do more than pray until you have prayed." Prayer is foundational to the Christian life.

JESUS: OUR EXAMPLE IN PRAYER

The best way to learn to pray is by studying how Jesus prayed. The Gospel writers recorded a request from the Lord to teach them. They did not ask, "Lord teach us *how* to pray," but "Lord teach us *to* pray" (Luke 11:1). We learn best from his example. How did Jesus pray?

- He modeled prayer (John 17).
- He spent time in personal prayer (Mark 1:35).
- He prayed at important events (Matt. 26:36–44; Luke 6:12).
- He taught the importance of prayer (Matt. 6).

I love watching commercials. I enjoy sitting with my kids and discussing how stupid and dishonest they are. I especially love commercials that mock other commercials. In particular, I love the ads of one soft drink that reacted to the "Image is everything" themes in one ad campaign. Their theme was, "Image is nothing. Thirst is everything: Obey your thirst." Jesus gave an example of this truth. He spoke of a man who prayed so people could see his "piety." Jesus then described a man who was penitent and broken, crying out to God alone in his anguish. "Image is nothing," Jesus could have said, looking at the Pharisee, "Thirst is everything," and, looking at the broken man, "Obey your thirst."

PRAYER AND SPIRITUAL WARFARE

The New Testament teaches the reality of spiritual warfare. However, we can make too much of spiritual warfare. Our focus in prayer should always be on the reality of knowing God and the strength we gain from him. Still, there is a real Satan and a legion of demonic powers, not to mention our battle with our own sinful nature and the lure of the world.

Paul compared the Christian life to a battle (see Eph. 6). However, many have failed to note the link between the armor of God and prayer and evangelism: "Praying always with all prayer and supplication in the Spirit, being watchful to this end with all perseverance and supplication for all the saints" (Eph. 6:18). Paul concluded his powerful teaching on spiritual warfare with an earnest appeal for the Ephesians to pray for the effective propagation of the gospel.

Andrew Murray said, "Prayer is the power by which Satan is conquered and . . . through prayer the church on earth has access to the powers of the heavenly world."[8] The Bible is emphatic about praying that engenders intentional evangelism:

- Jesus said we should pray for laborers (Matt. 9:36–38).

- The early church prayed for boldness to witness (Acts 4:29–31).

- Paul requested prayer for those who needed salvation (1 Tim. 2:1ff).

Scripture indicates two ways that Satan attacks people. He *blinds* the minds of the unsaved, those who don't believe (2 Cor. 4:4). He also *corrupts* the minds of the saved (2 Cor. 11:3). Oswald Chambers said an unguarded strength is a double weakness. We must guard our minds. The devil needs only one sin to destroy us, and a passive mind is as dangerous as a perverted mind in the hands of Satan.

The key to spiritual warfare is not to focus on Satan and what he might do, but on Christ and what he will do. Bold prayer that focuses on snatching people from the kingdom of darkness into the kingdom of light is the secret to spiritual warfare. Note the words of Ralph Herring:

> That Satan trembles when he sees the weakest saint upon his knees, why not make him tremble? Why not storm the very gates of hell? Nothing could please God more. In the conflict that is upon us, certainly we can ill afford to neglect one weapon Satan does not have in his arsenal and the one he fears the most—prayer.[9]

PERSONAL PRAYER

Where you are as a Christian five years from now will depend on how you pray more than any other factor. There is no time more valuable than time spent with God. I learned this in a course during my first semester in seminary, through a valuable resource called the 2959 Plan developed by Peter Lord. This approach emphasized certain practical considerations related to personal prayer.

Let your gaze be on God, your glance on your requests. Calvin Miller reminds the believer to "never start praying before you've stopped to look at God."[10]

Let prayer be your first choice, not your last. One of the worst statements uttered in the church is, "There is nothing we can do but pray." Can we do any better than pray? We can do more, but not better. Yes, there are occasional times when the followers of God are told to stop praying and get moving (as in the crossing of the Red Sea; Exod. 14), but in most cases too little praying is the greater problem.

Pray retail, not wholesale. In other words, pray for specific needs. We don't live in generalities; we live in a specific place with specific needs. A prayer list helps in this regard.

Pray more from conviction than from crisis. Daniel is a great example in prayer. When Daniel received the news that he would be thrown into the den of lions, notice how he responded. He faced Jerusalem, and prayed morning, noon, and night just as he had done previously (Dan. 6:10). What consistency. Daniel could respond like this because he was accustomed to talking to God out of conviction—not just when he faced a crisis. Crises are not times to get acquainted with God! We should walk with God before the crises.

The reason for personal devotional time is to develop intimacy with God. Billy Graham said the minister who does not have a daily quiet time will fall away in ten years.

A warning: Devotion time is not a spiritual rabbit's foot. Calvin Miller issues a threefold warning of an unrealistic focus on God:

- Loving the time to meet God more than loving God himself. This breeds a sort of inner addiction: "I've always wondered if many of these who go off with the rhetoric of holiness but never took the time to minister."

- Developing an otherworldly aloofness: "When someone translates as hyper-godly, most of us become hyper-nervous around them."

- Succumbing to the "sweet-little-Jesus" syndrome with "the sac-charine Christ of gooey pietism."[11]

In your devotional time, certain tools help in keeping a fresh, inti-mate walk with God:

- Daily Bible reading keeps our focus on God.
- Keeping a journal has been practiced for centuries by saints from John Wesley and George Whitefield to countless believ-ers today.
- Include names, specific concerns, and answers in a prayer list.
- A devotional book can be helpful as well.

FEATURES OF PRAYER

As we pray, certain features can guide our time to enhance our intimacy with God.

PRAISE

This is our response to the person of God. We praise him for who he is. A little girl attended a prayer service with her mother. She sat on the back pew while her mom and a few others knelt at the altar to pray. She listened closely while the adults cried out to God, some weeping. Finally she could sit still no longer. She stood on the pew, looked up into heaven, and cried, "Dear God! A, B, C, D, E, F, G, H, I, J, K, L, M, N, O, P, Q, R, S, T, U, V, W, X, Y, Z. Amen!" Then she sat down.

The mother, a bit embarrassed, asked her, "Honey, why did you say that?"

"Because you were all praying such beautiful prayers, and I wanted to talk to God. I didn't know the words, so I thought if I gave God the letters, he could make the words come out right."

This might not work for a forty-year-old believer, but I believe there is something about a sincere child's prayer, just with the let-ters, that brings praise to God. When we do not know the words to pray, God still hears the cries of our heart. Let us never become so sophisticated in our spirituality that we are afraid to offer God praise.

Praise is not noise, just as reverence is not silence. It is the acknowledgment of God's greatness. It is recognizing he is "hallowed," or "holy," as the Model Prayer tells us (see Matt. 6:9).

THANKSGIVING

This is our response to the goodness of God. Thank him for what he has done. "Enter His gates with thanksgiving" (Ps. 100:4). "In everything give thanks" (1 Thess. 5:18). An attitude of gratitude should permeate our lives.

CONFESSION

Confession is our response to the holiness of God. Our sins will hinder our praying (see Ps. 66:18). As we pray, we can ask the Holy Spirit to reveal each sin in our lives. Then we can confess the sin (see 1 John 1:9). When broken relationships are involved, we should seek to make them right as well.

INTERCESSION

This is our response to the love of God. When we ask of God, Foster reminds us, We are not "trying to manipulate God and tell Him what to do. Quite the opposite. We are asking God to tell us what to do. God is the ground of our beseeching . . . Our prayer is to be like a reflex action to God's prior initiative on the heart."[12]

PETITION

Petition is our response to the love of God for us. It is appropriate and necessary for us to ask God to meet our needs. However, in our consumer-driven culture, we can learn from this prayer of petition from an anonymous soldier:

> I asked God for strength that I might achieve;
> I was made weak that I might learn humbly to obey.
> I asked God for health that I might do greater things;
> I was given infirmity that I might do better things.
> I asked for riches that I might be happy;
> I was given poverty that I might be wise.
> I asked for power that I might have the praise of men;
> I was given weakness that I might feel the need of God.
> I asked for all things that I might enjoy life;

I was given life that I might enjoy all things.
I got nothing that I asked for—
but everything I had hoped for.
Almost despite myself, my unspoken prayers were answered.
I am among all men most richly blessed.[13]

LISTENING

There is another aspect about prayer that must not be missed: listening to God. You may not be aware of it, but wherever you are as you read this book, noises are all around you. Rock-and-roll music is all around you. Rap tunes are playing. People are discussing various topics from sports to finance. The only thing you need to hear these voices is the proper receiver. A radio will suddenly usher into your presence a bevy of sounds.

Prayer operates the same way. God is constantly speaking to us, teaching us, leading us. The question is not whether God is speaking but if we are listening. God consistently speaks to us through his Word, but do we hear him? He occasionally speaks to us through circumstances and other people. He also speaks at times through the still, small voice of his Spirit. Are we listening? If you walk with God, you will be prompted by him to witness. This cannot be taught as much as it is learned through the school of prayer taught by the Holy Spirit.

CONSECRATION

Consecration is a prayer of commitment to God. Often in Scripture believers made specific, fresh acts of consecration: Jonah in the whale's stomach (Jon. 2:1–10); David, following his sin with Bathsheba (Ps. 51); Paul, our Lord, and others. In our times of prayer, we are often confronted with the need to make a fresh, new commitment to God.

PRACTICAL TIPS FOR AN EFFECTIVE QUIET TIME

1. Establish in your heart and mind the importance of the devotional time. One of the most liberating lessons I learned from the school of prayer is that we must disciple ourselves to pray in all circumstances. I once thought great men and women of prayer loved to pray so much that it was a constant joy to be

in the presence of God. But then I read Foster's comments: "We must never wait until we *feel* like praying before we pray."[14] Prayer is a discipline. Many times we pray out of a desire to be with God. Other times we pray out of a sense of holy desperation. But at other times we pray not because it is convenient or comfortable but because it is *right*. Sometimes I am not in the "mood" to pray in the morning. But I have discovered that if I don't take time to pray, my mood gets worse as the day goes by!

2. Designate a time and place for your time with God. Guard the time.

3. Do whatever is necessary to be spiritually prepared. I need a fresh cup of coffee!

4. Adjust your time occasionally to avoid monotony.

5. As you pray, make the Scriptures a part of your time. Praying Psalm 51, the prayer of David after his sin with Bathsheba, should help us understand the seriousness of our sin and the greatness of our God.

Here are some other tips on prayer:

- Change your prayer time, mix it up; begin with Scripture sometimes, with prayer other times.

- Read a book on prayer annually.

- Talk to other Christian friends.

- Read the journals and biographies of great Christians.

LINKING PRAYER WITH EVANGELISM

The great man of prayer, E. M. Bounds, said, "Prayer does not stand alone. . . . It lives in fellowship with other Christian duties."[15] This is particularly true about evangelism. You cannot evangelize effectively on a consistent basis without prayer. In his research of growing churches, Thom Rainer discovered prayer ranked with biblical preaching and teaching as one of the major reasons churches in the survey reached lost people.[16]

Notice this prayer of the early church that links prayer and evangelism:

> Now, Lord, look on their threats, and grant to
> Your servants that with all boldness they may speak
> Your word, by stretching out Your hand to heal, and
> that signs and wonders may be done through the
> name of Your holy Servant Jesus. And when they
> had prayed, the place where they were assembled
> together was shaken; and they were all filled with
> the Holy Spirit, and they spoke the word of God
> with boldness (Acts 4:29–31).

Chris Schofield made a vital point about this passage. "The prayer for 'boldness' (from *parrhesia),* which has already been associated with the apostolic witness in 4:13, is significant in at least two ways. First, notice that the apostles are not seeking revenge or the end of the opposition but rather courage and freedom of speech. Second, they were seeking this boldness that they might proclaim the gospel. . . . Their motive was centered on God's redemptive work."[17]

Another key passage is Ephesians 6:18–20. Paul followed his discussion of the armor of God with a request for believers to pray for bold proclamation of the gospel. Prayer is seen as an indispensable part of the armor of God. Praying "in the Spirit" is not a reference to praying in tongues, but to prayer "in the presence, control, help, influence, and power of God's Spirit."[18] Paul exhorted the Ephesians to pray for "utterance," or *parrhesia,* an openness to preach the gospel. This is the expression translated "boldness" in Acts 4:29, 31. Paul was in prison as he wrote these words, asking for courage to share Christ.

Certain truths emerge from these two chapters, Acts 4 and Ephesians 6:

- *Boldness* to proclaim the gospel is a legitimate request to bring before God.
- Such boldness comes only from God. It cannot be "worked up."
- Such boldness comes through the prayers of God's people.

PRAYING FOR THE UNSAVED

Robert Speer, a Presbyterian missionary leader, said, "The evangelization of the world . . . depends first of all upon a revival of prayer. Deeper than the need for men; deeper, far, than the need for money; deep down at the bottom of our spiritless lives, is the need for the forgotten secret of prevailing, worldwide prayer."[19]

Korea is a great example of the impact of prayer. In 1966 about 11 percent of the Korean population was Christian. By 1978, it was 19 percent; 1981, 22 percent; now in the 1990s over one third of the people in Korea are believers. Korea also has the largest Presbyterian, Methodist, and Assemblies of God churches in the world.

The secret to this Korean explosion is prayer. Many Koreans pray early every day. Some pray all night on Friday nights. I once heard a Korean pastor say that the average Korean Christian prays an hour a day. One reason the Korean church prays so much is the threat of North Korea. Our problem today is we don't see the threats of worldliness, carnality, culture, ungodliness, and apathy that should motivate our prayers.

Charles Sullivan tells of a time when he gave the invitation and a man in his seventies came forward to give his life to Christ. His wife came down the aisle behind him with the glow of God on her face. After Sullivan counseled the man and prayed with him, he reached for a membership card to fill out, as we Baptists do, but the wife stopped him. She told Sullivan that he wouldn't need a card. She reached in her Bible and pulled out an old, yellow, tattered card.

"Forty years ago, I made a commitment to pray for my husband's salvation daily," she explained. "As a sign of my commitment, I filled out a membership card with my husband's name, and checked 'profession of faith' and 'baptism.' The only thing we need to complete is the date." God had answered her prayer.

A bedridden woman in London, England, had been able to cultivate the life of prayer. She had read in the papers about evangelist D. L. Moody's work in Chicago. She didn't know Moody or anyone associated with him. Placing that paper under her pillow, she began to pray, "Lord, send this man to our church." Moody did go to London in 1872 when his church building was in ashes back in Chicago.

While Moody was speaking to the YMCA, a pastor invited him to preach to his congregation. Nothing happened the Sunday morning Moody preached. After the service, the sister of that invalid woman had informed her that a Mr. Moody of Chicago had preached and that he was to speak again that evening. The invalid woman declared, "Oh, if I had known, I would have eaten no breakfast, I would have spent all the time in prayer. Send me no dinner, leave me alone, lock the door. I'm going to spend the whole afternoon and evening in prayer."

That evening the building was packed to hear Moody. The atmosphere was different, and the power of God fell on that place. Five hundred people gave their lives to Christ. Great revival began, and Moody's career as an evangelist multiplied because of that sick lady's prayer.[20]

The title of this chapter comes from an evangelistic prayer seminar called Praying Your Friends to Christ. The following suggestions on praying for the lost come from a booklet distributed in this seminar:

- Ask God to open their spiritual eyes (2 Cor. 4:4).

- Ask God to set them free from spiritual captivity (2 Tim. 2:25–26).

- Ask God to give them ears to hear (Matt. 13:15), faith to believe (Acts 20:21), and will to respond (Rom. 10:9).

- Ask God to send people into their lives to witness to them (Matt. 9:38).

- Ask God for ways to build caring relationships (1 Cor. 9:22).

- Ask God for opportunities to witness (Col. 4:3).

- Ask God for boldness to witness (Acts 4:29).

- Ask God for an opportunity to invite them to a harvest event (Luke 14:23).[21]

Prayer can give us a yearning to share the gospel with others. A seminary student was taking his son to preschool one morning when he noticed a man walking along the side of the road. The student, named Joel, was prompted to pray for that man. He promised that he would share Jesus with this man if he were still on this road on his return. However, after leaving the preschool complex, he thought nothing of the man.

After a stop at the grocery store, Joel headed home. As he neared home, he saw the young man again. As he pulled into his driveway, Joel realized all the seminary in the world didn't matter if his faith was silent. "I returned to the young man," Joel recalled, "and gave him a ride."

As Joel drove the stranger home, he remarked that "the man upstairs" had looked out for him. Joel began to share with him the good news of Jesus. The conversation flowed freely as God opened the man's heart to the gospel truth. They stopped along the road, and he repented of his sin and asked Jesus to save him. God will use us in witnessing for him *if* we walk with him in communion through prayer.

CORPORATE PRAYER

Martin and Ginter, in *Power House,* make a distinction between prayer ministries and the church as a house of prayer. "A prayer ministry involves a portion of the congregation in ministry, as with a youth ministry. . . . Such a ministry may take the form of missionary prayer circles; times of prayer open to the whole church such as a Wednesday night prayer meeting; or men's/women's/youth's prayer meetings; a prayer room; an intercessory team; prayer ministry before/during/after the church service; or a prayer chain."[22]

In contrast, a house of prayer "will have prayer saturating every aspect of its individual and corporate life. Having significant prayer will be seen as the first thing to do when planning, when meeting, etc. There will be teaching on prayer from the pulpit, in Sunday School classes, and in small-group settings. People will think of prayer as a major factor to be used at first to solve any problem."[23]

In other words, the goal is to have a church where prayer permeates its fabric—and where lost people receive a high priority in its praying. Not every church is a house of prayer, but every church can have an effective prayer ministry.

APPLICATION

Ponder the following words by men of prayer, Charles Spurgeon and Leonard Ravenhill, as you reflect on your own life of prayer.

Spurgeon's words relate to ministers but can be applied to any believer:

> Of course the preacher is above all others distinguished as a man of prayer. He prays as an ordinary Christian, else he were a hypocrite. He prays more than ordinary Christians, else he were disqualified for the office which he has undertaken. . . .
>
> Among all the formative influences which go to make up a man honoured of God in the ministry, I know of none more mighty than his own familiarity with the mercy-seat. All that a college course can do for a student is coarse and external compared with the spiritual and delicate refinement obtained by communion with God. . . . All our libraries and studies are mere emptiness compared with our closets. We grow, we wax mightily, we prevail in private prayer.[24]

Ravenhill's words give a similar exhortation:

> So the minister of a congregation should be seriously earnest to be right because his people will imitate him. *Like priest, like people.* The sheep will follow the shepherd. What need there is that the pastor should order his steps aright lest he lead a whole flock astray! If the town clock be wrong, half the watches in the place will be out of time. . . . One of the few thus blest leaves this record: "As he [John Hyde] came before the people . . . he spoke three words in Urdu and three in English, repeating them three times: 'Ai Asmani Bak, Oh, Heavenly Father.'" What followed, who can describe? It was as if a great ocean came sweeping into that assembly. Hearts were bowed before that Divine Presence as the trees of the wood before a mighty tempest. It was the ocean of God's love being outpoured through one man's obedience. Hearts were broken before it. There were confessions of sins, with tears that were soon changed to joy, and then to shouts of rejoicing. Truly, we were filled with new wine, the new wine of heaven.[25]

BIBLIOGRAPHY

Bounds, E. M. *Power Through Prayer.* Springdale: Whitaker House, 1982.

Bright, Bill. *The Coming Revival.* Orlando: New Life, 1995.

Carson, D. A. *A Call to Spiritual Reformation: Priorities from Paul and His Prayers.* Grand Rapids: Baker, 1994.

Elmore, Ted. *Praying the Heart of God.* Dallas: Baptist General Convention of Texas, 1994.

Ginter, Diane and Glen Martin. *Power House.* Nashville: Broadman & Holman, 1994.

9

God the Evangelist: The Work of the Holy Spirit

Those involved in evangelism know the crucial need of the Holy Spirit's power and presence. "Evangelism without the Holy Spirit," observes Delos Miles, "is like a body without a soul."[1] "No alternative to the Holy Spirit is available for the Christian leader,"[2] states Duewel, who adds, "We are in danger of being better trained and equipped on the human level than we are empowered by the Spirit."[3]

Charles Finney exhorts, "I would repeat, with great emphasis, that the difference in the efficiency of ministers does not consist so much in the difference of intellectual attainments as in the measure of the Holy Spirit they enjoy."[4]

As a teenager in the 1970s in a Southern Baptist church, I was a lot like the disciples of John mentioned in Acts 19; I was not sure there was a Holy Spirit! The charismatic movement had emphasized the Spirit, but it was very divisive as well. This overemphasis on certain gifts led non-Pentecostals to deemphasize the Spirit. Since the birth of Pentecostalism at the beginning of the twentieth century, in particular the Azusa Street Revival in 1906, there has been an increased interest in pneumatology. One thing is clear: the Holy Spirit's role in evangelism can hardly be overestimated.

THE PERSON OF THE HOLY SPIRIT

Why have we often overlooked the vital work of the Spirit of God? The Holy Spirit has too often been neglected. For some the Trinity has been more of a duality, with the Holy Spirit's vital role overlooked. There are several reasons for this. He is intangible, a Spirit. We tend to confuse personality with corporeality. We can relate to God the Father, for we know what a Father is. We have pictures of Jesus . . . well, not really! But we can relate to our Lord because he became like us. The Spirit is more difficult to visualize.

Another reason he is overlooked is ignorance. Very little emphasis is given to studying the work of the Spirit in many churches. Extremism by those who do emphasize the Spirit is another factor in his neglect. Some emphasize certain gifts or attributes to an extreme, or they associate certain phenomena with his work.

What do we know about the Spirit of God? First, the Holy Spirit is a person, not an "it." In our songs and discussions, we tend to refer to the Spirit almost like the "force" of Star Wars. How do we know he is a person? When speaking of the Spirit, Jesus referred to him as a person: "the Spirit of truth, whom the world cannot receive, because it neither sees Him nor knows Him; but you know Him, for He dwells with you and will be in you" (John 14:17).

Further, the Spirit does personal acts (John 14:26; 15:26; 16:13). He has all the attributes of a person except *a physical body* (Rom. 5:5; Acts 1:8; 1 Cor. 2:10–13). He can be *treated* like a person (Acts 7:51; Eph. 4:30; Acts 5:9).

THE WORK OF THE HOLY SPIRIT IN THE BELIEVER

THE SPIRIT INDWELLS AND SEALS AT CONVERSION

The Spirit indwells and seals the believer at conversion (Eph. 1:13–14). Seals were commonly used on documents in the first century. Drummond offers the following ideas to demonstrate the significance of this expression for Christians. First, we wear the stamp of God, as his personal possession. Second, the seal brings the mark of authenticity. It also emphasizes security, for a legal document with a seal in the first century was considered secured. Thus, the term *seal* implies the security of the believer in the new covenant relationship with God. Finally, the seal means service for God is expected. The Holy Spirit who seals us will also guide us.[5]

THE SPIRIT FILLS THE BELIEVER FOR SERVICE

He fills the believer with power and boldness to witness (Acts 1:8; 2; 4). Whenever a believer was filled, he or she witnessed as a result.

When Jesus declared that his followers would receive power after the Holy Spirit had come upon them and that they would be witnesses, he meant that we could be effective witnesses—but not in our own strength. Effectiveness comes through the power of the Holy Spirit. The key to effective witnessing is not in our technique or our strategy. The key is in the power of the Holy Spirit working within us. The question is, Do we really trust the Holy Spirit? Do we believe he will use someone just like us, and are we walking in that confidence?

Being filled means to be controlled. The question is not so much, How much of the Holy Spirit do you have? but, How much of *you* does the Holy Spirit have? Are we yielded to him?

Being filled is to be normal, consistent, and obvious (Eph. 5:18ff). The word for being "filled" with the Spirit in this passage is *eplesthesan*. The filling of the Spirit does not refer to a "second blessing" subsequent to salvation. The expression is most often found in Luke and Acts. The term and its derivatives have two main uses. First, being filled with the Spirit refers to the normal, consistent control of the Spirit in the believer's life. This is seen in the Lord Jesus (Luke 4:1); the early deacons (Acts 6); Stephen (Acts 7:55); and Barnabas (Acts 12:24). So the fullness of the Spirit is the expected lifestyle of any believer. After all, Paul reminds us that our bodies are the temple of the Holy Spirit (1 Cor. 6:19).

We see this clearly in Ephesians 5:18. Paul commanded believers *not* to be filled with wine. How can you tell a person is drunk? By his speech, walk, and appearance. Paul also commanded believers to be continuously filled with the Spirit, in a consistent manner. The term is *pleroo,* "fullness." This is the only time Paul refers to the fullness of the Spirit.

The verb is passive, emphasizing the role of God in the filling. The present tense notes the continual aspect of the Spirit's control. Further, Paul's emphasis to the church of Ephesus is on the corporate body, not a particular few. Kostenberger summarizes this verse in its context. Paul's expression, "in contrast to being drunk with wine enjoins believers to exhibit a wise, maturing lifestyle which is to be expressed in corporate praise and worship as well as in proper Christian relationships."[6]

If a pastor entered the pulpit intoxicated, you could tell. It would be obvious. You probably would not listen to him! However, Ephesians 5:18, which contrasts intoxication with the Spirit-filled life, tells us that it is just as great a sin to preach without the Spirit's control as it is to preach drunk! Lest you think I am picking on preachers, let me say that it is as wrong for a Christian parent to live before their children devoid of the Spirit's control as it is to be a drunkard!

There is another way the term *eplesthesan* is used. It refers to a "sudden, special filling or anointing."[7] Green says this second use did not refer to "the settled characteristics of a lifetime but to the sudden inspiration of the moment."[8] We see this in Peter (Acts 4:8), the early church (Acts 4:31), and in the life of the apostle Paul (Acts 9:17; 13:9). Believers should live in such a way that the Spirit guides and controls their lives. Still, at times the Holy Spirit gives unusual unction for specific tasks, notably evangelism.

How can you know you are filled? The filling of the Spirit does not generally happen through an ecstatic experience or other phenomena. Years ago, I heard pastor James Merritt give this simple test. Produce the *fruit* of the Spirit, as seen in Galatians 5:22–23, and perform the *function* of the Spirit, to bear witness to Christ. Jesus tells us the Spirit "will glorify Me, for He will take of what is mine and declare it to you" (John 16:14).

Hindrances to the filling. Scripture tells us we can grieve the Spirit (Eph. 4:30) or quench the Spirit (1 Thess. 5:19). We grieve by the act of commission, and we quench by omission. My colleague Andreas Kostenberger notes that these passages are not injunctions directly "linking confession of sins to the filling of the Spirit."[9] While this is true, the Spirit is indeed the *Holy* Spirit, and our sins of omission (quenching) and commission (grieving) can hinder the Spirit's control in our lives. We are to confess our sins, says Kostenberger, "in order to enjoy continued fellowship with the Spirit and with other believers."[10]

Thus, while there is no formula or other biblical teaching that directly links the filling of the Spirit with confessing of sins, the filling of the Spirit implies a desire to be sensitive to the reality of sin.

How does a person receive the filling? As noted, there is no set formula that will work, but certain principles do apply. Further, we should never seek the filling; we should seek to be obedient believers (Luke 11:13).

Desire the Spirit to control your life. Confess and forsake sin, trusting his leadership in your life. Notice in the New Testament we are never told to *ask* for the filling of the Spirit. The early believers never prayed for such an experience. Typically, the filling of the Spirit is the normal accompaniment of a life yielded to Christ. The filling of the Spirit is mentioned in reference to a request (Acts 4:31), but the request was for boldness to witness—not the filling of the Spirit. Yield yourself to the Spirit and believe he will use you to the glory of God.

THE SPIRIT GIVES BELIEVERS GIFTS

There is an increasing emphasis on the role of spiritual gifts in the American church. Space does not allow a detailed discussion, but here are significant factors.

- Gifts are not talents. They are Spirit-given abilities for Christian service in the body of Christ.

- Every believer has one or more gifts (1 Cor. 12:7; Eph. 4:7–8).

- Gifts are varied, and they are given to those in the body of Christ for the good of the body (1 Cor. 12:7).

- Believers are to exercise their gifts. Part of God's will is getting to the place where you exercise his gifts.

There are many spiritual gift inventories designed to assist a believer in determining his gifts. However, I believe such tools tend to identify convictions or preferences more than spiritual gifts. They can be helpful, but I would not use them as the primary means of determining the gifts of the Spirit.

Here are a few tips to help you determine your spiritual gifts.

- Study the lists in Scripture, asking God to confirm those gifts that he has given to you (see Rom. 12:3–8; 1 Cor. 12:8–10, 28–30; Eph. 4:11).

- Be a responsible Christian until those gifts are made clear. Don't sit around and do nothing because you haven't found your gift! You find the will of God by doing what you already know to be his will, not by sitting on the sidelines of life. You also discover your gifts by faithful service.

- Listen to the wise counsel of other believers who know you well.

- Exercise those gifts you believe are yours, seeking God's affirmation.

What about the "gift of evangelism?" Much of the literature on evangelism and church growth uses this term. However, the *Bible* does not say anything about the gift of evangel*ism*. It does speak of the gift of evangel*ist*. Further, some people have argued that in the average church only 10 percent of the people have the gift of evangelist.[11] Others have picked up on this idea. This is a cop-out.

Certainly, some people are more effective than others in witnessing. We need to start where people are. Nevertheless, the New Testament mandate is the total penetration of an area with the total participation of the church members. Jesus never told 10 percent of his followers to win the world to Christ; he commanded believers to do that—*period*. Every believer must become involved at some level in evangelism.

The New Testament term for *evangelist* in Ephesians 4:11 might convey the idea of a harvest evangelist where we think of a Billy Graham, a Bailey Smith, or a Luis Palau. It could also indicate a person who preached or shared the gospel where it had never been heard, as in the case of Paul. Or one could argue from the New Testament usage that the gift of evangelist, since it refers to equipping the saints for ministry, is a person gifted in teaching and inspiring others to evangelize.

We have to be careful to distinguish between our duty as Christians and our specific gifts. I'm not denying some people are more effective in evangelism than others, even as some men are better preachers than others. But the New Testament does not say some believers are to witness while others are not. The Great Commission is for every believer. Every believer ought to be able at least to administer spiritual CPR. If they meet somebody who wants to be saved, they should be able to tell them how to come to Christ.

Pastor Johnny Hunt of the First Baptist Church of Woodstock, Georgia, discussed the place of spiritual gifts in a message on his philosophy of church growth. He makes a distinction between "servant" gifts and "sign" gifts:

> God has given us servant gifts. Let me tell you churches that are filling them up today: Churches . . . that are dealing with sign gifts. "Ah, I want to be there where somebody speaks in tongues. I want to be there where there is interpretation of that. Oh, I want to be in a service where there's prophecy." You want to get into that mystical movement of the Spirit of God. Friend, if you want to get down where the rubber hits the road, you leave those sign gifts and get into the serving gifts. They are laid out for us clearly in the word of God in Romans 12:3–8. Let me just mention them to you: Wisdom, teaching, helps, hospitality, giving, government, mercy, faith . . . Those are gifts that God has given the church, and He's given them to us.

During this message, Hunt then went into the congregation to note individuals with particular gifts:

- a Sunday school teacher with an uncanny ability to prepare others to teach;

- an usher who serves others;

- a man with the gift of faith, who challenges the church to build bigger buildings and dreams greater dreams; and

- an individual with obvious organizational giftedness, who organizes the many international mission trips taken by the church.

Hunt then exhorted his people:

> If I could get all the people in this church to exercise their spiritual gift, we'd turn this town upside down for God. . . . Listen to this. Every person here has a supernatural gift. . . . I as pastor can touch only so many people. I'm one, but I'll tell you what I will do. I will spend my life preparing this book every week in order to address this congregation Sunday by Sunday with word from God. . . . If every person here that names the name of Jesus would find out

what their spiritual endowment is and employ it in service, the world would stand up in amazement. Hey, *USA Today* would come and say that this is a religious phenomenon. . . . We're a body, and we function effectively when we exercise our gifts.

THE HOLY SPIRIT IN THE BELIEVER'S WITNESS

- He empowers us to witness (Acts 1:8).
- He gives us wisdom (Luke 12:12).
- He gives us *boldness* (Acts 4:31).
- He helps us in our praying (Rom. 8:16).
- He gives us the burning desire to see people saved (Acts 4:29–31).

It was a rough day—four hours of driving—and I was late to a meeting. After I arrived, the meeting yawned on for five hours. Finally, I got to bed. I was staying at a military base. I had just drifted off to sleep when someone knocked at my door. The lady at the door said, "There's a bomb threat. We need to evacuate the building immediately."

A bomb threat? On a military base? I got dressed and headed out the door. I asked her, "Does this sort of thing happen all the time?"

"No. There's a package underneath a car in the parking lot and we don't know what it is. You need to get out to the field quickly." We went out to the field, and I could see armed military personnel along the perimeter. Security vehicles, a fire truck, and other vehicles arrived. Lights were flashing everywhere, and soldiers walked around talking on walkie-talkies. There was a sense of urgency.

Fortunately, there was no bomb. And we were able to go back to our beds. But I thought about that—urgency. There is a ticking going on. It's not the ticking of a bomb. It's the beat, beat, beat of hearts—hearts of people one heartbeat away from eternity without Christ. Do we sense that urgency? The Spirit of God gives us the urgency to share Christ.

The Holy Spirit teaches believers truth. The Holy Spirit, Jesus said, would bear witness to Jesus—not to himself, not to others—to be witnesses to the truth of the gospel, the truth of the Christian faith. John's Gospel tells us that we will know the truth and the truth will set us free. Jesus also said that the Holy Spirit would guide us in the truth. The Holy Spirit helps us to gain victory over sin: "So I say, live by the Spirit, and you will not gratify the desires of the sinful nature" (Gal. 5:16 NIV).

Temptation is not sin; temptation is an enticement to sin. The thought that comes across our mind—the attitude that we think about—is not sin. The Holy Spirit helps keep us from fulfilling that temptation to the point where it becomes sin in our lives. The Holy Spirit works to bring into our lives the risen life of Christ.

Some passages in the New Testament talk about the work of the Holy Spirit in us, and other passages talk about Christ in us, the hope of glory. There's no contradiction in the Godhead. The Holy Spirit works in us to bring alive the resurrected Christ in our lives.

THE WORK OF THE HOLY SPIRIT IN THE UNBELIEVER

THE SPIRIT PRECEDES THE WITNESS (ACTS 10:1–15)

On a hot summer day in Evansville, Indiana, my witnessing team was about to quit for the day. We decided to knock on one more door. A thirty-one-year old man answered. He listened, without showing much interest. Sensing our fatigue, he finally invited us inside. He seemed totally uninterested, but I shared Christ because I believe in the power of the gospel. When I got to the point of offering him the chance to repent and believe, he suddenly burst into tears. "I am a paramedic," he said, "and the last two weeks I have thought about death every day." The Holy Spirit had been drawing him to Christ, and we didn't even know it!

THE SPIRIT CONVICTS THE LOST PERSON

"Nevertheless I tell you the truth. It is to your advantage that I go away; for if I do not go away, the Helper will not come to you; but if I depart, I will send Him to you. And when He has come, He will convict the world of sin, and of righteousness, and of judgment: of sin, because they do not believe in Me; of righteousness, because I go to My Father and you see Me no more; of judgment, because the ruler of this world is judged" (John 16:7–11).

The term *elegcho* is translated "convict" or "convince." The Spirit of God, our Comforter *(parakletes)* of the converted, becomes the prosecutor of the unconverted, convicting the lost of three things:

1. *Sin.* Spurgeon, commenting on the conviction of the Spirit in his life, said, "When the Holy Ghost made sin to appear sin, then I was overwhelmed with the sight . . . A naked sin stripped of all excuse, and set in the light of truth, is a worse sight to see than the devil himself."[12] It is the work of the Spirit, not our argumentation, that convinces a lost person of his sin.

2. *Righteousness.* The Holy Spirit convicts the world that righteousness before God comes not by human effort. Only God can impute righteousness into a sinful creature.

3. *Judgment.* The world, as well as Satan, will be judged (see John 16:11; 1 Cor. 1:18). Those individuals not convinced of the truth of the gospel will see it as a stumbling block or foolishness (1 Cor. 1:18). But for those who respond to the Spirit's conviction, the response is like that of my favorite contemporary hymn:

Oh mighty cross, my soul's release,

The stripes He bore, have brought me peace;

His sacrifice love, on Calvary

Has made the mighty cross a tree of life to me.[13]

THE HOLY SPIRIT REGENERATES (JOHN 3:5–6)

"Not by works of righteousness which we have done, but according to His mercy He saved us, through the washing of regeneration and renewing of the Holy Spirit" (Titus 3:5).

On a busy day at an airport, one man was particularly rude. He had more bags than allowed, they were overstuffed, and the skycap mentioned this to him. He demanded that his bags be checked. The skycap went about his business, and the man didn't give him a tip. A couple standing next in line said to the skycap, "You certainly seemed cool. That man was so rude to you, it's hard to believe you didn't retaliate." The skycap smiled and said, "No big deal. That man's going to New York, and his bags are going to Brazil." The skycap had total control over the bags. In the same way, the Holy Spirit—not you or me—changes the eternal destiny of people.

THE HOLY SPIRIT IN THE WITNESSING ENCOUNTER

The Holy Spirit takes a willing witness and a seeking sinner and brings them together to make a new believer. Philip and the eunuch are biblical examples (see Acts 8).

The Holy Spirit will lead us to divine appointments if we are sensitive to him. Pastor Ronnie Stewart was on an errand. A man approached Ronnie and noticed the name of the church on the van. After learning Ronnie was the pastor, he said he was going through some serious problems in his life and had several major decisions to make.

Ronnie was in a big hurry, but he agreed to take time to talk with the man. This stranger shared his heart and the decisions he faced. Ronnie had just learned a memorized presentation (Continuing Witness Training), so he shared the gospel with the man. When he asked the question, "Are you willing to turn from your sin and place your faith in Jesus right now?," the stranger immediately said, "Yes." He trusted Jesus as Savior and Lord. The Lord had already prepared his heart.

APPLICATION

The greatest illustration I have seen to explain how the Holy Spirit uses the witness of different believers is the Spider Principle.[14] I have found this to be a great confidence-booster when shared with those who are apprehensive about witnessing.

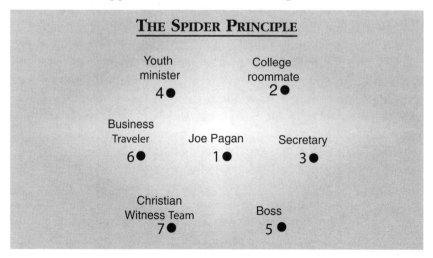

THE SPIDER PRINCIPLE

Joe Pagan [draw a circle around Joe Pagan on the transparency]. Joe Pagan was born into an unchurched family that rarely spoke of spiritual things. He was not an atheist or an agnostic. He just had little exposure to Christianity and never heard the story of Jesus.

College roommate [draw a line from 1 to 2]. When Joe went to college, his assigned roommate turned out to be a "Jesus Freak." He was extremely excited about being a Christian. He would do Jesus yells in the shower and have a devotional time at six o'clock in the morning, even on Saturdays. He constantly prayed about everything from tests to world peace. Joe had never known anyone who took religion so seriously. They had some interesting conversations from time to time, but Joe never made any kind of response to the gospel. For the first time in his life, however, he did begin to ask himself what he believed about God. They only roomed together a semester.

Secretary [draw a line from 1 to 3]. After college graduation, Joe got a corporate job. He had a secretary who was a Christian. She kept a small sign on her desk that read "Prayer Helps," and every Monday morning she came to the office and talked about the Sunday worship music, the sermon, or a special event at church. From time to time she would invite Joe to bring his family to her church, but he always made an excuse not to come.

What Joe noticed most about his secretary was her disposition. She always seemed happy, and she never talked about people in the office. She did her best with every responsibility, and her uplifting spirit was contagious. Occasionally, Joe would say something about wishing he could bottle and sell her optimism, and she would respond by saying that "Jesus likes to give my kind of joy away to any person who really wants it." Joe didn't agree with her religious beliefs, but he did like the impact they made on her and his office.

Youth minister [draw a line from 1 to 4]. Joe eventually joined a health club. One day he was looking for a racquetball partner, and the club teamed him up with another member. His opponent was very competitive and they made a good match. When they were visiting casually in the locker room afterward, Joe was shocked to learn that this guy was a youth minister from a local church. He had always thought that ministers were religious professionals who spent all their time in church. They began playing together and became friends. Joe became interested in what the youth minister did at the church, and occasionally they got into theological discussions. The youth minister answered some of Joe's questions about God, but Joe still had little interest in church or thinking seriously about a personal faith.

Boss [draw a line from 1 to 5]. After a few years, Joe was transferred to another office on the West Coast. His boss, one of the top producers in the company, turned out to be a committed Christian. Once or twice he would invite the office to his home. Without fail, the boss would say something to the group about the role Jesus played in his life. Often he invited Joe and his family to church and occasionally Joe would go. It was not as stuffy and formal as he thought it would be.

For the first time, Joe was with a superior who was a committed Christian. Joe always thought of religion in terms of your private beliefs about God, but this man was deeply affected by his faith at many levels of his life. Joe greatly respected this man's work habits and abilities, and he began to understand that religious convictions were a major factor in defining his boss's character.

Business traveler [draw a line from 1 to 6]. One spring Joe was flying across the country to a national convention. The lady next to him was going to the same convention. They began chatting and suddenly Joe found himself opening up and telling her about some serious problems. His marriage was about to fall apart, and he was feeling like a rat trapped in a maze with no place to go.

The woman listened for a time and then told him that he sounded just like she and her husband did three years ago. They were going opposite directions in their careers and were about to file for divorce when a friend shared what Jesus could do for her. The lady said she became a Christian, and slowly Jesus began putting the pieces of her life in order.

Now she was happier than ever before, because she knew that God loved her and that he had the power to help her.

Joe was deeply moved. He had never thought of God as one who would get involved in the personal lives of people. He began to realize that what he believed about God could affect far more than his theological opinions. It could impact his daily life.

Church witness team [draw a line from 1 to 7]. A few weeks later, Joe was home alone when his doorbell rang. Two people from an area church had come to ask him if they could tell him about Jesus. Joe invited them in, and forty-five minutes later he gave his life to Christ. Although the witness team led Joe to Christ, they were only the final strand in a web of witnesses that the Holy Spirit used.

The Spider Principle

The Holy Spirit connects our witness to that of other believers and creates a web that draws people to salvation. Your attempt to share Christ with a person may be the first, middle, or last strand in a web of witnesses. Each opportunity to share is important!

Evangelism is adding your strand to the web.

BIBLIOGRAPHY

Chaney, Charles L. *The Secret of the Spirit-Filled Life*. Wheaton: Tyndale, 1985.

Wells, David. *God the Evangelist*. Grand Rapids: Eerdmans, 1987.

Tell Your Story: The Testimony of the Christian Witness

W hat you do speaks so loudly that I cannot hear what you say." These familiar words of Ralph Waldo Emerson ring true in our day. The testimony of the believer, both in word and deed, is crucial to sharing Christ. How can we tell others with confidence, as did Peter, "the things which we have seen and heard"? (Acts 4:20). Believers excited and grateful for the change in their lives by the gospel can be powerful tools in the hand of God.

ASSURANCE OF SALVATION

Following my freshman year of college, I spent a summer selling books door to door. Most of the time I sold a reference book for schoolchildren. It was a good product overall; however, I soon learned that I was best at convincing people with limited resources to buy the product. As the weeks passed, I became convicted that the value of this product was not worth what some people were willing to pay.

Confidence is critical in selling a product. It is even more important in sharing the gospel. Please note, the gospel is not about selling a product—we are offering a gift! But one hindrance to a confident Christian life is a lack of certainty about our own salvation. The apostle Paul was certain of his (see Phil. 1:6). John talked as well of the confidence of knowing Christ: "These things I have written to you who believe in the name of the Son of God, that you may know that you have eternal life" (1 John 5:13).

I remember the first time I visited the First Baptist Church of Woodstock, Georgia, a perennial leader in evangelism. I stayed with a family of church members. The wife was obvious in her love for Christ. When I asked her about her joy in the Lord, she said, "It is amazing how much joy you can have when you are really saved." She had been an active church member for many years but had never been converted. After meeting Christ, the change in her life was obvious to her and to others.

Billy Graham has said that the greatest field of evangelism in America is the church pew. I am convinced that we who lead churches must exhort our people consistently to be sure they are in the faith. Confidence in one's conversion brings enthusiasm in evangelism! Here are eight keys to assurance of salvation.

1. *Memory of one's conversion.* While some believers may not remember the exact date of their conversion, most can remember the time they met Christ. We ought to cherish that day when we passed from death unto life.

2. *Promises of Scripture.* Passages from the Bible on the certainty of salvation include Acts 16:31; John 3:16, 18; and Romans 5:9–10.

3. *The Spirit's presence.* Romans 8:9, 16, speak of the fact that the presence of the Spirit is indicative of a genuine Christian.

4. *Righteous living.* First John tells us we are not to continue in sin if we are Christians. This does not refer to sinless perfection but to a state of life not characterized by habitual sin. We will still sin even as Christians, but the pleasure of sin is not enduring.

5. *Sound doctrine.* A true Christian will be convinced of the truth of Scripture. A young Christian may not understand much about doctrine, but a believer cannot consistently deny the truth of the revealed Word of God. I was a child when I came to Christ. I did not know what a virgin was, let alone the

virginal conception of Jesus. But I am fully confident in this biblical truth now. Can a believer be deluded by false teaching? Certainly. But the mark of a believer is his or her recognition of the truth.

6. *Answered prayers.* First John 5:14–15 gives evidence.

7. *Discipline by God.* Hebrews 12:8 tells us God disciplines his children.

8. *Love for other Christians.* First John 3:14 tells us believers will love one another. In fact, the assurance of salvation is the theme of the First Epistle of John.

SHARING YOUR CONVERSION TESTIMONY

BIBLICAL EXAMPLES

The Bible gives several examples of the personal testimony. For example, we read of the man born blind (see John 9). After the remarkable physical and spiritual changes in his life, the man was confronted by the Pharisees. "I was blind," he declared, "but now I see" (John 9:25 NIV). He told his story. The Samaritan woman went into her community saying, "Come see a man" (John 4:39).

On two occasions in the Acts, the apostle Paul gave his testimony (see Acts 22; 26). Peter and John also declared, "We cannot but speak the things which we have seen and heard" (Acts 4:20). Obviously, the early believers communicated their salvation to others.

WHY A CONVERSION TESTIMONY IS EFFECTIVE

Every Christian has a testimony. A personal testimony is something every Christian can share. I once thought my testimony was insignificant because it was not dramatic. If you feel that way, remember the fact of conversion is more vital than the circumstances surrounding it.

It is relevant. A testimony is not past history; it is something that happened in our lifetime. People are looking for living, real, spiritual experiences. Johnny Hunt, pastor of First Baptist Church, Woodstock, Georgia, came to Christ in a powerful way. His best friend was an agnostic. Some time after Johnny's conversion, his friend said to him, "I have a problem. I am an agnostic. I'm not sure there is a God or if you can know there is a God. So here's my problem—what happened to my friend?" Johnny's friend was saved and is now in the ministry.

It is unique. You are an authority on your testimony. You may not be on anything else, but you are an authority on what God has done in your life. You may not know the answer to every question, but you know what happened to you.

TV talk shows, talk radio, the World Wide Web, the Internet, and chat rooms demonstrate the hunger that people have to communicate with one another. I spend a little time every week or so on the Internet, chatting with people, and seeking opportunities to witness. One of the things I've discovered is that people are interested in learning about other people.

It holds up a mirror to the person with whom you share. Your testimony gives people something to which they can compare their lives. The focus is on Christ and the change he has made in your life, but it still is a mirror for that person. When my former professor, James Eaves, was pastor at the First Baptist Church, Albuquerque, New Mexico, years ago, a waitress was converted. She sent out invitations to her friends to attend her baptism, followed by a party at a friend's home. She also invited her pastor to the party and gave him an opportunity to say a few words. More than seventeen of her friends were converted as a result of her conversion and witness.[1]

GUIDELINES FOR WRITING YOUR TESTIMONY

1. Write out your testimony, seeking the Spirit's guidance.

2. Give adequate but precise details showing how Christ became your Lord and Savior and how Christ meets your daily needs.

3. Use language the nonbeliever can understand.

4. Relive your testimony as you tell it. This will enable you to present it with loving enthusiasm.

5. Relate your testimony to the Scriptures, using pertinent verses as they are needed.

6. Speak distinctly and in a natural tone, avoiding any mannerisms that might detract from the presentation.

7. Be brief (two or three minutes). People are interested in your testimony but not your life story!

8. Ask the Holy Spirit to help you present Christ so the unbeliever will want to know him and will come to know him personally.

9. Share your Christian testimony regularly with other Christian members of your family, then with Christian friends, until it becomes a natural part of your daily conversation. Then share it with your lost friends and others.

10. After sharing your testimony, ask, "Has anything like this ever happened to you?" This question is a simple way to move into the gospel presentation.[2]

PUBLIC CONFESSION

Jesus said that if we are ashamed of him, he will be ashamed of us. Let us never be ashamed of telling others what God has done through Christ for us. Often on youth nights in revival services, I will pick out a young lady in the audience (I try to get an extrovert!). I ask her, in interview format, to describe the perfect guy, including naming the most popular guys on TV. I encourage other young ladies in the crowd to help. After getting this description, I then ask her how she would feel if this "perfect guy" started coming to her school and asked her to be his girlfriend. Of course, the response is something like "Fabulous!"

Then I make my point: "But suppose there was one catch: suppose he said he wanted to be your boyfriend, but you couldn't tell *anyone*—it would be a secret. No holding hands, separate cars on dates, going to places where nobody would see the two of you. What would you think of him?" Without exception, they reply, "I would think he was ashamed of me, and I wouldn't like it!" Then I say, "Are we like that toward Jesus? Are we open about him at church but ashamed everywhere else?"

The more you share your testimony, the more comfortable you will become. You will learn to adapt it to the audience to whom you are speaking. For example, when speaking to a teenager, I emphasize the changed lives of youth from my past and the impact they had on me. To a person reared in church, I will emphasize the fact that I grew up in church but realized church involvement was not my primary need. Adapting is *not* embellishing. Avoid the temptation to add details that did not actually happen. Have confidence that God can use your story just as it happened.

SHARING A RECOVERY TESTIMONY

The reason the organization known as Mother's Against Drunk Driving makes such an impact is that the founder lost her son to a drunk driver. Chuck Colson's passion for prison ministry is fueled in large measure by his own time spent in prison. The difficulty my wife and I experienced before we had kids, coupled with the severe illnesses both our children faced in childhood, has given us a special burden for infertile couples and those who have lost children. It is amazing how many people have common struggles. A recovery testimony is the story of how God has helped you through a difficulty since coming to Christ. It gives praise to God for his work in bringing us through a crisis.

SHARING YOUR SPIRITUAL AUTOBIOGRAPHY

Another way your story can have an evangelistic impact is through your spiritual autobiography. The spiritual autobiography includes the following features:[3]

1. The autobiography should exalt God above all else.

2. The autobiography for evangelism should include intimate knowledge of God and personal religious experience.

3. The spiritual autobiography is easily communicated through different media. Some of my students have begun to print copies of their personal testimonies in more detail—something like an autobiography that I'm describing here. As they go door-to-door, meet people, or write people to whom they are witnessing, they include copies of their autobiographies. A personal experience of a changed life will gain a hearing with some people when a sermon in a church building would not.

4. The information in a spiritual autobiography will be more effective when you share it with people in your own cultural

context. The spiritual autobiography is effectively used in a public church setting or a public gathering where you have time to give more than your testimony. The testimony is brief and to the point, demonstrating the change brought by the gospel when you were first converted. The spiritual autobiography goes through much more detail, looking at the different aspects of your life before and after you came to Christ. Include both high and low spiritual marks, giving an honest, personal description of your life in Christ.

Here is how Delos Miles shares his spiritual autobiography:[4]

I was born and reared on a tobacco farm in Florence County, South Carolina, where my father was a day laborer who could neither read nor write. He had to sign an X for his name. My mother did go to the third grade in school.

There on the farm I grew up in an atmosphere of both spiritual and physical poverty—spiritual poverty because my parents were not practicing members of any religious group, physical poverty because of my family's social and economic standing in the community. We were on the bottom rung of the social and economic ladder, if indeed on the ladder at all. I recall how my older sister and I would at times steal chickens from the people on whose farms we lived.

The first pair of shoes which I remember owning was a second-hand pair of brogans given to me by my first-grade schoolteacher. I was very proud of those shoes.

The first real crisis in my life came when I was seven. It was on the first day of the big Easter egg hunt at school, supposedly a very happy day. Yet, it turned out to be one of the saddest days of my life. At that time my father was working away from home during the week. When my older sister, younger brother, and I returned home on the school bus that afternoon, our first cousin met us. He told us that our mother had left home, taking our baby sister with her, and that she intended never to return. I can't describe to you how deeply that hurt me. At that time I couldn't understand any of my mother's reasons for doing a thing like that. It hurt me so much that I couldn't even cry about it. A root of bitterness sprang up in my heart toward my mother which required many years to remove.

My father got the three of us children together and tried to make a home for us. Then, shortly after my eighth birthday, another tragedy befell us. Daddy left home early on Saturday afternoon, the day before Pearl Harbor was bombed, with his brother and a friend with whom he had grown up—a big, husky man.

He told me and my sister and brother to go to our uncle's house and to wait for him until he returned home that Saturday night. But he never came home. The three men went to a little beer joint near Florence on U.S. 301 and got to drinking and having a "good time." As the evening wore on, my dad's friend got into a fight with another man. My father tried to break up the fight, but was knocked down to the floor. His friend got on top of him, pulled out his big pocket knife, and in his drunken stupor stabbed and cut my father to death.

My whole world caved in because when I lost my father I thought I had lost the only adult person in the world who deeply cared for me. And because of some things which my dad's friend had said about my mother when he came by our house on Saturday to pick up my father, I got it into my head that my mother had hired him to kill my father. You can imagine how twisted I was with hatred and hurt.

After a few months with relatives, moving from place to place, not really being wanted by any of them, something very good happened to me. I was invited to live with some folks whom I knew, but who were in no way related to me. For the first time in my life I had a bed of my own, three good meals to eat every day, and decent clothes and shoes to wear. Yet, more important than these material blessings, these folks were believers in Jesus Christ and members of the Baptist church in that rural community. They took me to church with them every Sunday morning, every Sunday night, every Wednesday night, and even once a quarter on Saturdays to attend the business conferences.

There in that little country church I discovered the Bible, a Book to which I was a total stranger, although I had been reared in what is called the Bible Belt. And I learned some things about God. When I was eleven years old, I felt separated from God. I had a miserable feeling inside of me. I was so unhappy that I felt like I was going to die unless something was done soon. I talked this over with my Sunday School teacher and with my foster parents. They all told me that I ought to confess my sins to God, ask him to help me, and place my life into his hands. As best I knew how, I followed their advice. That unhappy feeling left me. Peace and joy came into my life. Later, I went before the whole congregation and publicly confessed my faith in Jesus Christ as the Son of God and as my Lord and Savior and was baptized into the body of Christ by that congregation in Lynches River.

I grew in grace and in favor with God and men until my fourteenth birthday. Then, shortly before my fourteenth birthday, I was reconciled to my mother. I became convinced that she had nothing to do with my father's death and that she did, in fact, love me very much. So, on my fourteenth birthday I ran away from my foster home in the middle of the night, borrowed five dollars from a friend, walked eleven miles, caught a bus, and went to live with my mother and stepfather in Charleston, South Carolina.

Shortly after arriving in Charleston, I discovered that my stepfather drank a great deal. Life was unpleasant in that environment. So at the age of fourteen years and three months, I quit school prior to finishing the ninth grade and joined the United States Army. Of course, I lied about my age and persuaded my mother to sign for me.

I was just a kid thrust overnight into a completely adult world at Fort Jackson. And for some reason, I wanted very much to be accepted by the men in my company as one of them. I started doing the things which most of them did. I stopped going to church, ceased to read my Bible, and discontinued praying. I started drinking, smoking, cursing, gambling, and fighting. In short, I became a moral reprobate, broke God's covenant with me, and forsook my baptismal vows. I continued that wayward life for a little more than two-and-one-half years.

Then a great shaking of the foundations of my whole being came during the Korean War. I was a platoon sergeant of a rifle platoon in an infantry company. We had made our way deep into North Korea through the Changin Reservoir within about four miles of the Yalu River, the boundary between Manchuria and North Korea. Snow was many inches deep on the ground. Sometimes at night the temperature would drop down to twenty or thirty degrees below zero.

On the night of November 26, 1950, about midnight, we heard bugles blowing and rifles firing. My platoon was not under attack. But for the first time in the Korean War the Chinese Communists had entered the war in our section of the front.

Soon we got an order on the telephone to move our platoon out of position and to try to plug one of the holes where the Chinese had broken through our lines. We moved as rapidly as possible across the snow, engaged the enemy until about mid-morning on November 27. Then they broke off the battle.

We discovered that during the night the Chinese had completely encircled our position and cut us off from the First Marine Division some twelve to fifteen miles behind us. There was no way to get our dead or wounded out, and no way to get food and ammunition supplies—both of which were running low. On that particular day the overcast was too heavy for an airdrop.

So we regrouped, placed our men two of the hole, and dug in a few feet apart on the forward slope of the mountain for the attack which we felt would certainly come when darkness fell. I was in the platoon command post with our lieutenant and our platoon medic and messenger. Our command post was a large bunker which the North Koreans had dug into the side of the mountain. It consisted of two parts. Each part was about six by six feet and was covered with poles and dirt; and the parts were connected with a trench about four feet deep.

About dusk the Chinese began to probe our lines. They shot flares into the air and charged our position in successive waves at the sound of a bugle. The lieutenant and I were in the trench which connected the two parts of our bunker, firing at the Chinese and giving orders to our men, trying to encourage them to hold fast. To our right in one part of the bunker were our medic and messenger passing ammunition to us and taking care of our telephone contact with the company command post.

Bullets were flying all around us. There were so many of the Chinese that we couldn't stop them. When I saw they were going to overrun us, I turned to the lieutenant and said: "Sir, what are we going to do?"

He said: "Sergeant, you know what the orders are." We had orders not to withdraw under any circumstances. In a matter of moments the lieutenant was shot. He fell over in the trench and groaned for a while before he died.

I didn't know what to do. But the thought came to me to throw down my M-1 rifle in the snow and to jump back into the vacant end of our bunker and to play dead. I lay down on my back, sort of on my right side, facing the entrance to the hole.

Almost immediately a Chinese soldier came into the bunker firing his rifle. He didn't see me at first because of the darkness. However, one of his bullets hit me in my right little finger, entering at the end joint and going out at the knuckle. It scared me. I thought I was going to die. I had not prayed for a long time. But I began to pray silently in my mind to God.

As the soldier came on into the hole and found me, he shook me with his hand and shouted something in Chinese. Then, I guess he wanted to make sure I was dead. So he placed his rifle on my forehead. When I felt that cold steel, I thought it was the end. I don't remember everything I said to God, but as best I recall, my thoughts went something like this: *Lord, if you are all powerful like I've always heard you are, you can bring me out of here alive. If you will save my life, I'll do anything you want me to do.* I was so desperate I was trying to bargain with God for my life. And, God is my witness, when the soldier pulled the trigger, instead of going through my head, the bullet went down past my right ear. It did not knock me out. In my memory, as I reflect back upon it, it seems like a red hot iron had been placed against my head and left there. There was that burning sensation.

He went on out. After an hour and a half or maybe two hours, the firing ceased. Two Chinese came into the hole with me. They slept and rested a couple of hours. Then two more would come in. All night long there were two in the hole with me. The next morning two of them came in and searched me. They removed my gloves from my hands, took everything from my pockets, ran their bayonets up my arm and took my military watch. They pushed several layers of clothing up on my stomach and felt around, and pulled my pants out of the top of my combat boots where I had them bloused. This was another difficult time for me.

To make a long story short, I lay there in that hole for more than eighteen hours slowly bleeding and freezing to death, without consciously moving a muscle in my body, reliving my past life in my memory and imagination. I confessed all of my sins to God and made the most solemn promises I knew how to utter. If God would just get me out of there alive, I would serve him the rest of my life; I would do anything he wanted me to do.

God did bring me out with a strong hand. After three days and three nights and more sorrows and horrors, I finally got back to the First Marine Division, where I was flown out to a hospital. Seven men came out alive from my entire company. I spent almost nine months in various hospitals, undergoing treatment and surgery. During the first few weeks of those months, I thought I might never walk again. My feet had frozen and turned black all the way up to the ankles. I had a long time to reflect upon those experiences and the vows which I had made to God.

Finally I was discharged. I was still only seventeen, though I had spent three years, five months, and nineteen days in the Army. I knew that I had to try to follow through on the promises which I had made to God. So, before getting my discharge, I took the GED tests, a series of five competitive tests, and was able to get the equivalent of a high school diploma. But even with that, Furman University wasn't anxious to have me as a student because of my poor academic background. I can appreciate that much more now than I could then. Nevertheless, my pastor interceded for me, and Furman agreed to let me in on a trial basis for one semester. That was the most difficult semester of my life. Some nights I studied until two or three o'clock in the morning. Occasionally, I studied all night long. Seldom did I go to take a test or an examination without preparing to do my best and asking God to help me. Because of this strong sense of mission, I graduated along with the top of my class, magna cum laude.

For ten years I served as a pastor in South Carolina and Virginia. Since 1963 I have worked full time in the field of evangelism for Southern Baptists, three of those years in Virginia, twelve in my native state of South Carolina, and the rest teaching evangelism at Midwestern and Southeastern seminaries.

I share these experiences with you in order to bear witness to the reality of God. God is real. I know he is real because he has made himself known to me. I did not come to believe in God through any of the classical arguments for his existence. I came to believe that God is through a personal encounter with him. I believe Francis Thompson was right in his great autobiographical poem when he referred to God as the Hound of Heaven and said he is on the trail of every person. Sooner or later every person must meet God, if not here, then hereafter.

Second, I share these experiences with you in order to bear witness to the greatness of God. God is great. He is omnipotent, almighty, all-powerful, a God who can do anything he wills to do. I know God is great because his great power has changed my whole life. Only a truly great God could have changed me from what I was into what I am now in the process of becoming. And I am convinced that God in answer to my prayers literally turned the course of that bullet, or else my body would have long since turned to dust on a Korean mountain. The God in whom I believe is a miracle-working God.

Third, I share these experiences with you in order to bear witness to the goodness of God. God is good. I know he is good because his goodness has literally led me to repentance time and time again. And especially can I never forget his exceeding goodness to me in Korea. When there was no other human being to help me, I called upon God in my distress. As far as I can tell, God was under no obligation to hear my prayer. If I had received what I deserved at that point in my life, it would have been wrath, judgment, death, and perhaps even hell. But God did not give me what I deserved. He heard my prayer, brought me out safely, and delivered me from my enemies. God does not always deal with us according to his wrath and after our sins. Most of the time he deals with us according to his great love and with an infinite patience.

Now, what does all of this have to do with you? Well, for one thing, I hope you can see in these excerpts from my own life story a microcosm of needs which we Christians should seek to meet through Jesus Christ. Poverty, illiteracy, a broken home, crime, alcoholism, war, physical suffering, loneliness, lostness, and the struggle of the human soul for acceptance, dignity, and meaning—each of these needs you may see in my own pilgrimage. And each of these needs, along with a thousand more, we Christians should seek to meet day by day in the name and through the strength of him who is the Lord of life. God did not save us that we might become more Dead Seas. One Dead Sea in the world is enough. He has saved us that we might become a channel of blessing to humanity.

What does all of this have to do with you? What God has done for me and for others, he can do for you. And he will, if you will let him. But God will not force himself upon you. God is not like some cosmic policeman who walks the beat of the world with a blackjack in his hand, knocking persons over their heads and dragging them against their will into his kingdom. Rather, God is like the Hound of Heaven who pursues us relentlessly down all the labyrinthine ways of life and who pays us the supreme compliment of letting us choose between life and death.

The autobiography takes fifteen to twenty-five minutes to share, a testimony ninety seconds or so. The autobiography is probably ten pages, double-spaced.

It would be appropriate for you as a church leader to share your autobiography occasionally with those you lead. Pastor, tell it to your church annually, or at times. Sunday school teacher, tell your story to your class. It may encourage them to do the same. Even if you never have the opportunity to give your spiritual autobiography in a public place, just writing it out can be a great spiritual exercise. When my wife and I were going through the missionary approval process for the Home Mission Board, we had to write our autobiography. What a wonderful experience it was for me to reflect over my entire life and remember how good God has been.

APPLICATION

In the witness training that I lead, I require each participant to write his or her personal testimony. On more than one occasion, individuals in the training have discovered they had no testimony and were converted! A simple exercise you can do in a Sunday school class or an evening service, for example, is to provide paper and pencils and ask participants to write their conversion testimony. You might use Paul's testimony in Acts 26 as a biblical guide, followed by the sharing of your own testimony. Then challenge the participants to share their testimony with someone during the next week.

BIBLIOGRAPHY

Ford, Leighton. *The Power of Story: Rediscovering the Oldest, Most Natural Way to Reach People for Christ.* Colorado Springs: NavPress, 1994.

Stanton, Jack. *Evangelism for a Changing World,* eds. Timothy Beougher and Alvin L. Reid. Wheaton, Ill.: Harold Shaw, 1995.

Part 3

WHAT WE MUST DO: THE METHODOLOGICAL BASIS OF EVANGELISM

E rnest Shackleton led an unsuccessful attempt to reach the South Pole. In 1900 he published the following advertisement in a London newspaper: "Men Wanted for Hazardous Journey: Small wages, bitter cold, long months of complete darkness, constant danger, safe return doubtful. Honor and recognition in case of success."

So many people responded to the ad that Shackleton later declared, "It seemed as though all the men in Great Britain were determined to accompany me, the response was so overwhelming."[1]

Evangelism is not exactly like conquering Antarctica, though some may fear the task in the same way! But evangelism can motivate us to make the impact for which we were created. A friend once gave me this definition: "Witnessing is a conversation between two people, both of whom are nervous." Any believer who takes seriously the command to share Christ will do so with some level of fear. This book recognizes that fear. Many of us have knocked on a door while witnessing, only to pray, "God, please don't let them be at home!"

Knowing how to go about the practice of evangelism brings great confidence. This final section of the book covers the methodological approaches necessary to reach the world. It builds upon Parts 1 and 2. Methods are effective only when built on a biblical foundation and when applied through the life of passionate Christians.

11

The Need of the Hour: Personal Evangelism

D id you hear about the three pastors who met in an account- ability group? One day they told one another their greatest hidden sins. The first said, "Don't tell my congregation, but I'm an alcoholic." The next confessed, "If my people knew I'm a compulsive gambler, they would fire me." The third said, "I hate to admit it, but I'm addicted to gossip, and I can't wait to get out of here!"

It is obvious that most American Christians are better at talking about evangelism than actually doing it. In this chapter, we will focus on some specific ways to witness to others. But first let's address the problem of fears. How do we get people in our churches to overcome their fears?

CONFRONTING OUR FEARS

Paul told young Timothy, "God has not given us a spirit of fear." In my witness training through the years, two primary fears surface again and again: the fear of failure and the fear of rejection.

THE FEAR OF FAILURE

If you have attempted to witness, you know about this fear: "I don't know what to say." "What if they ask a question I can't answer?" The fear of failure is real. How do we cope with it?

This fear may exist because we misunderstand our task. We are called to faithfulness. Faithfulness to share is our measure of success. Our Lord Jesus did not win every person with whom he shared. We are ambassadors. Ambassadors do not speak on their authority but for another. We must remember that God holds us accountable for obedience, not perfection. If we enjoy fishing as much as catching, we will experience a lessening of this fear.

My kids are big Michael Jordan fans. Once Joshua asked me if Michael Jordan ever missed a shot. After all, he is the consummate basketball player. During the 1997 NBA playoffs, a Nike commercial featured Jordan musing over his career. *I've missed nine thousand shots . . . I've lost almost three hundred games,* he pondered. *Twenty-six times I have been trusted to take the winning shot and missed.* Then he concluded: *I've failed over and over in my life—and that is why I succeed!*

I used this commercial to show Joshua that Michael Jordan is not great because he is perfect but because he is *tenacious.* He won't quit. He won't let the fear of failure defeat him. The same season the commercial aired, in game one of the 1997 NBA finals against Utah, Michael Jordan was again trusted to take the game-winning shot, and he made it. He later hit the key shot in a game in which he played when he was sick with the flu. You can make it too as a witness—and what you are doing is far more important than a basketball game!

Where do we get the false notion that we should be able to answer any question a person raises? Nowhere in Scripture are we told that an effective witness must be a Bible know-it-all. I see this attitude in seminary students. "I am getting a Master of Divinity," they think, "so I must know all the answers." We don't have to know everything; we must know what *matters.* Our focus should be on the essential gospel, not the trivial chatter of society.

This leads me to the best practical solution for this fear: witness training. What a joy it is to show people how simple it is to use a tract to present Christ. "I can do *that*" they say. Believers who earnestly desire to serve Christ will find such training helpful.

Witness training that allows people to learn through classroom experience, role playing, and field experience helps them to see that they can do it!

THE FEAR OF REJECTION

Rejection is an inevitable part of witnessing. The most winsome person on earth will not convince everyone the truth of the gospel. I have yet to meet any person who loves rejection. *Facing* rejection rather than *avoiding* rejection is crucial. We must understand the reasons for rejection in order to face it to the glory of God.

The principle of transference. Transference states that in every new relationship, positive and negative feelings occur as a result of prior experiences. It is always present in new relationships; it is unconscious; and it can be positive, negative, or both. For example, you as a pastor might introduce yourself to a hospital patient. Before he even gets your name, he starts cursing you! Perhaps he didn't like something about some preacher somewhere—and he's taking it out on you. A lot of times you are the lightning rod for things that have nothing to do with you. When we share the gospel with people, they may not appreciate what we say, but we shouldn't take this personally.

While serving as evangelism director, I provided leadership in a witnessing conference. As part of the training, we went out in threes to visit. The chairman of deacons at the church took my team to the "meanest guy in town." His name was Mike. We sat in his living room, talking about sports. I transitioned to the gospel by asking, "Mike, do you know for certain you have eternal life and that you will go to heaven when you die?"

Immediately, Mike's hands went up as if to form an invisible wall. "I don't talk about religion in my house," he said. I could sense his hostility, so I said, "Mike, I understand that I am a guest in your house. But, several years ago, Jesus Christ radically changed my life, and I have never gotten over it. As passionate as I am about sports, my love for God is deeper."

For the next twenty or thirty minutes, we discussed spiritual things. Mike did not receive Christ, but he did listen. As we left, he told me I was the first preacher who treated him as a person, with respect. He had been negative toward me because of his past experiences. I am happy to say that he was eventually reached for Christ. We must not take it personally if a person rejects us.

The Engel Scale (see a simplified version in Figure 11.1) illustrates the reality that not every unsaved person will receive Christ on their first encounter with his truth.[1] They may be atheists, but your witness could cause them to begin to think of spiritual things. Another person may be having questions; your witness can give answers. While we want to win everyone with whom we share, the truth is we will not. But we can help each person to consider more clearly the claims of the gospel.

The role of rejection. We desperately need a paradigm shift in the American church. We must revisit the biblical teaching that *we are*

Figure 11.1

God's Role ↓	Communicator's Role		Man's Response
General Revelation		-8	Awareness of Supreme Being but no Effective Knowledge of Gospel
Conviction	Proclamation	-7	Initial Awareness of the Gospel
		-6	Awareness of Fundamentals of the Gospel
	R e j e c t i o n	-5	Grasp of Implications of Gospel
		-4	Positive Attitude Toward Gospel
		-3	Personal Problem Recognition
		-2	DECISION TO ACT
	Persuasion	-1	Repentance and Faith in Christ
REGENERATION			NEW CREATURE
Sanctification ↓	Follow-up ↓ Cultivation	+1	Post-Decision Evaluation
		+2	Incorporation Into Body
		+3	Conceptual and Behavioral Growth
		+4	Communion with God
		+5	Stewardship
		•	Reproduction
		•	Internally (gifts, etc.)
		•	Externally (witness, social action, etc.)
ETERNITY			

never more like the prophets or Jesus than when we are rejected. How could you identify a true prophet in Old Testament times? What they said came true, and they led people toward faithfulness to God. Another characteristic of a true prophet was that people didn't like what he said.

How do you know Micaiah was a true prophet? Because Ahab didn't like what he had to say! You know Amos was a true prophet because he was told, "Go back where you came from, buddy" (see Amos 7:12). They were rejected because they said the truth. So when we speak the truth, some people are going to reject us.

What did Jesus say in the Beatitudes? "Blessed are ye when men revile you. They speak all manner of evil against you falsely for my sake. Rejoice and be exceedingly glad, for great is your reward in heaven." If you want to be in grand company spiritually, take note of how much you have been rejected. Our Lord Jesus was despised and rejected. We should never seek rejection, but it must be understood as a part of authentic Christianity.

We need to replace our fear with a greater fear. There's an appropriate place for fear in the life of the Christian. The fear of the Lord is the beginning of wisdom (see Prov. 1:7). The apostle Paul declared that we must all appear before the judgment seat, the bema seat, the rewards seat of Christ (see 2 Cor. 5:10). We will receive rewards based on the things we've done, whether good or evil. The word *evil, dotkornea,* is the word that can be translated "trivial" or "worthless." Then Paul says, knowing therefore the *terror* of God, we persuade men (see 2 Cor. 5:11). Here we find a biblical motivation to share the gospel out of the holy fear of God. Having a healthy fear of God enhances our understanding of his love.

FEAR AND COMFORT ZONES

In the matter of witnessing, it's necessary for God to push us out of our comfort zones. My son Joshua comes to mind as a good example of this principle. He loved the training wheels on his bicycle, but the day came when I was sure he was ready to take off the training wheels.

Joshua was nervous about this. "Dad, I don't think so," he kept telling me. And I kept saying, "Joshua, you can trust me. Dad won't lead you wrong. You can do this."

After the training wheels came off and he learned to ride without them, I couldn't get Joshua off his bike. He rode so much faster, with so much control, that he couldn't believe how much fun it was.

Witnessing can be like that. We're nervous, we're afraid, but when we step out and do something that honors God, it is exhilarating and rewarding beyond description.

How sad it would be for a person to grow up in a church, attend faithfully, become a devoted follower of Christ—but never learn to share his or her faith. Could it be that there are many Christians, even key church leaders, who have never consistently witnessed? Is it possible that there are many longtime believers who have *never* shared with a single lost person their testimony of how Christ changed their life? Are we as leaders not robbing saints of great joy by failing to show them the pleasure of witnessing?

OVERCOMING FEAR

A former student and an effective evangelistic pastor named Jerry Devinney has taught me a couple of techniques to help people overcome their fear of witnessing.

First, when Jerry witnesses to people for the first time, he asks how many times anyone else has shared Christ with them. Most people to whom he witnesses have never had anyone witness to them. This gives Jerry—and it should give each of us—a greater sense of urgency. The reason many people have not given their lives to Christ is that no one has told them how!

A second thing Jerry has done is sobering as well. One year when his church led the local association in baptisms, he checked with a funeral director in his town to determine how many people had died the year before. He discovered more people died that year than the entire association baptized. That served as a powerful motivation for both Jerry and his church to tell others—in spite of the fears that go along with witnessing.

THE APPROACH TO A WITNESSING ENCOUNTER

When witnessing, many people have a difficult time guiding the conversation from the secular to the sacred. A good approach is helpful in doing this. The initial contact with a lost person, through words and actions, establishes enough relationship to allow a witness for Christ.

While teaching a required Old Testament course at Houston Baptist University in 1994, I noticed one young lady asked several questions about the course the first day. Most students just hoped to get through the syllabus so class would be over, but Allison continued to probe. Finally, she said, "I am a practicing Jew, in the nursing program, and I am very nervous about studying the Hebrew Bible at a Baptist school."

I assured her that she would be treated with respect. Speaking with her after class, I learned the reason for her anxiety. While a student at another institution, she was approached by Christian witnesses. When Allison replied she was Jewish and not interested, they replied, "Oh well, we know you aren't. After all, you Jews killed Jesus." This was *not* the best approach. I told Allison that not every Christian was like that and encouraged her to share her thoughts with the class.

As we moved into Exodus, I asked Allison to explain a Jewish Seder (Passover) service to us. She went crazy with excitement! She demonstrated the whole service, complete with leg of lamb, the candy, and the trimmings. The students were wowed, the professor was impressed, and Allison felt a part of the class and the school.

As the class continued, I shared openly with Allison due to our friendship. By the end of the course, Allison said, "You know, I think Jesus may be the Messiah after all." She even went to hear me preach. Although I moved and lost touch with Allison, the approach I took helped her become more open to the gospel. While this encounter occurred over a period of time, the same can be said about a one-time witnessing encounter.

REASONS FOR THE APPROACH

A good approach eases tensions of the lost person. It is more winsome if you build rapport prior to moving into the gospel.

It eases the fears of the witness. One definition of soul-winning is "a conversation between two people, both of whom are nervous."

HOW TO APPROACH A LOST PERSON

The most significant practical detail related to personal evangelism is this: In order to win lost people to Christ, we must talk to lost people! You can build rapport by finding something in common with another person in only a couple of minutes. A great start is to ask, "Where are you from originally?"

Approach the person in love. People are not stupid; they can tell if you care! You may stumble in the presentation. You may not answer every question they have. But your ability to look them in the eye and to lead them to sense that something important has happened in your life will overcome a world of mistakes. A concern for people will overcome other factors.

I have known people who stumbled through the presentation, even breaking into tears—partly because they were nervous, partly because they knew they were messing up—and still they led somebody to Christ.

Paige Patterson, speaking to students on a mission trip, said there are four things lost people can tell about Christians:

1. If you know what you are talking about;

2. If you believe what you are talking about;

3. If you care about them; and

4. If you have the anointing of God on your life.

Herschel Hobbs tells the story of a hardened criminal awaiting execution. Several pastors and ministers tried to reach him for Christ. Typically, they focused on what a sinner he was and how he needed salvation. This only hardened his heart. Then a layman came to see him. He sat with him and said, "You and I are in a terrible fix, aren't we?" The humble layman's identification with the hardened criminal led him to weep, and soon he repented of his sins and trusted the Savior.[2]

Approach the person in a spirit of prayer. "For the Holy Spirit will teach you in that very hour what you ought to say" (Luke 12:12). Our efforts are in partnership with the work of the Holy Spirit.

Approach the person expectantly. Believe he or she will be interested. A student in Houston visited my office to ask about her grade. I asked Sabrina if she ever thought about spiritual things, to which she replied, "Yes." I shared Christ with her, and in a short while, we were on our knees in my office, as she gave her life to Christ!

Be sensitive to the Holy Spirit. The more you witness, the more you will learn to listen to the Holy Spirit. Even if you give a terrible approach, God can still use you. Bill Bright said we fail in witnessing only if we fail to witness. We learn to witness by doing it. And I will say it again—evangelism is *caught* more than *taught.*

In Claremont, New Hampshire, I met Eileen, an apartment finder for the town. I asked her, "You know the area well; what is the greatest need?" Immediately, she said, "There is a lot of hopelessness here." I handed her a tract that said "Here's Hope" on the cover (*that* got her attention!). I told her, "We are here to tell others of the hope of Jesus." She was a recovering alcoholic and said she did more counseling than apartment finding.

I shared my testimony, and she replied with a nebulous belief in a nebulous God. She had never heard a clear presentation of the gospel. After sharing with her, I said to her, "Jesus Christ radically changed my life." She replied, "I can tell he has!" I did not lead her to Christ, but it was another example that many people will talk about spiritual matters.

MODELS OF A GOOD APPROACH

Learning some basic models can give confidence. The approach one takes can be *formal,* as with Jesus and Nicodemus. Don't be afraid to be direct. I have told students to take gospel tracts and simply say, "I have this crazy professor who says I have to read this booklet to someone. Can I read it to you?" One student did that, then came to class in tears. This direct approach opened the door for him to lead a person to Christ. Or we can be *informal* as Jesus was with the Samaritan woman (see John 4) and with Zacchaeus (see Luke 19).

Here are three simple ideas for approaching people to witness. It may be summarized in three words: *Explore, stimulate, share.*[3]

1. *Explore.* Get to know the other person. Ask questions, listen, be alert.

2. *Stimulate.* Raise their interest. Simple questions are effective:

- If you ever want to talk about the difference between religion and Christianity, let me know.

- When you attend church, where do you attend?

- Have you thought more lately about spiritual things?

- Would you say you have a personal relationship with Jesus Christ, or are you still in the process? This question has been very effective!
- In your opinion, what is a real Christian?
- What do you think of _____? (God, Jesus, the Bible)
- Who do you think Jesus Christ was?
- We've been friends for a while. Could I share with you a very important part of my life?

The last question is good for somebody you've known for years but to whom you've never witnessed. I had a businessman in Tennessee who said to me, "I've been on the job for several years, and people know that I'm a Christian, but I've got friends to whom I've never witnessed. How do I go about witnessing to them?" I sensed he really wanted to know. He had one person in particular in mind. I will call him Bob.

"Let me tell you what you need to do for Bob," I replied. "First of all, you need to go to church tomorrow. Go forward to recommit your life to Christ and say that you've not been the witness you need to be. Tell the entire church that. Monday morning find Bob and ask him if you can speak to him for a minute. Then tell him, 'Bob, I need to apologize to you because of something I haven't done. Yesterday I told my church that I've not been right, and I'm sorry. I want you to know the greatest thing that ever happened to me.' Then go right into your testimony."

3. *Share.* Respond to their needs. Apply the gospel to where they are.

An acrostic is a simple memory tool to help you with your witnessing and sharing approach. Both Evangelism Explosion (EE) and Continuing Witness Training (CWT) use this. (See the following page for how CWT uses the acrostic.)

Personal Testimony

The personal testimony is the best way to move into a gospel presentation. You might ask, "Where are you from originally?" After their answer, say "That's interesting. I am from . . . ." Move into your testimony, followed by, "Has anything like this ever happened to you?" If they cannot give a clear testimony, move into the gospel.

Continuing Witness Training[4]
Model Presentation

F.I.R.E. Acrostic:

A. Family

[Do you have any special hobbies?]

1. Interests

[When you attend church, where do you attend?]

2. Religious Background

[Let me ask you a question.]

3. Exploratory Questions

a. Have you come to a place in your life that you know for certain that you have eternal life and that you will go to heaven when you die?

[The Bible says, . . . (1 John. 5:13). Now I know for certain I have eternal life and when I die I will go to heaven. Let me ask you another question.]

b. Suppose you were standing before God right now and he asked you, "Why should I let you into my heaven?" What do you think you would say?

[God loves us and has a purpose for our lives. The Bible states it this way, . . . (John. 3:16). God's purpose is that we have eternal life.]

SERVANTHOOD EVANGELISM

A simple act of kindness provides a marvelous way of introducing the gospel. This particular approach is explained in detail in the following chapters.

EFFECTIVE TOOLS FOR PERSONAL EVANGELISM

MARKED NEW TESTAMENT

The first way I trained anyone to witness was by showing them how to mark a New Testament. There are many excellent Bibles already marked to assist the witness in sharing Christ. A more recent example is the *People Sharing Jesus* New Testament.

CWT Model

Gospel

A. God's Purpose

1. We receive eternal life as a free gift (Rom. 6:23).
2. We can live a full and meaningful life right now (John 10:10).
3. We will spend eternity with Jesus in heaven (John 14:3).

   [As I searched for real meaning in life, I discovered that my sinful nature kept me from fulfilling God's purpose for my life.]

B. Our Need

1. We are all sinners by nature and by choice (Rom. 3:23).
2. We cannot save ourselves (Eph. 2:9).
3. We deserve death and hell (Rom. 6:23).

   [God is holy and just and must punish sin, yet he loves us and has provided forgiveness for our sin. Jesus said, . . . (John 14:6).]

C. God's Provision

1. Jesus is God and became man (John 1:1, 14).
2. Jesus died for us on the cross (1 Pet. 3:18).
3. Jesus was resurrected from the dead (Rom. 4:25).

   [The only way Jesus can affect our lives is for us to receive him. The Bible says, . . . (John 1:12).]

D. Our Response

1. We must repent of our sin (Acts 3:19).
   a. Repentance is not just feeling sorry for our sin (Acts 26:20).
   b. Repentance is turning away from our sin and turning to God through Jesus.
2. We must place our faith in Jesus (Eph. 2:8).
   a. Faith is not just believing facts about Jesus (James 2:19).
   b. Faith is trusting Jesus.
3. We must surrender to Jesus as Lord (Rom. 10:9–10)
   a. Surrendering to Jesus as Lord is not just saying we give our lives to Jesus (Matt. 7:21).
   b. Surrendering to Jesus as Lord is giving Jesus control of our lives.

[As evidence of giving Jesus control, we will want to iden-tify with him. The New Testament way is to confess Jesus publicly and to follow him in baptism and church mem-bership.]

Leading to a Commitment
A. Commitment Questions
  1. Transition Question:"Does what we have been discussing make sense to you?"
  2. Willingness Question:"Is there any reason why you would not be willing to receive God's gift of eternal life?"
  3. Commitment Question:"Are you willing to turn from your sin and place your faith in Jesus right now?"
B. Clarification—To receive Jesus you must:
  1. Repent of your sin.
  2. Place your faith in Jesus.
  3. Surrender to Jesus as Lord.
     [Let's bow our heads, and I will lead in prayer.]
C. Prayer
  1. Prayer for Understanding
     [The Bible says, . . . (Rom. 10:13). If you truly want the Lord to give you eternal life, tell him out loud.]
  2. Prayer of Commitment
     [Welcome to the family of God. You have just made the most important decision of your life. You can be sure you are saved and have eternal life.]
  3. Prayer of Thanksgiving
     [Receiving Jesus into your life is only the beginning of a wonderful experience. Let's read the booklet "Welcome to God's Family" and see how you can be sure you have eter-nal life and how you can grow as a Christian.]

Immediate Follow-up

TRACTS

With the first person I ever led to Christ, I used the *Four Spiritual Laws* booklet produced by Campus Crusade for Christ. Spurgeon said more people are in heaven because of tracts than any other means. They are valuable not only because they keep the witness on track with the gospel but because you can leave them with people for later reading and reflection.

Here are six useful principles for using tracts in witnessing.

1. Never use a tract you haven't read. (Some are weak theologically.)

2. Brevity is desirable.

3. Use tracts that are attractive.

4. Be enthusiastic about the contents.

5. Be sure the tract sets forth the facts of the gospel.

6. The tract should explain the process by which a person becomes a Christian, particularly emphasizing repentance and faith.

MEMORIZED PRESENTATIONS

The best examples of memorized presentations are from Evangelism Explosion (EE) and Continuing Witness Training (CWT). A new approach called FAITH, uses this word as an acrostic to assist in sharing Christ.

Some people criticize memorized presentations because they are "canned." In my experience, *any* presentation of the gospel—a marked New Testament, tract, or testimony—is canned, if the person sharing Christ doesn't care about the person hearing the message. But the discipline such an approach offers has aided many believers in their growth in personal evangelism. (See the CWT Model.)

Regardless of whether you use CWT, EE, FAITH, Billy Graham's materials, or any other approach, make sure the presentation you use emphasizes the need of the lost person, as well as the work of Christ, and the biblical response (repentance and faith). A person cannot be saved unless he realizes he is lost and in need of saving. The law of God has a purpose—to show us our need for salvation and our insufficiency to save ourselves. We are not trying to get someone to "pray the prayer." We are attempting to help individuals meet the God who created them.

Let me encourage you to train others to witness. A helpful way to teach believers to witness is through role-playing. I wish someone had taught me as a teenager how to witness and to role play sharing the gospel. I believe I could have won twenty or thirty of my friends to Christ because I was a leader, I was well-liked on the campus, and I was a Christian. I had many friends, both Christians and non-Christians, but I didn't know how to communicate the gospel clearly one-on-one. I could get people to come to church, and I saw some of my friends come to Christ, but how I wish someone had trained me. When I was a freshman in college, somebody taught me how, and it changed my life.

When I served at a local church, at times I would use a service for practical training. I would give everyone a tract, then have them spend some time role-playing with one another.

I had been a pastor and was on staff at a church before I had ever watched anyone witness. I am convinced of the importance of watching somebody else. Sometimes I'll go out witnessing with a pastor and say, "Let me watch you one time. I still have a lot to learn. Then you watch me and let's talk about it." That's what I love about CWT. You're actually out there witnessing. The people can watch you. You can watch them. Then you can talk about it. This leads to effective learning and effective witnessing.

THE GOSPEL PRESENTATION: LEADING TO A DECISION

We are obligated to God and the other person to ask for a decision whenever possible. At times this can't be done because of time factors or interruptions. But the gospel presentation is incomplete without a call to decision. Intellectual awareness of the gospel is not salvation. We need to look for opportunities to draw the net.

In assisting people in their commitment to Christ, we must remember we cannot always determine what is happening in their hearts. We must explain the message, pray for them, and trust the leadership of the Spirit. The questions used in the CWT presentation are repeated here because they are extremely helpful. (See "Leading to a Commitment.)

Leading to a Commitment

A. Commitment Questions
  1. Transition Question: "Does what we have been discussing make sense to you?"
  2. Willingness Question: "Is there any reason why you would not be willing to receive God's gift of eternal life?"
  3. Commitment Question: "Are you willing to turn from your sin and place your faith in Jesus right now?"
B. Clarification—To receive Jesus you must:
  1. Repent of your sin.
  2. Place your faith in Jesus.
  3. Surrender to Jesus as Lord.
     [Tr.: Let's bow our heads and I will lead in prayer.]
C. Prayer
  1. Prayer for Understanding
     [Tr.: The Bible says ... (Rom. 10:13). If you truly want the Lord to give you eternal life, tell him out loud.]
  2. Prayer of Commitment
     [Tr.: Welcome to the family of God. You have just made the most important decision of your life. You can be sure you are saved and have eternal life.]
  3. Prayer of Thanksgiving
     [Tr.: Receiving Jesus into your life is only the beginning of a wonderful experience. Let's read the booklet "Welcome to God's Family" and see how you can be sure you have eternal life and how you can grow as a Christian.]

Explain the commitment the person is to make. When using a tract, read the prayer to the person, asking if it expresses their desire to know God. Remind the other person that Christianity is a relationship, not a ritual. They are to talk to God personally.

The third approach should be used sparingly and with caution. The Scripture does not give a prescribed "sinner's prayer," so a formula is not required. However, the Bible does teach a lost person to cry out to God in prayer for salvation (Rom. 10:9, 13), so a sinner's prayer can be deduced from Scripture. The danger is in emphasizing the reciting of words more than the attitude of the will.

Further, I would avoid such terminology as "accepting Jesus into your heart," a concept that is not found in Scripture. Repentance and faith are the conditions; further, receiving the gift of salvation is a biblically valid expression. The question is not, do I accept Jesus, but does Jesus accept me? Thankfully, the response is *yes*, when we come in repentance and faith.

FOUNDATIONS FOR EFFECTIVE FOLLOW-UP

When a person becomes a believer, he or she is birthed into the kingdom of God. But he is a baby spiritually and in need of nurture. Immediate follow-up can help a new believer in her or his time of spiritual infancy. Churches have neglected follow-up. We have left a generation of baby Christians stranded, unsure of how to grow.

In his book on this subject, Waylon Moore makes the following point concerning follow-up.

> Follow-up is the conservation, maturation, and multiplication of the fruit of evangelism. Winning and building are inseparably linked together in the scriptures. There is no continuing New Testament evangelism without follow-up. They are God's "two-edged sword" for reaching men and making them effective disciples for Christ.[5]

There are two extremes we must recognize in dealing with the subject of follow-up. First, there is the extreme that emphasizes follow-up so strongly that witnessing occurs only in the most ideal settings—settings in which the growth of the new Christian is virtually ensured. We must remember that Philip shared Christ with the eunuch (Acts 8), although he was not able to stay with the Ethiopian to assist his growth. On the other hand, there are those who are extremely evangelistic but who give little regard for the nurture of new Christians. This extreme emphasizes *decisions,* not *disciples* as Jesus did.

PRACTICAL STEPS IN IMMEDIATE FOLLOW-UP

Help the new believer with assurance. Immediately after a person repents, pray a prayer of thanksgiving, then ask the other person to thank God in his or her own words. I have heard wonderful, simple, earnest prayers uttered by baby Christians. Then go over their commitment with them briefly. Encourage them by reminding them that heaven rejoices in their commitment.

Give specific guidance in the Christian life. Many tracts do this well). Help the new believer discover the best time for Bible study and prayer, the name of persons who would rejoice in this person's salvation, and the names of those who need to hear the gospel.

A BIBLICAL PATTERN FOR FOLLOW-UP

Waylon B. Moore lists four ingredients in New Testament follow-up:

1. Personal Contact

2. Personal Prayer

3. Personal Representatives

4. Personal Correspondence[6]

Follow-up begins with a proper understanding of evangelism. A church functioning with a definition of evangelism that focuses on decisions rather than disciples will not emphasize follow-up. Follow-up is helped by building a gregarious fellowship. A program alone is not the cure. Build a spirit of friendliness in the congregation. Statistics indicate that if a new believer doesn't make seven friends during the first year in the church, he or she likely will not stay there. New Christians need good role models.

Be the type of people with whom new converts want to be. A joyous, aggressive church provides a great atmosphere for follow-up. In addition, take new believers out witnessing. This is great follow-up. Also look for ways to enhance current structure for effective follow-up: the Sunday school, more ministry, etc. CWT has an approach for follow-up called the Encourager Plan through the Sunday school.

Provide tools for the new converts, such as *Beginning Steps,* a booklet with instructions in the Christian life. The following points are covered in this resource:

• Assurance
• Baptism/church membership
• Bible study
• Prayer
• Corporate worship/fellowship
• Witness
• Discipleship

APPLICATION

I heard a speaker tell a story about the late entertainer Jimmy Durante, who often entertained troops during wartime. On one occasion, he was visiting a military hospital. The administrator asked him to stay for a short show in the auditorium. Durante said he had to leave for appointments, but the administrator insisted. "Five minutes," Durante agreed, "but then I must go."

The sick and wounded were brought into the auditorium. Durante did a brief routine, and the crowd clapped and cheered profusely. Instead of leaving, the comedian continued—for a full hour. The elated administrator asked him why he stayed so long.

"When I did the first routine," Durante replied, "I noticed two men in the front row. The one on the left had lost his right arm. The one on the right had lost his left arm. When they clapped, they clapped as one. I was so moved, I couldn't leave."

When we learn that what we give in evangelism does not compare to what we will receive, we will share the gospel.

Is presenting the gospel a part of your lifestyle? Suppose for a moment that you are the only Christian in your world. No one you know is saved—neighbors, work associates, family, or friends. What are the odds of any of these coming to Christ if you continue to witness at your current level?

BIBLIOGRAPHY

Fay, William and Ralph Hodge. *Share Jesus without Fear.* Nashville: LifeWay Press, 1997.

McCloskey, Mark. *Tell It Often, Tell It Well.* San Bernardino: Here's Life, 1985.

Little, Paul. *How to Give Away Your Faith.* Downers Grove: InterVarsity Press, 1966.

Robinson, Darrell. *People Sharing Jesus.* Nashville: Thomas Nelson, 1995.

"Eternal Life" booklet. Available through the North American Mission Board, 4200 North Point Parkway, Alpharetta, GA 30022-4176.

12

Out of the Sanctuary into Reality: Mobilizing for Personal Evangelism

P ersonal evangelism is the ultimate good news/bad news situation. It reminds me of the story of a bachelor who had lived alone for many years. One day he called his father.

"Dad," he said, "I have good news and bad news."

"Tell me the good news first," his father replied.

"I finally got married."

"That's good, son."

"But, Dad, my wife is really ugly."

"That's bad, son."

"But, Dad, my wife is rich."

"Why, that's good, son."

"But my wife is very stingy."

"Oh, that's bad, son."

"But she built me a big, beautiful house."

"That's really good, son."

"But the house burned down."

"That's too bad, son."

"But my wife was in the house when it burned."

The father didn't know what to say! In the same vein, many Christians believe in the Good News but act as though sharing it is bad news. I believe many Christians want to witness, but they just don't know what to say. But even more significant is the number of Christians who know what to say but never witness. How do we get saved folks out of the sanctuary into reality?

When it comes to personal evangelism, believers are at different levels of commitment. Many people who are nominally affiliated with a given church are not interested in witnessing. This group consists of those who are unequipped church attendees (Figure 12.1).

FIGURE 12.1

```
┌─────────────────────────────────────────────────┐
│   ┌─────────────────────────────────────────┐   │
│   │      Unequipped Church Attendees        │   │
│   └─────────────────────────────────────────┘   │
└─────────────────────────────────────────────────┘
```

For these people, Christianity is a *pastime*—not a *passion*. There is no consistent fruit; in fact, more than a few of these could be unconverted and thus ought to be the subject of evangelism themselves. Others are spiritual infants, and still others are living carnal lives. This group needs to realize that Christianity calls for radical Christian living. They will never be consistent witnesses without a passion for God. They need deep, biblical revival! That's why evangelism in the local church must be built on the foundation established in the first two sections of this book and why spiritual emphases, such as prayer conferences, must be tied to evangelism.

The next group consists of those believers who have genuinely met Christ. They love him, but they have never really been taught how to share him with others (Figure 12.2). Personal evangelism has never been a priority for them, mainly because they don't see it as their job or they simply don't know how to witness. Their number is legion. I am convinced this group holds the key to whether we will reach America and the world for Christ. These people need consistent, ongoing motivation and training in soul-winning. More about the need for witness training later.

FIGURE 12.2

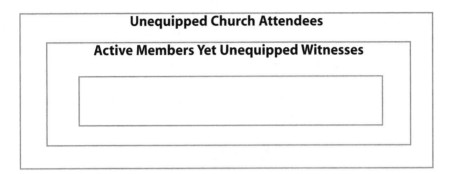

There is another group that represents the greatest opportunity for an immediate, significant impact. These are the multitude of active, born-again members of evangelical churches who not only know Jesus but also believe it is imperative to make him known (Figure 12.3). *At some point they have been equipped to witness—*through Evangelism Explosion, CWT, a Billy Graham school, or another tool. If pressed into a corner, they could lead someone to Christ.

FIGURE 12.3

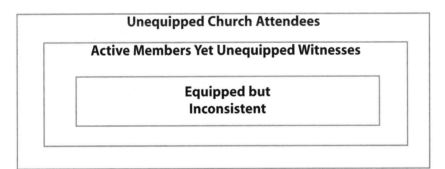

There is only one problem with this third group: although they know how to share Christ, most of them just don't do it. Just imagine if this army of believers suddenly marched into battle? I have conducted witnessing training for people like this hundreds of times. The greatest obstacle we face is not our training methods; it is the discovery of a mechanism to get people motivated to go into the highways and hedges. Thus, getting the prepared army to go into battle is probably the greatest challenge facing church leaders.

There is a final group—a small minority, statistically speaking, consisting of 3 to 5 percent of believers—who share their faith consistently. The goal is to move people in each group forward until more and more are part of the core group of witnesses (Figure 12.4).

FIGURE 12.4

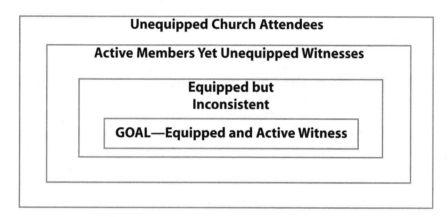

Unequipped Church Attendees

Active Members Yet Unequipped Witnesses

Equipped but Inconsistent

GOAL—Equipped and Active Witness

How can a church move believers forward in their witnessing knowledge and action? How do we get the prepared laborers off the front porch and into the harvest field?

TRADITIONAL MEANS OF ENGAGING WITNESSES IN THE HARVEST

Personal evangelists have traditionally been released into the lost world in three different ways: (1) *assignment visitation* (visiting prospects, door-to-door surveys, etc.), (2) *relational evangelism* (building relationships with individuals with a view toward helping them come to Christ), and (3) *lifestyle evangelism* (sharing Christ on the go with people we meet). These three approaches are biblical and effective. However, I want to describe another approach, which may be conducted through these three methods. This concept is the most exciting thing to affect personal evangelism in many years. It is called *servanthood evangelism*. It is the simplest, most transferable, and most enjoyable approach for moving believers closer to a biblical lifestyle marked by consistent witnessing.

SERVANTHOOD EVANGELISM

Servanthood evangelism is a combination of simple acts of kindness and intentional personal evangelism.[1] I wish I could say I created the concept. I would like to say my discovery came from years of academic study, from marvelous experiences, or from a knack for innovation. But it came from none of that. Actually, this approach is as old as the New Testament. I first used it out of necessity in a personal evangelism class at Southeastern Seminary. David Wheeler, evangelism director for the State Convention of Baptists in Indiana, told me about it after meeting Steve Sjogren, pastor of the Cincinnati Vineyard Church, who started and built a megachurch based on servanthood evangelism.[2]

My students in that class went nuts over this approach. Part of class time became lab time as the class went out in small groups to evangelize. What did they do? Some bought sodas and gave them to shoppers in our small town's business district. Others went door-to-door in an older community with replacement batteries to check residents' smoke detectors; one student with batteries led a person to Christ for the first time in his life. One group had a free car wash (FREE—no money was accepted) at a local church. People would try to give money, but the students refused. "We're just showing the love of Christ in a practical way," they said. At that car wash a man from a Hindu background was saved.

Some students went door-to-door, giving away free lightbulbs: "You'll probably have a lightbulb go out sometime, so here's one," they said. "By the way, Jesus said he is the light of the world." It was amazing to see how open people were because of these simple gifts. I came upon two students giving away quarters at the laundromat. Two women met Christ through their witness.

Another student, who served as youth minister at a nearby church, took his youth group to do a free car wash. A man came to have his car washed. The youth minister led him to Christ. "I've been thinking about how I need to know God for the past several days," the man said. The youth group was so excited that several of the young people are now sharing their faith consistently.

Servanthood evangelism is not new. Churches have used it for generations. However, the concept is critical for our day for two reasons: First, it fits our times—it is a powerful medium for reaching our contemporary, post-Christian culture. Second, we are seeing more and more churches whose entire ministry is built on this concept with great success.

It's not where you are, but where you are headed. Servanthood evangelism will head believers in a direction of greater excitement and commitment for evangelism.

Simple acts of kindness and intentional evangelism fit well together. Like so many profound truths, this one is so simple it is easily missed. Get a group of believers, say at a local church, and begin practicing simple acts of kindness. These acts of kindness open the door for the greatest act of kindness a Christian can give: the gospel.

Matthew's Gospel gives a summary of Jesus' ministry (see Matt. 4:23; 9:35). Jesus was described as having a ministry of preaching, teaching, and healing. This threefold ministry—preaching the Good News, teaching about himself, and acts of profound kindness—marked our Lord's ministry. His acts of healing and other kindnesses undergirded his ministry of teaching and preaching but never superceded them. Jesus performed other acts of kindness: talking with the Samaritan woman, forgiving and protecting the woman caught in adultery, and receiving children. The greatest act of kindness we can do today is to present the glorious gospel to lost people, but we can do it through the ministry of deeds of kindness.

Does the servant side of Jesus have a role in your church or ministry? Do you emphasize the victorious Christian life without noting the humble servanthood of our Lord? (Mark 10:45). Servanthood evangelism not only presents the gospel but also reminds us of a central feature of the church.

Please understand what I mean by kindness. I don't mean just telling people what they want to hear so they will feel good. Some churches have so compromised the gospel that the only thing they do is help people on the way to hell with a smile on their face! Servanthood evangelism is more than acts of kindness. There are valuable ministries, such as taking a loaf of bread to newcomers, that are helpful, but they are not explicitly evangelistic. Servanthood evangelism is intentionally evangelistic, but it is not pushy and coercive.

When doing an act of kindness, the witness says, "I am showing the love of Jesus in a practical way." Then the witness asks for the opportunity to share Christ. If the other person refuses, the witness goes no further, except to offer a gospel tract. However, we have discovered that people are more likely to allow a witness when evangelism is coupled with an act of kindness.

Servanthood evangelism consists of two parts: acts of kindness *and* evangelism. Wouldn't it be cruel to offer to wash a person's car and then fail to tell him or her about the water of life? To give a lightbulb without telling about the light of the world? To clean a toilet without telling of the only One who can cleanse their hearts from sin?

SERVANTHOOD EVANGELISM COMPARED TO MINISTRY-BASED EVANGELISM

Servanthood evangelism is not to be confused with another excellent approach to presenting Christ: *ministry-based evangelism.* The concept, used with great effect by Charles Roesell and the First Baptist Church of Leesburg, Florida, has its own strengths.[3] This church has scores of wonderful ministries that are intentionally evangelistic and have reached multitudes. See the chart for a comparison of these two approaches.

MINISTRY-BASED EVANGELISM	SERVANTHOOD EVANGELISM
Ongoing ministry	Short-term ministry
Meets deep needs (housing, food, medicine, etc.)	Meets simple needs (acts of kindness)
Involves some well-trained people with volunteers	Involves little detailed training, only volunteers
Involves significant organization and oversight; best when done following some planning	Involves little organization, can be done almost spontaneously
Weakness: Without care, can move easily away from intentional evangelism	Weakness: Can become a gimmick if the church doesn't truly care about people

Strengths of Servanthood Evangelism

Servanthood evangelism is characterized by several strengths that help to launch believers into the harvest.

1. *In a post-Christian culture, servanthood evangelism offers a demonstration of the gospel coupled with an explanation.* Too many people have rejected a caricature of Jesus. Their concept of Christianity needs to be changed. A simple deed of kindness helps to build rapport with people like this. Sjogren has noted that servanthood evangelism is heart-to-heart witnessing versus head-to-head. The verbal message is linked to a demonstration of compassion. This is more effective than an academic dissertation on the truthfulness of the faith.

2. *Servanthood evangelism is personal evangelism in a corporate setting.* Servant evangelism often involves a whole group washing cars, offering sodas at a park, etc. The body of Christ can be on mission in the community. This allows many believers to share in the experience.

   A student at Southeastern Seminary manages a local gas station. He allows students to pump gas, check the oil, and wash the windows of his customers' cars. During one semester, four people gave their lives to Christ as a result of this outreach. Many of the customers asked, "Why are you doing this for me at a self-serve station?" "We're just trying to show the love of Christ in a practical way," they replied. This immediately opens the way for conversation about the gospel.

3. *Servanthood evangelism is low risk.* A witness doesn't need unusual communication skills, an outgoing personality, a slick sales pitch, or multiple hours of training. This approach places the emphasis on the true Lord of the harvest. We are called to share, not to convert. Some folks are too afraid to witness, but they can wash a car and hand out lightbulbs! This allows timid witnesses to learn from watching others. Evangelism is more caught than taught.

4. *Servanthood evangelism can be an essential part of the church's mission.* In chapter 3, I spoke of the New Testament concept of total penetration of a community through total participation of the membership. We are accountable for reaching our

Jerusalem! Every person at some point thinks about God. When they do, you want them to think of your church. Servanthood evangelism gets church people among unchurched people.

5. *Servanthood evangelism is fun!* We must remember that we serve Christ not because it is fun but because it is essential. God's desire is not to make us *happy* but to make us *holy.* But evangelism is so frightening to so many people that the idea of having a good time witnessing is liberating. I have had pure enjoyment sharing Christ through car washes, cleaning up after hurricane Fran, giving away lightbulbs, and serving at laundromats.

6. *Servanthood evangelism involves everyone in witnessing.* While one person may do the witnessing, everyone takes part in the experience. The person pumping gas is praying as another person witnesses. Those who prepare gift packages to be delivered door-to-door contribute to the person who is led to Christ by those delivering the gift.

7. *Servanthood evangelism follows the model of Jesus: preaching, teaching, and healing.* Jesus demonstrated unusual kindness to the woman at the well—kindness coupled with the gospel.

8. *Servanthood evangelism allows laypeople to use their own creative minds to initiate ministry opportunities.* I have seen believers use their own ingenuity to discover means of communicating Christ through servanthood evangelism. For example, two men at Faith Baptist Church bought cleaning materials, then asked to clean a store's toilet! It made quite an impact!

9. *Servanthood evangelism requires few resources and can be done anywhere in any setting.* You might have to buy a few lightbulbs, sodas, or cleaning supplies, but you can begin by determining what you already have and using it to minister to the community. This approach has been used to share Christ from suburban areas of Raleigh, North Carolina, to impoverished regions of Croatia.

10. *Servanthood evangelism is warm and friendly.* Traditional evangelistic approaches still work. I still love to go door-to-door. Those who criticize this approach haven't tried it much. But servanthood evangelism is a *better* means of mobilizing a church to reach its community. Many believers do servanthood evangelism door-to-door!

CAUTIONS ABOUT SERVANTHOOD EVANGELISM

Anything with the potential for good also has the possibility for harm. Three cautions must be expressed about servanthood evangelism.

1. *We must be intentionally evangelistic.* We should not be pushy but ready for opportunities to share. You may not get to witness on every occasion, but you need to be ready. Our evangelism must be biblical, for the legacy of liberalism is its emphasis on meeting social and physical needs without including the power of the gospel.

2. *We must care about people.* Unless we have compassion such as Jesus displayed (see Matt. 9:35–38), servanthood evangelism is a gimmick. We cannot limit our acts of kindness only to those who will let us talk.

3. *We must use equipped personal witnesses.* Every individual who participates does not need to be a trained witness. But each participating group or pair must include someone who can lead people to Christ. Servanthood evangelism is not complete in itself; it assumes witness training has occurred. It is a vehicle for *releasing* trained witnesses.

Servanthood evangelism can also be effective as part of planting a new church. A group of students helped start a church in 1997 in Claremont, New Hampshire. As one of the team leaders, I was recovering from hip surgery, so I was unable to do the more rigorous door-to-door work. I thought about how I might use servanthood evangelism. I noticed the local high school was next to a park. Two members of our team and I bought some sodas, filled ice coolers, and offered the passing students free sodas. We gave them a brief information piece about the new church and a gospel tract. We told them we were sharing the love of Jesus in a practical way.

The response of the youth was overwhelming. Almost everyone we talked to spoke of the need for the youth to receive some attention. The next day we were swarmed by youth, and almost none wanted a soda. They were impressed by our presence and had many spiritual questions. We talked to students of every persuasion—from Satanists to existentialists. Six met the Lord!

If you want to see your church develop a passion for evangelism, let me encourage you to offer them a vision for reaching their community that is less intimidating to them and to the lost community around them—servanthood evangelism.

ASSIGNMENT VISITATION

Servanthood evangelism is an exciting and effective way to mobilize believers to witness. But it is only one way. Servanthood evangelism can be used with other effective methods.

One of these is assignment visitation. The early believers went "house to house" (see Acts 5:42; 20:20). This approach is biblical, and it is also effective. Kirk Hadaway discovered that 76 percent of Southern Baptist churches *which are growing* conduct weekly visitation.[4] Assignment visitation today is conducted in two primary ways. First, it occurs through local churches that develop a list of prospects, systematically sending witnessing teams to see these persons. Churches that conduct ongoing evangelism training are effective with this method.

Jesus, in a general way, assigned the church to witness, beginning in Jerusalem (see Acts 1:8). He was also more specific (see Matt. 10). The angel assigned Philip to witness to the eunuch (Acts 8:26). Ananias was "assigned" to talk to Saul (Acts 9:10). Although Philip had been in Caesarea (Acts 8:40), the Lord sent Peter to Caesarea to share Christ with Cornelius (Acts 10).

Assigning believers to witness to individuals has a clear precedent in Scripture. Such an approach is systematic in its effect. An up-to-date prospect file, easily maintained on computer, is essential for an effective assignment-based evangelistic ministry. The first rule of cultivating prospects is to be among unsaved people. Following are six proven ways to discover prospects.

1. *Annual church survey.* Use a Whodo card or FRAN card (friend, relative, associate, or neighbor). Distribute these cards

WHODO CARD [5]

Who do you know who would be a prospect for our Sunday school?

Name _____

Address_____Phone _____

Mailing Address (if different)_____

Date of Birth_____School Grade _____

Please check with me if you need additional information.

_____

Name of Person Giving Information_____Phone _____

once a year in the worship service. Encourage members to note unchurched people whom they know.

2. *Door-to-door prospecting.* Some churches go door-to-door annually, primarily to discover prospects. Some churches actually pay college students during the summer to do this work. First Baptist Church, Jacksonville, Florida, takes their young people by busloads during the summer through the community to discover prospects.

3. *Register guests at all services.* Some churches have effective events that may not win many people to Christ, but they are an excellent way to discover prospects. Many people will attend a Christmas presentation or an Easter music special. Register *everyone,* then note the guests.

4. *Telephone survey.* This is similar to a door-to-door survey. Some churches call every home in their church field periodically to discover prospects.

5. *Sunday school or church roll.* You can sometimes find unchurched prospects on the Sunday school or church roll, particularly by discovering relatives of those already enrolled.

6. *Newcomer or utility lists.* These lists can be purchased in most communities.

The first way to conduct assignment visitation is by sending witnesses to visit specific people. A second way this is carried out is through door-to-door evangelism. This, too, is supported by Scripture. Jesus sent his disciples to homes (see Matt. 10). He stipulated they were to visit the houses inhabited by Jews (Matt. 10:5–6). He also warned them of the difficulties they would face. The early Christians preached Christ "in every house" (Acts 5:42). Paul testified that he witnessed door-to-door (Acts 20:20).

Perhaps no evangelistic approach has been attacked more than this one. I would simply like to introduce the "experts" who say door-to-door evangelism is dead to people whom I have led to Christ "cold turkey" by using this method. Many churches have been started this way. The reason this method doesn't work for many is because they don't try it!

Going door-to-door is not the only way to reach a community, nor is it necessarily the best way. Further, some gated communities won't allow such an approach. But too many have given up on it too quickly. It remains a biblical, effective method. Why has this method fallen on such hard times? One reason is the false assumption that people are turned off by anonymous visits. The same people say telemarketing doesn't work; apparently it does or my phone wouldn't be ringing off the hook!

Perhaps we don't like this method because we don't want to look like the cults. Jehovah's Witnesses and Mormons are famous for their house-to-house efforts. The fact that these groups are growing so rapidly—although they have an aberrant message and a low popularity in the general population—should tell us something. If error paraded so consistently reaches some people, how many more could we reach by sharing the Truth?

Someone told me we need more Christians who look like this: the head of a Baptist, showing sound doctrine (you would expect me to say Baptist, wouldn't you?); the heart of a Pentecostal, excited about praising God; and the feet of a Jehovah's Witness, consistently telling others! The cults use a New Testament *method* to tell others about a false god; we have the New Testament *message,* but we too easily forsake biblical methods.

This leads me to another reason many believers forsake door-to-door witnessing: It is hard work. I have done it a lot. Take it from me, it is exhausting. But I have seen many people come to Christ this way. It is simply un-American to do something that requires such hard work, given our hunger for easy everything.

Another reason we neglect door-to-door evangelism is the high rejection rate. But Philip left a revival to talk to one eunuch, remember? Jesus went to a hard-to-reach area (Samaria), and Paul listened to a Macedonian call rather than consulting a demographic study! We should research our area and use the minds God gave us, but let's not try to outsmart the Spirit of God. I led a Mormon to Christ once simply because I had been more consistent going door-to-door than the Mormons in that area had. The woman was impressed by our efforts.

The older I get, the more sophisticated I want to be. Too many of us want to avoid the grunt work of ministry. But many people won't hear about Christ unless we knock on their door. Let me state this positively: *Everyone, sooner or later, thinks about God.* When they do, you want them to think of you. By consistently saturating your community, through door-to-door witnessing and a variety of other methods, you can increase people's God-consciousness.

A final reason many people have overlooked this approach is that it is not the latest thing going. It is old news. We want the latest, most effective, most helpful approach that will get the gospel to people.

We need a paradigm shift in our churches that elevates the place of personal evangelism. Sharing Christ, impacting eternity, can become a joyful experience for many. In 1989 I worked with several other people to assist a church in Oklahoma City on a door-to-door campaign. I was teamed with two women in their seventies who were lifelong members of that church. They were nervous, telling me they had never done this before. But did we have fun! The women were so encouraged by this experience that they made a commitment to do the same thing once a week from then on. Imagine, they were almost octogenarians and were lifelong church members, but they had never done that. God help us to teach people the *joy* of serving Christ through evangelism!

We never know who we might meet behind the next door. In 1992 I was responsible for helping lead the Crossover Indianapolis effort prior to the SBC. Prior to the major door-to-door emphasis just before the convention, during the spring we had teams come from all over the country to this pioneer area to go door-to-door witnessing with our churches.

One church in Indianapolis had a team go out door-to-door. They met a lady who was like Lydia. The Lord opened her heart, she was open to the gospel, she was prepared, and they led her to Christ. The next day the team went by to see her on a follow-up visit. She told them that the very afternoon they came to visit her, she was considering suicide. She had already made plans for her kids, she was going to purchase the gun, everything was in order—and then the group came by to lead her to Christ. "My circumstances haven't changed," she told them, "but my attitude has." This illustrates the urgency of getting out and telling people about Christ.

Here are seven ways to increase your success at door-to-door witnessing.

1. *Smile, smile, smile, always smile.* A pleasant face begets a pleasant response.

2. *Be polite, regardless of the response.* You cannot tell how the Holy Spirit will honor your efforts.

3. *Use an effective survey tool.* Here are some examples.

New Hampshire Personal Opinion Poll

1. Are you currently active in a church? YES   NO
2. What do you feel is the greatest need in this area?
3. Why do you think people go to church?
4. If you were looking for a church, what would you look for?
5. What advice would you give me or a pastor of a new church?
6. Can I share with you how Jesus Christ has changed my life?
   If answer is no, say thank you. If answer is yes, share your testimony, then ask, **"Has anything like this ever happened to you?"**
   If answer is yes, say "great!" and ask them to tell you about their testimony.
   If answer is no, or if they give an unclear testimony, say **"God loves you."** Then go into a presentation of the gospel.

220 INTRODUCTION TO EVANGELISM

How Saddleback Began: "A PERSONAL Opinion Poll"[6] (Five Questions to Ask)

1. Are you currently *active* in a local church?
2. What do you feel is the greatest need in this area?
3. Why do you think most people don't attend church?
4. If you were looking for a church, what kind of things would you look for?
5. What advice would you give me? How can I help you?

4. *Offer a gift, as in servanthood evangelism*—free lightbulbs, carnations at Mother's Day, a Christmas ornament, etc.

5. *Have clearly designated areas, good maps, and instructions to avoid overlap and confusion.* The folks going out are nervous enough, so don't add to their anxiety.

6. *Train the surveyors to take good, clear information.* I wish I had a nickel for every survey form filled out in such a way that no one could use it. The surveyors should ask themselves, *If a total stranger picked this up in a month, would it help him or confuse him?*

7. *Cover an area well.* It is better to survey half of your church field well than to cover the entire area poorly.

There are significant strengths of door-to-door evangelism.

- It is biblical.
- It saturates the community.
- It requires little training and therefore allows greater involvement.
- It will win some people to Christ.
- It will uncover excellent prospects.
- It recognizes that some people are ready to receive Christ.
- It will honor God and be blessed by Him.

Many pastors have told me about door-to-door witnessing efforts that seemed to bear no fruit, but it planted a seed that eventually led to a rich harvest. God is looking for people who are anxious to tell others his good news!

We must admit that door-to-door witnessing also has certain weaknesses.

- It allows little time to build rapport.
- Follow-up is much more difficult.
- Not every community can be reached this way.

LIFESTYLE EVANGELISM

C. B. Hogue defines lifestyle evangelism as "a life-sharing, life-giving evangelism which includes a verbal life-sharing of what Christ means in a person's heart."[7] Lifestyle evangelism is sharing Christ with people whom you may never see again: a waitress in a restaurant, a passenger on an airplane, a plumber repairing your sink. Jesus often encountered people in this manner as did Paul.

Sharing Christ with waiters and waitresses, especially when the restaurant is not too crowded, can be very effective. Sometimes, after building a little rapport, I will ask the waitress, "Has anyone told you today that God loves you?" Generally, nobody has! I have been able to share Christ this way on many occasions.

I will never forget an occasion during a national witness training seminar in southern Indiana. Three participants in the seminar were having lunch, laughing, and having a good time. Their sweet spirit made an impression on the waitress. She enjoyed serving them so much she offered them dessert on the house. One of the pastors said to her, "The reason we are having such a good time is because of Jesus." They began to share Christ. When he neared the place of offering her a chance to respond, she was called to another table. After serving them, she came back, pulled up a chair, and sat down! One member of the group began to serve tea to the other tables, and they led her to Christ!

R. A. Torrey gave two important rules to remember when witnessing in public:

1. Obey the Holy Spirit.

2. Never embarrass the person to whom you are witnessing. Don't get him or her in trouble with the employer, for example, when you share.

A friend of mine was leaving a restaurant one day. A woman was on her knees, scraping the sidewalk. He was prompted to say,

"Ma'am, while you are on your knees, why not give your life to Christ?" She looked at him in deep conviction, and he led her to Christ right there on the sidewalk!

RELATIONAL EVANGELISM

Relational evangelism consists of ongoing witnessing encounters with people we know—family members, coworkers, and friends. Relational evangelism allows repeated opportunities to witness. Andrew shared Christ with Philip (John 1:40–41), and Philip shared with Nathaniel (John 1:45). Many people will be won to Christ only after a significant relationship is built up over a period of time.

THE POWER OF INFLUENCE

The central issue of getting people involved in witnessing is leadership. Let me give you a sad example of this. I participated in a witnessing effort in a church in the southwest. The young pastor was obviously nervous about door-to-door evangelism. He read the passage about Jesus sending out the seventy where Jesus said, "I saw Satan fall like lightning from heaven" (Luke 10:18). Commenting on this statement, he said, "Some people interpret this to mean that the witness was so powerful that it caused Satan to fall." (By the way, that's the way I interpret that.) He went on to say, "That's not how I interpret it." Then he spent about five minutes explaining that Satan was going to give everyone a hard time, people would not be interested, and so on. That's the most blatant example of defeatism I've ever experienced. By the time he finished his explanation, I was so discouraged I almost didn't want to go out witnessing.

This young man didn't like to go out and witness. It was uncomfortable for him. This is not typical, but it is certainly true that pastors can hold their people back. Soul-winning pastors beget soul-winning churches. Here are some ways you can encourage your people to get into the fields.

- Talk about your witnessing. If you would simply share an example of witnessing to someone once a week, those you lead would understand your passion for evangelism.

- Let your people know that success is as much in the witnessing effort as it is in actually winning people to Christ. Get them to love fishing as much as catching.

- *Do not* tell only your favorite few stories from days gone by. Instead, tell current, live accounts: "Just yesterday, I shared Christ with the paperboy."

- Tell these stories in a way that emphasizes the work of God over your ability.

APPLICATION

Try this in your church or class: Ask how many people have ever had a Mormon or Jehovah's Witness knock on their door. Usually, it is 90 percent or more. Then ask how many have ever had anyone approach them to share Christ. Usually the number is more like 10 percent. This is a striking reminder that we have been too reluctant to share Christ with others.

BIBLIOGRAPHY

Hanks, Billie, Jr. *Everyday Evangelism.* Waco: Word, 1986.

Hybels, Bill and Mark Mittelberg. *Becoming a Contagious Christian.* Grand Rapids: Zondervan, 1994.

Reid, Alvin and David Wheeler. *Servanthood Evangelism.* Alpharetta, Ga.: North American Mission Board, 1998.

Sjogren, Steve. *Conspiracy of Kindness.* Ann Arbor: Servant, 1993.

13

Friends of Sinners: Reaching the Unchurched

I heard the story of an encounter between a great preacher and a skeptic. The skeptic said, "You Christians talk about the God of Moses, Abraham, and Elijah. Where is this God?"

The preacher replied, "Sir, your point is well taken, but it is misplaced. The question is not, 'Where is the God of Elijah.' The question is, 'Where is the Elijah of God?'"

I would add, "Where are those who are willing to confront the contemporary culture with the timeless gospel?" While every individual is either saved or lost, there are two groups of people who have not responded to the gospel: (1) those who have heard the message but have rejected it; (2) those who haven't clearly heard. The first group must be confronted at the point of their excuses or objections for rejecting the gospel. The major issue for them is one of *volition*. The second group must hear the gospel in a manner that communicates the message clearly. Their need is for *information*. We must increasingly consider how to contextualize the gospel, even in the United States.

What the church needs today is not more buildings, more dollars, or more new ideas—not a marketing strategy or a new technology. What the church needs today is an army of apostle Pauls, who serve

God with a passion and who are burdened for reaching those who have never clearly heard the glorious gospel.

Let me use the apostle Paul as an analogy. He was called to be the apostle to the Gentiles, although he sought to reach Jews as well. I think of the Jews of Paul's day, who had a religious heritage from which Paul could begin his witness, as analogous to the millions of nominal Christians in the United States—those who have been to church and heard about God but who have never been changed by the gospel. Like the first-century Jews, they have some awareness, but they still need the gospel's personal touch (see Figure 13.1).

FIGURE 13.1

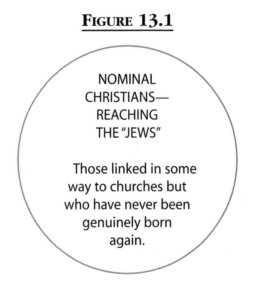

NOMINAL CHRISTIANS— REACHING THE "JEWS"

Those linked in some way to churches but who have never been genuinely born again.

The Gentiles in the first century were those who knew nothing about the gospel message until someone like Paul told them. They had no heritage of Scripture as the Jews did. Some were religious; some were not. They are analogous to the millions of people in our country who have little knowledge of Christianity. They know what a clerical collar is, and they recognize a church building, but they have no functional knowledge of the gospel. I call these people the *radically unchurched*. They may be devoutly religious, as some first-century Gentiles were, or they may be irreligious. They may be Muslim or Hindu or New Age or Mormon, or they may be agnostic.

The difference between these people and the nominal Christians—the "Jews," to use my analogy—is that any idea they have of Christianity is obscure or flawed. These people recognize the golden arches of McDonald's much more quickly than a cross as a symbol with meaning (see Figure 13.2).

Figure 13.2

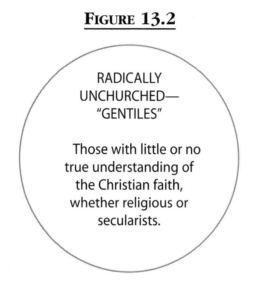

RADICALLY UNCHURCHED— "GENTILES"

Those with little or no true understanding of the Christian faith, whether religious or secularists.

The evangelical church has had some success reaching the "Jews"—or those with some knowledge and background in the faith. They are more likely to be like us. Our evangelism tools are almost exclusively geared toward them. Most evangelism methods are geared toward harvesting, and those who have some background in the faith are obviously closer to harvest time. But the "Gentiles"—the radically unchurched—are a different story. Many of them are not ready for the harvest, although some certainly are. They are what Billy Graham called "an unseeded generation." They see the church as irrelevant and an enemy to progress. They are ignorant of the truths of Christianity. We can honor God by seeking ways to present the gospel in a way that will be understandable to them.

Figure 13.3 portrays these two groups of people—the "Jews" and the "Gentiles" with a third group that can make a difference in their lives: born-again Christians who are committed to bearing their witness for Christ.

FIGURE 13.3

Christians and churches in our nation are much more effective at reaching the "Jews" than the "Gentiles." We need more churches who seek to reach the radically unchurched. Let's consider the importance of confronting the objections raised by the "Jews."

DEALING WITH THOSE WHO RAISE OBJECTIONS

I'll never forget the first time I taught CWT in a local church. That was the spring when a national evangelical religious personality fell into sin. Week after week we would visit, and people would say, "Look at that guy. I don't need to be around a bunch of hypocrites." At first, I was defensive, but then I changed my approach. As we talked to a man whom I'll call Bob, he raised this scenario.

"Bob," I said, "You are right. Not every preacher lives a life that honors Christ. There are hypocrites. In fact, Jesus spoke against hypocrites more than anyone else. Let me ask you a question. How would you describe a real Christian?" Bob's reply was *not* that he believed Christianity was false due to the testimony of a fallen preacher. Rather, he replied that a Christian is someone who goes to church, is moral, etc. He did not disbelieve the faith; he was only using this fallen preacher as an excuse.

I then said to Bob, "Can I explain to you what a real Christian is according to the Bible?" He then allowed us to share Christ. He did not respond, but the gospel was proclaimed.

Most people have never been confronted with the truth of the gospel in a personal encounter with a loving witness. But most have wondered about spiritual issues that cause them to think about ultimate realities. From tragedies to cults to psychic hotlines, various events cause everyone to think about God at some point. When an objection is raised, we have to ask, Are they rejecting Christ based on a clear knowledge of the gospel, or are they ignorant or misinformed about Christianity? We must get beyond the excuses that people give to the real reason they object to the claims of Christianity.

I'm convinced that many of the objections people raise are smoke screens. They are attempts to set aside the main issue—a volitional commitment to God—under the guise of intellectual excuse. This is not new in our day. Michael Green, in *Evangelism in the Early Church,* describes a street preacher of the second century who was talking to a group of philosophers. One of them asked him why a small mosquito has six feet and wings while the elephant, the largest of all animals, is wingless and has only four feet. The question was an attempt to stump the preacher much as some questions are asked in our day. But listen to Green's comment on his response:

> The preacher is unabashed. "There is no point in telling you the reason for the different structure of mosquito and elephant, for you are completely ignorant of the God who made both." He could . . . answer the frivolous questions if they asked them sincerely, but he refuses to get sidetracked by bogus issues like these impelled as he is by the concern to fulfill his commission. The preacher says further, "We have a commission only to tell you the words of him who sent us. Instead of logical proof, we bring before you many witnesses from among yourselves . . . it is of course open to you either to accept or disbelieve adequate testimony of this sort but I shall not cease to declare unto you what is for your profit: for to be silent would be loss for me just as to disbelieve would mean ruin for you."[1]

Part of the struggle we face as witnesses is dealing with questions we can't answer. I heard a student say he hated door-to-door evangelism because he feared being confronted with an issue for which he had no reply. But note this: *nowhere in Scripture are we told that we must answer every question a person has.* Even the Bible doesn't do that! It doesn't tell us everything we *want* to know but everything we *need* to know. It doesn't tell us where Cain got his wife;

that is not a significant issue. It does tell us how sin entered the human race because this is important! We can spend so much time trying to be relevant that we fail to be significant. We may not be able to tell people all they *want* to know about spiritual things, but we can tell them what they *must* know to be converted.

I have learned that the best way to deal with objections is through a Socratic method, as opposed to the rote memorization of pat answers to complex questions.[2] Here are four general principles to keep in mind:

1. Recognize the objection while keeping the conversation focused on the gospel.

2. Remember, the Holy Spirit will give you guidance. Trust him.

3. The gospel itself will answer many honest questions.

4. Many objections will not be raised *if* you maintain a proper attitude.

Here are five guidelines to help you avoid emotional confrontations without compromising the gospel.

1. *Negotiate; do not argue* (think win/win).

The approach that CWT uses gets to the heart of the matter. Whenever possible, we should agree with the person raising the objection to make it a win-win situation. For example, R. A. Torrey said he was talking with a man who said he was too great a sinner to be saved.[3] Instead of talking him out of that sentiment, Torrey agreed with him and directed him to 1 Timothy 1:15 where Paul said he was the chief of sinners but Christ came into the world to save sinners. The man replied, "Well, I am the chief of sinners." Torrey said, "Well, that verse means you then." If it is a legitimate concern that people have when you agree with them and show them the scriptural answer, this makes all the difference in the world as you lead them toward conversion.

2. *Avoid emotional confrontations.*

3. *Accept the other person as an equal.* Remember that we are not *better* than unsaved persons; the difference is that we have met

Jesus! And so can they! A holier-than-thou attitude is quickly discernible.

4. *Exercise gentleness.* The goal is to present truth, not win a debate.

5. *Check your motivation.* Love should be your guide.

The material used with Continuing Witness Training has helped many witnesses in dealing with objections. The basic approach can be summarized in the following steps:

1. *Use a transition statement.* "You've obviously given this some thought." Most people have given some thought to spiritual matters, so your first statement is affirmative, not confrontational. Then you can address the specific objection.

2. *Convert the objection to a question.* The question should deal with the objection raised, as illustrated below. If you are not sure what to ask, two general questions are, When did you begin believing this? or, Why?

3. *Answer the person's question.*

4. *Continue with the gospel presentation.*

Example 1: "The church is full of hypocrites. I don't need it."

Transition: "You've obviously given this some thought. I would agree that hypocrisy does exist in churches. Jesus warned against hypocrisy."

Convert to a question: "Let me ask you a question. What is a real Christian like?"

Typical answer: "Lives a good life, not judgmental, etc."

Answer: "The only way to discover what a real Christian is would be to see what the Bible says."

Example 2: "I believe there are many ways to God."

Transition: "You've obviously given this some thought. I would agree that there are many religions with many devout followers."

Convert to a question: "Let me ask you a question. Have you ever considered the unique claims of Christianity?"

Answer [following their response]: "The Christian faith is unique in that it is less a religion than it is a relationship."

R. A. Torrey used a similar approach. If he encountered a skeptic who said, "I don't believe the Bible," he would say, "Are you saying the Bible is foolishness?" And if he said yes, (by the way I've met people like that), you can say, "Well, that's what the Bible says about itself. First Corinthians 1:18 says the preaching of the cross is to them that perish foolishness." And then you can say, "But you don't have to be perishing."[4]

If someone says the Bible is full of contradictions, the best thing to do is hand a Bible to him and kindly ask him to show you one.

PEOPLE IN CULTS AND OTHER RELIGIONS

The proliferation of cults and new religious sects has been an unmistakable part of American society during the past thirty years. Thousands of new religious groups, ranging in membership from less than fifty to hundreds of thousands, have sprung up. Other groups such as Mormons and the Jehovah's Witnesses have been around much longer. Other world religions are also growing in the United States. In particular, the rise of Islam has caused a great rise in pluralism and syncretism, with the merging of faiths and other challenges to the Christian faith.

What is a cult? Brooks Alexander, cofounder of the Spiritual Counterfeits Project in California, gives a theological definition of a cult.

1. A cult has a false or inadequate basis of salvation. In other words, their soteriology is wrong. This comes out of a faulty Christology.

2. A cult has a false basis of authority. Biblical Christianity is founded on the Bible as the Word of God, while a cult looks for other authorities—a messianic figure, a David Koresh-like leader, or other writings such as *The Book of Mormon* or *The Pearl of Great Price*.[5]

There are certainly other religious sects as well: Zen Buddhism, Hare Krishna, and the Unification Church. Evangelicals in America must confront Mormonism and Jehovah's Witnesses more than any other single group or groups. We must admit that cults represent "the unpaid bills of the church."[6]

PRINCIPLES FOR WITNESSING TO A PERSON IN A CULT OR ANOTHER RELIGION

Here are five principles for witnessing to people in cults and other religions.

1. *Commit to a relationship with this person whenever possible.* These people, if they are devout, will not be won to Christ upon their first contact with the gospel. As a pastor, I had the privilege of leading a Mormon to Christ, but I led her to Christ out of a relationship that I had established with her family. I have also led Muslims and one Buddhist to Christ. In every case, I got to know them and spent time with them. They saw the change Christ has made in my life.

2. *Know your faith and theirs.* None of us can be an expert in all the different cults. But if there is a dominant religious group in your area—Mormonism for example—you ought to know something about their beliefs so you can talk intelligently with them. The Interfaith Witness Department of the North American Mission Board and the Spiritual Counterfeits Project have excellent materials to help.

   My friend John Avant led a Mormon missionary to Christ. He knew Mormon beliefs, and he was able to demonstrate weaknesses in their theology. However, he didn't do this initially. After spending time talking with the missionary, finding points in common, he began to show the errors in Mormonism and was able to lead this person out of Mormonism into genuine Christian faith.

3. *Do not begin your witness by attacking the other person's beliefs.* This may seem contradictory to the example of John Avant, but the principle stands. If you start witnessing to a person involved in a cult by attacking the cult, for example, the person is not likely to have any respect for your views. Begin your witness by affirming anything you can about the group, building rapport as you would in any other witnessing situation. Then move to God's truth.

4. *Share your own testimony.* This is critical. I have had students from a Mormon background who were very effective in winning people to Christ out of Mormonism. One student, Larry, was a fourth-generation Mormon. He has won several to Christ over the Internet by sharing his testimony and telling how he came out of Mormonism.

5. *Explain the gospel clearly, noting especially the reality of sin and the need of a Savior.* Their soteriology is almost always a works-oriented view of salvation. They need to hear the gospel of grace.

PAUL'S EXAMPLE

There is a biblical paradigm that helps us in dealing with cults and other religions. The apostle Paul went to Athens to preach the gospel. He was overwhelmed by the number of idols in that city. The religious pluralism was abundant. He was provoked when he saw the city was given over to idols. He reasoned in the synagogue with the Jews and the Gentiles and in the marketplace, talking to them about their relationship to God and their need for him (Acts 17:17). Then he was taken to Mars Hill and asked to speak on what he believed.

Paul said, "Men of Athens, I perceive that in all things you are very religious." The King James Version translates that last word as "superstitious." Paul affirmed the reality of their search for God, building a common ground with them. He affirmed their search, recognizing they were seeking truth.

Paul also knew their beliefs. He even quoted two of their poets (see Acts 17:28).

Paul moved from their error to the truth. He noticed an inscription on an idol—"To the Unknown God" (Acts 17:23). He started talking about God in general terms as Creator and moved on to the specific reality of Jesus as the Son of God. Paul did not compromise the gospel. Instead, he began where they were and took them to the place where they could be.

Paul clearly presented the gospel. If he had not done this, we could accuse him of selling out the gospel by speaking of a general god. He moved from a general understanding of God to the specific claims of the cross. He also talked about the judgment of God and the resurrection (Acts 17:23–31). At Paul's mention of the resurrection, the people began to back off. In fact, in this passage, we see three ways people respond to the gospel. Some believed the gospel, and others rejected it, while others said, "We want to hear more about this." That's the way people respond. If we follow these principles in witnessing to people in cults and other religions, we can expect these same kinds of responses.

REACHING SECULAR PEOPLE

There are 120 million functionally secular people in the United States. Millions more are caught up in cults and other religious systems. How do we communicate the gospel to them? Before dealing with specific groups, let me say again that any witness is better than no witness. A friend of mine named Saleim grew up a Muslim. He knew Christians in high school, but they never witnessed to him. They apparently thought he was unreachable. Saleim finally came to Christ in college. He told me he could have been saved earlier if someone had taken the time to share the gospel with him!

The landscape of American culture has changed radically over the last generation. In our day we are called to share Christ in a culture with no consensus on *heritage*, as seen in our ethnic diversity; no consensus on our *moral code*, as evidenced by debates over abortion, homosexuality, and euthanasia; and no consensus on *religious belief*, as seen in the growth of other world religions and the explosion of cults.

In any generation, apologetics—or the defense of the faith—has a role in evangelism. The two were combined in the lives of Paul, Justin Martyr, and Augustine, and in our day we see them wed in the lives of such people as Ravi Zacharias and the late Francis Schaeffer. Apologetics has been founded on propositional truth, and this remains essential. However, I agree with Calvin Miller that we need "sensory apologetics" to reach a postmodern culture.[7]

For example, Mormonism's impact in contemporary culture is not due to success on epistemological grounds. They use the arts well (their TV commercials are without peer in touching the emotions). They don't reach people with *truth* claims; they use sensory appeal. Now just imagine if the church, without compromising any commitment to the epistemological basis of the faith, appeals to the arts to help declare its truth?

This is why drama has become effective in many churches. We live in a sensory, TV-dominated age. How can we share the timeless truths with a postmodern culture? We must do it the same way the Bible does it. The Bible is primarily narrative, easy for a person to relate to. It is *relational*—the story of how God relates to man. For example, the story of the prodigal son may be more effective in reaching some people than the Roman Road witnessing approach. The truth is the same, but the approach is different.

In the sixties, some people said, "God is nowhere." Now God and gods are everywhere. Spiritual experience is of great interest in our day. Rick Warren has a church member give a testimony every Sunday as part of his message, coupling the preaching of the Word with an experience from today.

Music is the best example of the use of the arts in the church, but we must find ways to integrate the arts into our gospel witness. Drama, or personal interviews, can add to a service, for example. At the same time, we must relate everything we do to the timeless truths of Scripture.

Miller has noted the cultural shift we face today:

- The Reformation era to 1950 was the "It" generation. This was the era of the text.

- The 1950s to the 1970s was the "You" generation, or the era of the imperative.

- The 1980s was the "Me" generation, or the era of Narcissus.

- The 1990s are characterized as, the "We" generation. It is the era of multiculture, postmodern values.[8]

George Hunter defines a secular person as one not substantially influenced by Christianity.[9] Secular people generally have three responses to Christians:

1. Do Christians really believe this?

2. Do Christians really live this?

3. Does it really matter?

In the sixties secular people were turned off by the church because it was too spiritual; now they are turned off because it is not spiritual enough.

There are more than 350,000 churches in the United States. Eighty percent of them are stagnant. Of the 20 percent that are growing, most are doing so by biological/transfer growth. Less than 1 percent are growing by conversion growth. We are not reaching secular people.

How do we relate to changing culture? We must distinguish between pop culture and traditional culture. Hunter defines pop culture as much the same everywhere; it varies little across space but changes rapidly across time. Some popular music in Tokyo can be found in Chicago. Changes are called *fads*. Traditional culture varies greatly across space, but it changes very little across time. Changes do occur and are called *trends*. In relating to a changing culture, Hunter states:

- Some things should be abandoned—hymns that are not understandable, mimeographed bulletins, irrelevant announcements.
- Some things should be kept—preaching, singing, prayer, giving.
- Some things should be repackaged—worship style, worship order.[10]

REACHING BUSTERS

The so-called Baby Buster generation provides great challenges and opportunities for the church. This is an angry generation, and who can blame them, given the names they are called. They are Busters because they came after the glorious Boomers when everything was going "bust." They are also called "Generation X," which sounds alarmingly like "Brand X." Further, they have been called the "Thirteenth Generation." How would you like to be known for the number thirteen?

I taught this generation at a university, and I now teach many in seminary. They have been labeled, reduced, and marginalized. I personally disdain such labels, but I will use the term *Buster* simply to differentiate this group, born roughly between 1965 and 1981, from the Boomer Generation, those like myself born from 1946 to 1965.

Busters are characterized by relativism and subjectivism. They are less gender specific than people in the United States have been in the past. Emotional issues loom larger, for so many come from broken or dysfunctional homes. They live in an increasingly violent society where security is elusive. They are becoming adults in an obsessive-compulsive culture where calendars are too filled and lives are too empty. Absolute truth has been lost as a core value for most.

Kevin Graham Ford, in a book on evangelizing Busters, noted three fundamental assumptions of this generation:[11] (1) the world is not user-friendly; (2) the world is not simple; and (3) the world has no rules. Ford also notes significant values of Busters and the things they distrust:

VALUE	DISTRUST
Simplicity	Authority
Clear action	Systems and structures
Tangible results	Talk rather than action
Bottom line	Symbolism rather than substance
Survival through	The Boomers
self-sufficiency	
Boundaries	
Friendships and relationships	

Ford's book confirms the two things I believe are critical to reaching Generation X. First, personal evangelism is the essential medium. But specifically, this group is "highly suspicious of fakes and of people who want to exploit them."[12] I recently had a Buster student tell me how it drives her nuts when an evangelist spends too much time selling books and tapes in a meeting. This practice smacks of falsehood to them. Here lies the great inroad for the gospel. According to Ford, "Xers are hungry for the kind of authenticity and integrity that they can't find in the systems of this world."[13]

Here is an example. The question, Do you know for certain you have eternal life? can still be asked of many people. But asking Generation Xers about eternal life may bring blank stares or questions about reincarnation. A college student from New York replied to that question with, "I just don't connect with that." I have found it much more effective to ask about a personal relationship with Jesus when talking to this group.

In a dramatized vignette, Ford illustrates this truth with a young man named Grant: "Do I think about death? Sure I do. All the time. But thinking about it doesn't make me live more carefully. It makes me want to live more intensely."[14]

Grant needs to know how the gospel can give him not only life to come but also *real* life in the here and now.

Busters demonstrate the fleshing out of the philosophical shift in culture from modernism to postmodernism. Modernism refers to the time beginning at the death of the Middle Ages and the Renaissance. This ushered in the Enlightenment, bringing scientific, philosophical, political, and theological revolution.

The beginning of the shift from modernism to postmodernism can be seen in the rise of quantum physics and Einstein's theory of relativity. Postmodernism flourishes in culture today, marked by a denial of absolute truth and a greater regard for subjective experience over objective reality. Stan Grenz offers four assumptions of postmodernism:[15]

1. *Feelings and relationships are more important than logic and reason.* The supernatural was largely rejected in the Enlightenment era, but it is accepted in a postmodern world.

2. *Pessimism.* Fueled by Darwinism, discoveries, and inventions, modernism continually saw a bright new world. Boomers wanted to save the world, but Busters simply want to survive.

3. *Holism/wholism/community.* Modernism exalted the individual, saying man is the measure of all things. Postmodernism desires community. *Star Trek* was about Captain Kirk's heroism, while *Star Trek: The Next Generation* is about the community aboard the *Enterprise.*

4. *Truth is relative.* Truth has shifted from the rational realm of the intellect to the subjective realm of experience.

There is a positive side for presenting the gospel. Without denying the timeless truths of Scripture, we can add the impact of Christianity on our lives in communicating to Generation Xers. We can touch the Busters at the point of the supernatural, emphasizing the level of community, emphasizing the failure of man to be autonomous.

Apologetics has a role for Generation Xers, but it is more important to believers for discipleship than unbelievers for evangelism. Ford says: "In our effort to reach Generation X, we would do well to spend less energy defending the 'fortress of truth' and more energy providing a safe and nurturing haven of relational stability."[16] We must be careful, however, not to compromise biblical truth in our desire to emphasize relationships.

Ford believes three approaches will reach Xers.[17]

1. *Embodied apologetic.* Like Calvin Miller's "sensory apologetic," there must be "a flesh-and-blood, living and breathing argument for God."[18] The question is not only, Can a Christian *prove* the faith? but also, Can a Christian *live* the faith?

2. *Process evangelism.* The question today is not, Is there a God? but, Which God? Process evangelism is what is normally meant by relational evangelism, which occurs incarnationally over time. Of course, there is the danger of never sharing Christ. Ford acknowledges that the current generation is quite similar to the first century; however, in the New Testament, process was always linked to *intentionally* sharing the Good News. There is no record to my knowledge of any New Testament narrative in which a believer intentionally refused to share the Good News for a long time. Jesus shared the Good News of the kingdom intentionally. Process evangelism cannot be divorced from intentionality.

3. *Narrative evangelism.* Rather than approaches that focus on methods or felt needs, narrative evangelism tells the gospel story in a way that intersects with our own personal story. When compared to the story of the gospel, we recognize the differences, and hopefully, the failures of our worldview compared to the truth of Scripture. Narrative evangelism, compared to the propositional approach (as in the Four Spiritual Laws and Evangelism Explosion), is more relational. Yet if told accurately and consistently with Scripture, it is powerful in reaching Generation Xers.

Narrative evangelism must contain the essential elements of the gospel, for truth is essential to Christianity. But it does more—it can speak to the heart and touch the soul. Just as a good sermon contains illustrations and stories that touch the heart, narrative evangelism changes both the mind and the heart.

For many people today, life is meaningless. The story of the gospel is critical. I was witnessing on the Internet to a Generation Xer. She was captivated by my testimony of how I came to Christ. Then I shared the simple truths of the gospel. I said, "Jesus died for us because of our sin." "So what," she replied, "I would die for my friends." "But Jesus raised from the dead," I continued. "OK, I can't do that," she admitted. She did not deny the possibility of the resurrection. She told me why—she could tell by my testimony that I was completely convinced of the truth of the resurrection. She was also convinced I was not loony or naive. My story impressed her in a way that my arguments would not.

Please note that this is not a matter of either-or. Propositional truth in the revealed Scripture is central. I am referring to the way we *deliver* that truth. Weaving the gospel into our story, or telling the stories of Scripture (the prodigal son, the woman at the well), speaks to this age. Stories or parables were a central part of the message of Jesus (Mark 4:33–34).

APPLICATION

Imagine that you are in a community with five thousand homes that you want to touch with the gospel. Using mass evangelism, the Sunday school, small group, visitation, outreach—all of these viable, traditional tools—you will reach many. But how many will we truly impact? There is a significant percentage of people you will never touch—the radically unchurched.

Let's assume you have a fruitful Sunday school campaign. You go out and enroll 10 percent of the population in Sunday school in three years (500 of those homes). Then you have evangelistic crusades each year. In three years 50 people a year (150 people) come to Christ. So you have reached 650 homes in three years.

Statistics show that one out of three unsaved people in our Sunday schools will eventually come to Christ. So out of those 500 people whom you enrolled in Sunday school, about 170 of those would come to Christ.

Now we have 150 people reached with the gospel through mass evangelism and 170 reached through Sunday school for a grand total of 320. Add to that the 80 who came to Christ by other means in three years. Four hundred people have come to Christ out of 5,000 homes. Outstanding, yes, but literally thousands of people in that community have still not heard the gospel of Christ.

Without taking anything away from these methods, the truth is the greatest single missing element of evangelism is total participation. Roy Fish has pointed out that the evangelistic methods we use, including contemporary worship, harvest events, and concerts, actually create a subtle reversal of the Great Commission. Instead of obeying Jesus' commission to "go tell," we emphasize "come and hear" or "come and see."[19]

We must get involved in the lives of the millions of unchurched people all around us if we are to reach America and the world. And when we do, we must tell them the timeless, unchanging gospel in a manner that they can understand.

BIBLIOGRAPHY

Ford, Kevin Graham. *Jesus for a New Generation*. Downers Grove: InterVarsity Press, 1995.

Hunter, George. *Church for the Unchurched*. Nashville: Abingdon, 1996.

_____. *How to Reach Secular People*. Nashville: Abingdon, 1992.

Kramp, John. *Out of Their Faces and into Their Shoes*. Nashville: Broadman & Holman, 1995.

Roof, Wade Clark. *A Generation of Seekers*. San Francisco: Harper-Collins, 1994.

These organizations provide information to help witness to persons in cults and other religions:

Christian Research Institute, P.O. Box 500, San Juan Capistrano, CA 92693-0500.

Interfaith Witness Department, North American Mission Board of the Southern Baptist Convention, 4208 North Point Parkway, Alpharetta, GA 30202.

Spiritual Counterfeits Project, P.O. Box 4308, Berkeley, CA 94704.

MTV and the Internet, or Jesus Christ and Fishing Nets: Evangelizing the Next Generation

I took a vow during the summer of 1996 never to serve again as pastor at a youth camp. This was not because I hate teenagers or camps—on the contrary, I *love* them. But at this particular camp, I ignored my age and physical condition and entered the mud volleyball tournament. My team, the counselors, beat the best youth team. I must have talked too much trash. After the game, I got *creamed* by about two hundred (OK, maybe six or eight) boys. When they got off me, I could hardly walk, but I was too proud to admit I was hurt. I think I said something like, "I have a rock in my shoe," to hide my pain.

For the next three months, I hobbled around until I discovered I had a broken hip. Soon I was facing two realities. First, a major hip operation was in my near future (this will ruin your whole day!). Second, I faced the fact that youth camps are hazardous to my health.

Unfortunately, it seems that the church as a whole has abandoned the opportunity of reaching young people with the same zeal I adopted toward avoiding youth camps. In my denomination, the SBC, we are not reaching youth effectively. And much of our efforts at reaching children have been misguided.

In the second century A.D., apologist Justin Martyr wrote: "Many men and women of the age of 60 and 70 years have been disciples of Christ from childhood."[1] Pliny, in A.D. 112, said that he found among the Christians not only adults but children as well. In his recent book, *The Bridger Generation,* Thom Rainer reminds us that 80 percent of people who are saved come to Christ before age twenty.[2] From the early church to the contemporary setting, reaching pre-adults has been a critical need for the church.

EVANGELIZING CHILDREN

There are few resources that give sound, detailed counsel concerning the evangelization of children. Yet in many circles, such as Southern Baptists, about one half of those making professions of faith are under the age of thirteen.

Roy Fish, the dean of evangelism professors, having taught at Southwestern Baptist Theological Seminary for more than thirty years, offers sage counsel on this vital subject.[3] Fish notes certain assumptions from Scripture concerning children. First, infants and young children are safe within God's care. Second, if they die, they will go to heaven. Delos Miles, my predecessor at Southeastern Baptist Theological Seminary, stated:

> The child is not a "miniature adult." Infants and young children who die before they are capable of conversion go to heaven. They are a part of God's kingdom. Based upon what the Bible tells us about the nature of God, He will not hold a young, immature child responsible for making a decision of which he is incapable.[4]

THE AGE OF ACCOUNTABILITY

Fish's third assumption is that there is a time when children become accountable to God. In other words, we must confront the issue of the "age of accountability." Miles defines this term: "Infants are safe in God's care until they become capable of responsible decision-making."[5] William Hendricks defines the age of accountability as "the moment of grace when one is brought to a decision for or against Christ by the Spirit."[6]

Of course, various traditions deal with this matter in different ways. Sacramental theology focuses on the role of sacraments such as infant baptism. However, the biblical text indicates a conversion theology, regardless of the age of the individual.[7] I agree with Fish, Miles, Hendricks, and others that there is no set age of accountability.

Because of biblical teaching on conversion and the practice of believer's baptism following conversion, the age of accountability is an important concept. Yet we must admit there is no singular biblical passage that clearly elaborates this concept. Romans 14:12 perhaps implies the idea: "So then each of us shall give account of himself to God."

Part of the reason for concern about evangelizing children is the alarming number of people who say something like this: "I didn't know what I was doing at age nine. I joined the church, but I didn't have the capacity for making an intelligent decision. When I was seven or eight nothing really happened, so I needed a later saving experience to be a real Christian." The fact that increasing numbers of adults have done this has caused some people to look suspiciously at the possibility of child conversion.

Further, increasing numbers of children being baptized at earlier ages has caused some to be alarmed at the rate at which we are baptizing children. The issue raises genuine concerns. This is reflected in the extremes that exist on this subject. On the one hand are those who question the possibility of evangelizing children. An example of one who looked suspiciously at this issue is Sam Southard in his book, *Pastoral Evangelism*. Relying heavily on the findings of both psychologists and theologians, Southard concluded that conversion requires a responsible, repentant attitude that is not possible until adolescence or the early teenage years.

On the other hand, some groups seek to evangelize children at a very early age. Fish noted that a former head of the Child Evangelism Fellowship (CEF) wrote that children should be evangelized from three to five years of age. The idea of a three-year-old understanding even the simplest implications of the gospel is extremely problematic, and this seems to me to be very close to infant baptism. And yet, at the other pole, there is too much reliance on psychology to the neglect of the Spirit. Hear Fish at this point:

> We ought not to pay a great deal of attention to secular psychologists who have no knowledge of the work of the Holy Spirit in Christian conversion. Conversion or regeneration is a miracle which defies explanation on a psychological basis. To declare that the Holy Spirit cannot convict children of sin, cannot reveal Christ savingly to them, and cannot work the miracle of regeneration in them is a prerogative no psychologist or theologian ought to assume.[8]

Fish recalled a conversation with Christian psychologist Clyde Narramore. In a message heard by Fish, Narramore related an experience out of his early life. He was converted at age eleven, but he suggested that he could have been converted much earlier. He came under conviction of sin at the age of five. He told about being in a backwoods church in California in a mountainous area. A little pot-bellied stove sat in the middle of the building. When he came under conviction, he discovered that he could sit behind the stove and miss the searching gaze of the preacher. This seemed to lessen the conviction he was feeling. They never took the stove down in the summer, so he had the year-round opportunity of sitting behind it. When the preacher would look to the right side of the pulpit, he would veer to the right side of the stove, and when the preacher would move to the left, he would move to the left of the stove.

Narramore said, "I escaped the searching gaze of the preacher for a number of years until finally God caught up with me, and at age eleven, I became a Christian."

As the men sat across the table at lunch, Fish said to him, "Dr. Narramore, I got the indication in your message that you could have become a Christian at quite an early age."

"Yes, indeed, I believe I could have."

Fish continued, "Some of our leaders are beginning to look suspiciously at child conversion. Where do you think they get it?"

Narramore is not the most nondirect man in the world. With a chuckle and a smile, he looked up and said, "Well, Roy, I think they get it from the devil."

BIBLICAL TEACHING ON EVANGELIZING CHILDREN

We must admit that the Bible says very little explicitly about the evangelization of children. The Old Testament offers examples of children serving the Lord. Samuel was quite young when he began to minister to the Lord under the tutelage of Eli. During the Old Testament era, the idea developed that Jewish children became responsible members of the worshiping community at age twelve. This is why Jesus was taken to Jerusalem to worship when he was twelve. This was not specified in the Old Testament; it simply evolved during the Old Testament era.

Certain passages in the New Testament are helpful on this subject. There is the implication that Timothy followed Christ from childhood (see 2 Tim. 3:15). Jesus said, "Let the little children come to Me, and do not forbid them; for of such is the kingdom of God" (Mark 10:14).

But the most definitive passage relative to the conversion of children in the New Testament is found in Matthew 18:

> At that time the disciples came to Jesus, saying, "Who then is greatest in the kingdom of heaven?" Then Jesus called a little child to Him, set him in the midst of them, and said, "Assuredly, I say to you, unless you are converted and become as little children, you will by no means enter the kingdom of heaven. Therefore whoever humbles himself as this little child is the greatest in the kingdom of heaven. Whoever receives one little child like this in My name receives Me. But whoever causes one of these little ones who believe in Me to sin, it would be better for him if a millstone were hung around his neck, and he were drowned in the depth of the sea.

> "Woe to the world because of offenses! For offenses must come, but woe to that man by whom the offense comes! If your hand or foot causes you to sin, cut it off and cast it from you. It is better for you to enter into life lame or maimed, rather than having two hands or two feet, to be cast into the everlasting fire. And if your eye causes you to sin, pluck it out and cast it from you. It is better for you

to enter into life with one eye, rather than having two eyes, to be cast into hell fire.

"Take heed that you do not despise one of these little ones, for I say to you that in heaven their angels always see the face of My Father who is in heaven. For the Son of Man has come to save that which was lost. What do you think? If a man has a hundred sheep, and one of them goes astray, does he not leave the ninety-nine and go to the mountains to seek the one that is straying? And if he should find it, assuredly, I say to you, he rejoices more over that sheep than over the ninety-nine that did not go astray. Even so it is not the will of your Father who is in heaven that one of these little ones should perish" (Matt. 18:1–14).

In this passage, Jesus used two words to describe little children. One of the words is *paidion* (vv. 2, 4, 5). The other is *micros* (vv. 6, 10, 14). The first word refers to a very young child and periodically refers to infants. It was used of Jesus as an infant. The second word, *micros*—the word we use in English in such words as microscope and microcosm—also refers to children of a young age.

FISH ON MATTHEW 18:1–14

Roy Fish offers the following commentary on this passage.

1. *Conversion occurs on the level of a child.* Jesus says, "Except you be converted and become as little children, you will by no means enter the kingdom of heaven." We typically think of salvation as something of an adult experience to which children must attain. But this passage indicates just the opposite. Not only is conversion possible for the child, but also any adult who would enter the kingdom must first become as a child. We say to children, "Wait until you're adults; then you can become Christians." Jesus said, "Oh, no, you've got it in reverse. You adults become little children, and then you can become Christians."

2. *Humility, the essential quality of greatness in the kingdom, already belongs to the child.* Jesus said, "Whoever will humble himself as this little child, the same is the greatest in the kingdom

of heaven." The word *humility* refers to a state of weakness and dependence that determines greatness. The older we grow, the more proud we become.

3. *A little child can believe in Jesus.* Jesus warned those who "offend one of these little ones who believe in Me." Fish is correct when he says this is the most important statement in Scripture concerning evangelizing children. It should settle the question once and for all as to whether a child can be saved. The word Jesus uses for *believe* here is the same word found in John 3:16, Acts 16:31, and Romans 10:9–10.

4. *Jesus says that to cause a child to stumble is an extremely serious thing.* If a person should cause those who believe in him to stumble, it would be better for him if a millstone were hung about his neck and he were drowned in the depths of the sea. How serious it becomes to reject a child who truly seeks Jesus. What a sobering word to a parent who would treat with indifference the spiritual interest of a little child.

5. *We should seek a little child, for the Lord Jesus as a shepherd seeks a stray sheep.* The sheep in this context refers to children, not adults. Both the preceding and following verses refer to a child. Jesus is saying that we should seek and find children for him as straying lost sheep are sought out by the shepherd.

6. *The Father's will is that no child should perish.* Although the phrase is couched in negative terms, if we turn it around, it declares that the Father desires that every child should be saved. This should cause us to double our efforts in prayer and tactful, careful evangelism that seeks to lead children to the Savior.

I want to conclude this final section by quoting Fish at length:

> In summary, there is a time when children do not need conversion, a time of innocence when they are not accountable or responsible to God. But if the Bible teaches that children, along with adults, respond to God negatively, they respond to what they know about God with rejection, it might be that *negative* and *rejection* are words all together too mild. They respond by rebellion against God. And

the New Testament teaches that when a man or a child responds negatively to God or what he knows about Him, he becomes accountable or responsible to God. In my thinking, this certainly is possible for children.

God does not have two ways of saving people— one way for saving adults and another for saving children. To what extent, then, should we attempt to put a child through the hoop of a dramatic adult experience of conversion? The answer is very simple. Only in the proportion as the child is an adult. The essential ingredients must be present in the salvation experience of a child, however minutely they might appear. Repentance to a child, though based on a limited awareness of sin, will involve a rejection of what in himself is displeasing to God. He should be taught some idea of the cost of following Christ, but to expect all characteristics of a dramatic adult conversion in the conversion experience of a child is being unrealistic. I would not want to soften the line of the necessity of a conversion experience for children. However, we must keep in mind that the New Testament demand is not so much for dramatic conversion as it is for repentance and faith.[9]

HISTORICAL EXAMPLES

There are notable examples of childhood conversion in Christian history. Polycarp, bishop of Smyrna, was converted at age nine, during the first century. He testified at his martyrdom in about the year A.D. 160 that he had been a believer for eighty-five years. He was martyred at age ninety-five. He may have been converted through the ministry of John the Apostle.

Isaac Watts, the father of English hymnody, came to Christ at age nine. Some of Jonathan Edward's biographers contend his salvation came at age seven. Commentator Matthew Henry was ten; Baker James Cauthen, for many years head of the Foreign Mission Board of the Southern Baptist Convention, was six. W. A. Criswell of the great

First Baptist Church, Dallas, Texas, was under ten when he met Christ.[10]

PRINCIPLES FOR DEALING WITH CHILDREN[11]

1. *Deal with each child individually.* This principle is true of adults as well but is so critical with children. Perhaps the reason many children made spurious decisions, or are unsure of genuine commitments, is because of the poor way they were counseled. Some children may in fact be ready, but others simply want to please others around them. Utilizing trained workers to deal at length with each child is essential. If children come forward as part of a group, some would do so because of peer group pressure. A large number of children are not coming because they are ready to make their commitment to Jesus Christ. But some are coming who are willing to make that commitment if only someone would counsel with them and show them the way.

2. *Avoid asking questions that expect a yes or no answer.* Children want to please. They will likely give you the answers they believe you want to hear.

3. *Consider the child's religious background.* My son Joshua at age six and one-half understood more about the gospel than many unchurched teenagers I have met. He had been nurtured in a Christian home where the Bible is read daily, where spiritual matters are discussed regularly, and where church involvement is a central part of our family life. In fact, by the time he was eight, he beat me in Bible Trivia (OK, I did ask him the children's level questions)!

If a child has no religious background, the first time he expresses interest in becoming a Christian, there's a high probability he or she is not ready to make that commitment. Very few children are truly converted the first time they hear the gospel (or adults, for that matter).

4. *Do not use fear as a primary motivation.* I believe fear is a viable part of the gospel for a person of any age. Many people come to Christ because they are afraid of the consequences if they reject him. But extreme methods should not be deliberately used to produce this fear. We must refrain from severe efforts to produce fear in the lives of boys and girls as a motive to get them to Jesus.

5. *Explain the gospel on a child's level.* A few times each year, I will have a small child shake my hand following a sermon delivered

in his or her church. The child will say something like, "I really liked your sermon," or "I understood that."

These compliments mean more to me than anything anyone else could say. If I speak in such a way that a child cannot understand me, it is not a sign that I am deep or profound; it means I'm a poor communicator!

You do not have to use terms like *reconciliation, justification,* or *repentance.* You need to explain such terms on a child's level. The meaning you communicate is more important than the specific words you use.

When you talk to boys and girls about becoming Christians, also talk to them in terms of Christian responsibility. Talk in terms of the lordship of Christ. If they're old enough to accept him as Savior, they're old enough to understand something of the responsibilities of the Christian life. The obligation to obey Jesus belongs as much to the young child as to the aging adult. Those who are old enough to trust are old enough to obey. The claims of the gospel, the law of God, and our need for him must be clearly stated to any person regardless of age.

Jim Elliff adds appropriate comments here in the context of a Christian parent's role:

> By carefully laying out the law (the demands of God on the conscience), by explaining the consequences of breaking that law, and by continually emphasizing the exclusivity of Christ in delivering the child from those consequences, the parents cooperate with the Spirit in this special preparation of the heart. . . . We can cooperate in the Holy Spirit's convicting process by teaching our children the awful consequences of sin as well.[12]

6. *Affirm the child regardless of his or her level of understanding.* You should *never* present a child as having received Christ if you have doubts about the genuineness of his or her confession. But we can affirm the child at some level. W. A. Criswell affirms children who come forward as taking a "step toward God."[13] When a child comes forward in a service, regardless of age, he or she ought to be greeted with these words: "I'm so glad you've come forward today." If an adult refuses to do this and ignores a child's interest, this can

be devastating to a child's growing faith as well as to his trust in adults.

Expression of interest on the part of a child does not mean he or she is ready for an experience of conversion. We must remember that the Holy Spirit can lead a person a step or two nearer to Christ without bringing him or her to new life. Preparatory work is sometimes long, but it's just as much the work of the Holy Spirit as regeneration.

7. *Distinguish between the internal experience of conversion and external expressions associated with it.* Children easily confuse the symbol for the real thing. The real thing happens when they trust the Lord Jesus as their Savior. But the symbol, the external expression, happens when they walk down an aisle and present themselves for church membership and baptism. Some boys and girls are prone to equate salvation with baptism and joining the church.

This is how it is when most children come forward. Little Johnny comes down the aisle. We're glad. He's age ten, but we haven't had a chance to talk with him about this matter. We ask him why he's coming, and he says, "I want to join the church." We quickly explain that he must trust in Jesus to be his Savior, and then we begin asking him questions before the congregation. "Johnny, you know you're a sinner, don't you? You know that Jesus died for you, don't you?" And we begin to nod our heads in an affirmative fashion. "And Johnny today you are trusting him as your Savior, aren't you?" By then our head is bobbing like a fishing cork when the fish are biting.

When children come forward, why not say something like this: "Johnny, I'm so glad you've come forward this morning. As best you can, tell me why you've come." Let him express to you his feeling about the matter. Don't rush in to counsel him or her at the altar. Schedule some time for this after the service. The salvation of a child is too important to rush. Use questions like these: Tell me what you've been thinking about in regard to becoming a Christian. Why do you want to become a Christian? What made you start thinking about it? What do you think a person has to do to become a Christian?

Keep in mind that children need only to receive Christ. They don't have to explain the gospel in detail. Children may not be able to explain why they have this need, but they must sense a need for

Jesus. They must understand that God's provision for meeting the need they feel is Jesus. They don't have to have all the theological answers, but they must understand that it is through Jesus that God meets the need they are experiencing. They also must know how to appropriate or to claim God's provision—through faith by trusting him as they commit their lives to Christ.

EVANGELIZING TEENAGERS

I am grateful that I grew up in a church with a strong youth group. Because of its influence, I was able to begin, with a Methodist friend, a Fellowship of Christian Athletes chapter and a Christian club at our public high school. I attended youth retreats that made a life-changing impact on my life. I participated in choir and mission tours across the country. Young people were important in our church, and we knew it.

I believe the greatest challenge confronting the church in the new millennium relates to youth ministry. We must address the issue of youth evangelism, both in terms of evangelizing teenagers and equipping students to witness to their peers. There is a critical need for youth ministry built on relevant, conviction-laced biblical teaching. The church has an open door to feed the idealism of youth with Christian truths and values.

Paige Patterson once spoke with a student who asked for advice on youth ministry. Patterson told him three things: (1) don't entertain; (2) teach the Bible and tell the young people he would teach them things even their parents don't know; (3) get the youth out witnessing. Patterson saw the student a couple of years later. That youth minister had founded his ministry on those simple truths and had built one of the strongest youth ministries in the state!

I love witnessing with young people. It is criminal to lead a youth group and fail to take the kids out to share their faith. In my informal observation from being in hundreds of churches and talking with scores of youth ministers, I get the impression that most churches treat young people like fourth-graders. We allow them to do certain things, but we really don't believe they can make a significant impact. They are "the church of the future," we say in condescending tones.

I am more inclined to agree with Kenny St. John, who served as minister to students at the First Baptist Church of Jacksonville,

Florida, for many years. He says youth typically achieve the level we expect of them. If we treat them like kids, they will act like kids. If we treat them as young adults with the potential and the ability to honor Christ, they will honor Christ.

THE POTENTIAL OF YOUTH

One of the overlooked features of modern spiritual awakenings is the vital role played by young people. While significant revivals were cited in chapter 4, the following survey examines specifically the role of youth in these acts of God.[14]

Pietism, the experiential awakening of the eighteenth century, grew through the impact of students who graduated from the University of Halle, then spread the experiential emphasis to points across the globe. Zinzendorf graduated from Halle. The one-hundred-year prayer movement begun through his influence at Halle was essentially a movement among young people.

The role of youth is abundantly clear in the First Great Awakening. Jonathan Edwards, commenting on the revival in 1734–35 under his leadership, referred to the role of youth in its origin: "At the latter end of the year 1733, there appeared a very unusual flexibleness, and yielding to advice, in our young people."[15] This happened after Edwards began speaking against their irreverence toward the Sabbath. The youth were also greatly affected by the sudden death of a young man and a young married woman in their town. Edwards proposed that the young people should begin meeting in small groups around Northampton. They did so with such success that many adults followed their example. Concerning the revival's effect on the youth, Edwards commented,

> God made it, I suppose, the greatest occasion of awakening to others, of anything that ever came to pass in the town . . . news of it seemed to be almost like a flash of lightning, upon the hearts of young people, all over town, and upon many others.[16]

Edwards also remarked on the role of youth in this revival in his treatise *Thoughts on the Revival,* while indicting older believers for their indifference:

> The work has been chiefly amongst the young; and comparatively but few others have been made

partakers of it. And indeed it has commonly been so, when God has begun any great work for the revival of his church; he has taken the young people, and has cast off the old and stiff-necked generation.[17]

Another feature of the First Great Awakening in relation to students was the log college of William Tennent. Tennent, a Presbyterian, built a log house to provide ministerial training. Three of his sons and fifteen other youth were the early students.[18] George Whitefield recorded the following thoughts in his journal after visiting the log college:

> The place wherein the young men study now is in contempt called The College. It is a log house, about twenty feet long and near as many broad; and to me it seemed to resemble the school of the old prophets, for their habitations were mean; . . . From this despised place, seven or eight worthy ministers of Jesus have lately been sent forth; more are almost ready to be sent, and the foundation is now laying for the instruction of many others.[19]

From the log college advanced several youth who became leaders in the First Great Awakening. These included William Tennents' sons Gilbert, the most prominent revival leader among Presbyterians, John, and William, Jr., along with Samuel Blair. In addition, many graduates established similar log colleges of their own. The log college, which ultimately evolved into the College of New Jersey (now Princeton University) has been called "the forerunner of modern seminaries."[20] Thus, the rise of seminaries, such a mainstay of ministry training in our day, can be traced to students in this great awakening.

In England, the Evangelical Awakening featured such notable leaders as the Wesley brothers and George Whitefield. Their ministries grew out of a foundation built in college through the Holy Club. Whitefield was only twenty-six when he witnessed remarkable revival in the American colonies. These young men never let their youthfulness hinder their impact.

The Second Great Awakening featured powerful revival movements on college campuses. Hampden-Sydney, Yale, Williams, and others serve as bold reminders of what God can do in our day as well. Churches could not have experienced the depth of revival they felt apart from youth. Bennett Tyler collected twenty-five eyewitness accounts of pastors during the Second Great Awakening. Twenty of these revival reports described the important role played by young people. Ten accounts noted that the revivals began with the youth, and five documented the fact that revival in their area affected young people more than any other group. Only one account out of twenty-five asserted that no youth were involved.[21]

Colleges experienced revival in the 1857–59 Layman's Prayer Revival as well. One pivotal feature of this revival in relation to young people was the impact it had on Dwight Lyman Moody, who was twenty years old at the time. In 1857 Moody wrote of his impression of what was occurring in Chicago: "There is a great revival of religion in this city . . . [It] seems as if God were here himself."[22] Biographer John Pollock reports that "the revival of early 1857 tossed Moody out of his complacent view of religion."[23] Moody went on to make a dramatic impact for Christ during the rest of the nineteenth century.

An aspect of Moody's influence regarding students that cannot be overlooked was his leadership in the Student Volunteer Movement. Although this movement's roots have been traced to the Second Great Awakening and the Haystack Prayer Meeting of 1806, it was Moody who invited 251 students to Mt. Hermon, Massachusetts, for a conference in 1886. As a result of these meetings, highlighted by A. T. Pierson's challenging address, one hundred students volunteered for overseas missions. In 1888 the Student Volunteer Movement was formally organized with John R. Mott as chairman. Over the next several decades, literally thousands of students went to serve as foreign missionaries.

According to J. Edwin Orr, the Welsh Revival of 1904–05 was greatly influenced in its beginning by a church in New Quay, Cardiganshire, and the testimony of a teenage girl. Pastor Joseph Jenkins led a testimony time in a service in which he asked for responses to the question, What does Jesus mean to you? A young person, fifteen-year-old Florrie Evans, only recently converted, rose and said, "If no one else will, then I must say that I love the Lord Jesus with all my heart."[24]

Her simple testimony caused many people to begin surrendering to Christ, and the fires of revival fell. The revival spread as young people went from church to church testifying. An itinerant preacher named Seth Joshua came to New Quay to speak and was impressed by the power of God. He then journeyed to speak at Newcastle Embyn College. The next week he spoke at nearby Blaenannerch, where a young coal miner named Evan Roberts, a ministerial student at the college, experienced a powerful personal revival.

Roberts felt impressed to return to his home church to address the youth. Seventeen heard him following a Monday service. He continued preaching and revival began there.[25] The revival spread across the country, and news of the awakening spread worldwide. Many colleges reported revival. A good example was the revival reported at Denison University in Ohio.[26]

Many colleges witnessed revival in the 1950s as well. In Minnesota, Northwestern School, St. Paul Bible Institute, and the University of Minnesota were touched. At the Northern Baptist Theological Seminary in Chicago, professor Julius Mantey observed: "Nearly every student that I have asked says he was deeply stirred. . . . We are all on a higher plane."[27] The year 1951 saw a notable spiritual stir on the campus of Baylor University. President W. R. White commented favorably about revival at this school.

Fred Hoffman recorded what happened during this period at Wheaton College: "Perhaps one of the most remarkable and powerful spiritual awakenings was the one experienced at Wheaton College in February 1950."[28] After numerous prayer meetings were inaugurated by student leaders the previous fall, the revival began when a student shared a testimony of his changed life in an evening meeting. Others began testifying, and this continued for more than two days. Asbury College in Kentucky experienced revival as well. One of the stronger movements in the period in the opinion of historian Clifton Olmstead was Youth for Christ, a parachurch movement that began in 1944.[29]

Finally, the Jesus Movement described in chapter 4 was actually a youth awakening. Many of the leaders of churches, denominations, and parachurch organizations were touched by this revival. A significant number of evangelistic pastors and other leaders trace their zeal for the Lord to the impact of the Jesus Movement on their life.

Students are perhaps the most fertile field for the working of the Spirit of God. If only churches would tap into the zeal of youth!

REACHING THE BRIDGER GENERATION

Is it possible that we have lost ground in evangelism in America because we are always playing catch-up? Do we work too hard to gear worship services to adults, provide materials for adults, and focus all our energies on those who pay the bills while neglecting the younger generation?

We have been deluged with information about Baby Boomers and Baby Busters. The oldest Boomers are in their fifties, and the youngest Busters are now adults. What group in America is under twenty years of age? It is the Bridger generation, born 1977–94.[30] Also known as the Millennials and the Echoboomers, this generation is the second largest in American history—72 million strong (Boomers numbered 76 million). So much has been written about Boomers—my generation, born from 1946–64. Boomers have been described as self-absorbed. We now see billions of dollars spent on reaching Busters, born 1965–76 (or up until 1980, depending on who you read). Have you seen those Generation Next Pepsi commercials, for example? But in the church, our efforts to reach Boomers and Busters have often come too little, too late. Generationally, we are losing the battle.

We must strategically seek to reach this generation. "The time to reach the Bridgers is now," says Rainer, "not 2010."[31] There has been a general decline in the Southern Baptist Convention over the past twenty-five years in the number and percentage of youth baptisms. Not since the Jesus Movement in the early 1970s have we as a denomination effectively reached youth. Now that the numbers of youth in America are increasing, will the church intentionally seek to reach them?

There is a great deal of talk in our day about revival. Many people are praying and fasting, and some hopeful signs are apparent. What is missed in most discussions regarding revival is the role that youth have played in past awakenings. What would happen if our churches stopped treating teenagers like fourth-graders and began to see young people less as *peripheral* and more as *essential* to what God wants to do in revival?

In the past three years, I have been in several churches where God moved in a mighty way with a touch of true revival. In every one of these situations, without exception, there was a strong youth group vitally involved in the life of the church.

We need a paradigm shift in how we do student ministry. A friend who is a prominent evangelist in our convention met recently with student ministers from some of the strongest churches in the SBC. He told me one of the admissions of the group is that they had lost sight of their need to be personal soul winners.

Youth *can* be reached. When I served in Indiana, I was grieved to find that our state declined in baptisms every year in the 1980s— youth baptisms declined the most. We made a strategic attempt to focus on reaching young people. The youth evangelism conference grew from two hundred to two thousand, and baptisms increased four consecutive years. Youth baptisms played a prominent role. Youth ministry must give chief importance to the building of biblical, evangelistic student ministries. These ministries must focus more on relevant biblical teaching than ski trips—more on evangelizing their peers than pacifying their parents.

On a larger scale, there remains a serious, urgent call for churches to shift in mentality concerning the very purpose of the church. The church is not a hotel for saints; it is a hospital for sinners. Our failure to reach youth is symptomatic of a larger failure in evangelism.

We must see technology as our friend in evangelism. Rainer notes that the Internet will affect the Bridgers the way television affected Boomers. Throughout history, the church at its best has been at the forefront of technology. Think of how the printing press was used to publish the Bible and how trade routes helped in worldwide missions expansion. In recent history, we have lagged behind. I have been privileged to lead someone to Christ through the Internet. The technology is available. Compare TV evangelists to MTV in terms of influencing culture! The Internet may become one of the most viable tools for reaching the Bridger generation.

We must use the media and the arts in biblical ways to declare Christ to this generation. Music and other arts play an influential role in the lives of Bridgers. Can we not use the arts to reach this group? No one epitomizes the Buster generation any better than singer Alanis Morissette. Her in-your-face, filled-with-angst lyrics speak volumes. If Morissette speaks for Busters, then the current Bridger-aged group, Hanson—all under twenty years old—speaks for many Millennials. You may have never heard of them, but their smash 1997 hit "Mmm-Bop," with its "nostalgic-for-a-simpler-time feel,"[32] demonstrates the surface happiness Bridgers show when contrasted with the more pessimistic Generation X. Through the arts, we can strike a chord among Millennials.

Hold to the cross and the truthfulness of Scripture. Rainer encourages us to confront the pluralism of the Bridger generation not with a compromised gospel but with the bold declaration that Jesus Christ is the only way to God. An uncertain ocean requires a strong hand and a sound rudder. We must confront the pluralism of the age with courage, not compromise.

Demonstrate intimacy with God and people. Youth crave intimacy. The Millennials are a fatherless generation. We must minister to youth, and to children for that matter, in the context of their families. Youth workers are ministers not only to teenagers but also to their parents. In this time of family disintegration, churches must step up their efforts to strengthen families.

The numbers of fatherless children (homes with no father present) have grown from 14 percent in 1970 to almost one third by 1993. Further, the percentage of mothers, with school-aged children, who work outside the home has increased from 39 percent in 1960 to 70 percent by 1987. Today, fifty percent of marriages end in divorce.[33] The crumbling of the home, coupled with the rise of youth gangs, points out the desire for intimacy.

As I drove down the Atlanta freeway recently, I flipped to a radio station and caught a DJ speaking to a mother. She put her child on the line—a young teenager. "What would you like to say to the DJ?" the radio personality asked. "Play more Hanson!" she answered. The song he played included these lyrics: "We'll be your friend now and forever," and, "We all need somebody we can cling to, someone who always understands." Then the chorus chimed, "When you have no light to guide you, no one to walk beside you, I will come to you." The Millennials are looking for guidance, closeness, and intimacy. We can show them true intimacy with the Light of the world, Jesus Christ.

APPLICATION

A subtle trend in local churches needs to be addressed—the segmentation of youth ministry apart from the church mainstream. For example, over the past two decades the number of vocational youth ministers has grown while at the same time youth baptisms have declined. This is not an indictment of youth ministers, but it may indicate that the growth of youth ministry as an entity of its own has helped to take young people out of the mainstream of the church. In many churches with significant youth ministries, the only time young people are noticed is when they return from camp or when a youth emphasis is scheduled during revival services.

Churches must place a higher priority on youth. They are not the church of the future; they are the church of today. Churches need both the wisdom of mature believers and the zeal of youth. During the Jesus Movement and the years following, youth choirs filled hundreds of churches. They were a focal point of the service and a source of great inspiration. Surely there are ways students can be brought into the heart of church life.

Your church bears a responsibility to guide students. Mature Christians should help young people channel their zeal in ways that honor Christ. We can affirm their concern for unsaved friends and encourage them to maintain convictions. The True Love Waits campaign is a beautiful illustration of the multitude of godly young men and women who seek to honor God with their bodies. The author is grateful to God for a church that affirmed and encouraged him to make a radical commitment to Christ as a teenager. In your church, delegate responsibilities to mature youth in the worship service. They can help take the offering, lead in prayer, and do dramatic presentations. An occasional word of affirmation from the pastor in the service is very affirming.

Finally, those of us who are older can listen to young people. They too can hear from God. At times they are more sensitive to the voice of the Spirit than many of us. May the following words remind us of the importance of youthful zeal, regardless of age:

> If we look at the ranks of middle-aged men and women we observe that there is all too often no spiritual fire, no urge to achieve things for God. That condition does not suddenly come upon people at that age; you need to be on guard against it now, whatever your age. *It is when one has found his niche that imperceptibly zeal flags and lethargy creeps in*. Oh, to keep burning brightly to the end![34]

BIBLIOGRAPHY

Fields, Doug, *Purpose Driven Youth Ministry*. Grand Rapids: Zondervan, 1998.

Fish, Roy. *Introducing Children to Christ*. Audiotape TC1794, Southwestern Baptist Theological Seminary, Fort Worth, Texas.

Rainer, Thom S. *The Bridger Generation*. Nashville: Broadman & Holman, 1997.

15

Relic of the Past or Uncut Jewel? Mass Evangelism

Have you ever played cerebral torment? Try this one: Which is correct: nine plus seven *is* fifteen, or nine plus seven *are* fifteen?[1]

Okay, let's try another: By removing six letters from the following line you are left with one word (English only, please!). What is the word?

B S I A X N L A E T N T A E S R S

Give up? Here are the answers: First, nine plus seven equals *sixteen,* not fifteen! Next, remove "SIX LETTERS"—the word is *bananas:* B S I A̲ X N̲ L A̲ E T N̲ T A̲ E S̲ R S

Most people don't get these right because they rush to discover the answer before seriously engaging the question. Let me ask you one more question related to ministry in the local church: What method has God used more than any other approach, except personal evangelism, to reach the lost? The answer: Mass evangelism. This is a bit of a trick question because technically all evangelism is either personal—one person witnessing to another—or mass—one person talking to more than one other person.

By mass evangelism I refer specifically to gospel preaching to a group of people, particularly traditional crusades in local churches or areas. In a general sense, mass evangelism refers to any gospel message presented to a crowd, including a musical, drama, block party, or some other tool. Mass evangelism has endured as a timeless method ordained by God in Scripture and used with incredible effectiveness throughout history. Also, itinerant evangelists have ministered from New Testament times until today.

The New Testament affirmed preaching the Good News to the masses; however, the approach varied according to the audience. John the Baptist vilified the Pharisees; Jesus preached repentance; Peter began with the Old Testament in speaking to Jews at Pentecost; Paul followed a similar approach with a Jewish audience, but he used another technique when speaking to Greeks in Athens.

MASS EVANGELISM IN HISTORY

The most effective times of evangelism throughout history also featured some of the most effective mass evangelists. Some were pastors; some were itinerants; still others were pastor-itinerants. In different eras, different means have been used to proclaim the gospel to a given audience.

In the modern era, gospel preaching marked the evangelical awakening in England, although earlier the Pietists in Europe had preached mass meetings of some kind. George Whitefield, John Wesley, and others preached the gospel outdoors, in the streets and fields, with great success. They struggled with this approach because it was so nontraditional in their day. Congregationalist Jonathan Edwards preached his famous sermon, "Sinners in the Hands of an Angry God," to another congregation, in a one-service mass evangelism event. Shubal Stearns, noted Baptist leader of the Sandy Creek Church, utilized protracted meetings, or extended evangelistic services. The camp meetings on the American frontier erupted spontaneously about 1800, providing an avenue for many to preach and thousands to be saved. Methodist circuit riders became the itinerant evangelists on the frontier.

Charles Finney utilized protracted meetings, at first extending services over several nights spontaneously after the fire of God fell in revival. In Rochester, New York, Finney preached ninety-eight sermons from September 10, 1830, to March 6, 1831. Hudson called Finney's meetings "the camp meeting brought to town."[2] By the 1830s, the term *revival meeting* was used to refer to a general protracted meeting, whether it was a camp meeting on the frontier under such men as James McGready or a protracted meeting under Finney in the urban areas of the East.

D. L. Moody signaled the next significant shift in mass evangelism. He was the first modern urban evangelist. He planned meetings with great preparation, set the date, stayed for many days, and involved the entire city. A whole caravan of evangelists followed after him, including Wilbur Chapman, R. A. Torrey, Billy Sunday, and Billy Graham—the best-known and the evangelist who has preached to more people than any other in human history. Whether it was field preaching, camp meetings, or citywide crusades, Wood has aptly concluded, "For every age God has a programme of evangelism."[3]

THE SIGNIFICANCE OF MASS EVANGELISM

In George Whitefield's day, mass evangelism practiced in the fields was rejected by most church leaders because it was an innovation. Today, some church leaders have stopped holding evangelistic meetings because they are considered too traditional! Why should a church consider mass evangelism?

A BIBLICAL CONCEPT

Mass evangelism and evangelists are biblical concepts. Both were God's idea. This doesn't mean that churches that fail to conduct annual or semiannual evangelistic campaigns are bad; it suggests that some have given up on the method prematurely. Unfortunately, some evangelists have given evangelistic meetings and evangelists a bad reputation. But there are many godly, effective preachers who are gifted as harvesters.

THE URGENCY OF EVANGELISM

Mass evangelism reminds believers that people are lost and must be reached. In a day when tolerance is a virtue and conviction is a vice, too many believers have lost a sense of their own lostness apart from Christ. Our culture has robbed us of the sense of people's lostness and the urgency of evangelism. Gospel preaching speaks not only to lost people; Christians need to hear the "old, old story."

AN EFFECTIVE METHOD

Mass evangelism still works. We can preach the timeless gospel in a changing world. The largest services in the history of Billy Graham's crusades are happening right now—on youth night! Graham has learned how to preach the timeless gospel in a changing world.

Some of my most precious memories are of evangelistic services: the father of a close friend coming to Christ in deep brokenness and tears; a married couple from different church backgrounds who moved from a religious system to a relationship with God; one fourth of a junior high school football team coming to Christ in one night; a church transformed by witnessing the power of God changing lives.

A recent study revealed that almost one half of evangelistic Southern Baptist churches use "revival evangelism" regularly. How has the method been so successful? First, extensive planning is done. Hard work and high expectancy mark these churches. Second, prayer is not on the periphery in these efforts. Third, these churches generally use vocational evangelists.[4]

As a young pastor, I used such an evangelist. We prepared diligently in our little church, using our Home Mission Board's materials. We prayed all night one Friday! We went out into the community again and again. And God blessed! More people came to Christ and were baptized in that church than had been reached for the past eight years. Don't give up on the method; it will work in our day if we make the right preparations.

Many evangelists hold crusades in local churches or areas. Bailey Smith preaches in local churches and areawide crusades, and he has preached to massive crowds around the world. Some of the most effective evangelists tell me that areawide crusades are still effective in small to midsized towns and cities.

Mass evangelism, or the preaching of the gospel to a group, permeates the New Testament. Peter's sermon at Pentecost is the most famous example; but Jesus, Paul, and others preached to large crowds. In modern times, more organized, structured evangelistic campaigns in local churches and great arenas have been the means for the conversion of multitudes. In the Southern Baptist Convention, years marked by simultaneous evangelistic crusades have led to some of the most significant increases in baptisms.

A. W. Tozer is known for his book, *The Pursuit of God,* which emphasizes godliness and holy living. What many people don't know about him is that as a seventeen-year-old walking home from his job at Goodyear in Akron, Ohio, he heard a street preacher say, "If you don't know how to be saved, just call on God." After that, he called out to Christ to save him. A. W. Tozer came to Christ through a street preacher. We should be careful about throwing out evangelistic methods.[5]

EVANGELISTIC PREACHING

In *Effective Evangelistic Churches,* Thom Rainer noted that preaching played an important role in virtually every church surveyed. More important than worship styles or ministries was the role of the pulpit. More than 90 percent of churches surveyed reported that preaching played a major role in the evangelistic growth of the church. Respondents also indicated that almost three out of four pastors of these churches preached expository messages.

Some people believe that to reach the current generation, expository preaching must be abandoned in favor of topical, needs-oriented sermons. However, studies indicate that expository preaching still plays a vital role in many evangelistic churches. We should remember that the Bible speaks to both *felt* needs and *real* needs! It takes more work to exegete a text and apply it to today's world, but the long-term effects are worth it. The Word of God is as relevant as tomorrow, for God already knows tomorrow's headlines! Instead of deemphasizing sound, biblical, expository preaching, we should work to eliminate *boring* preaching and replace it with *effective* preaching.

During my first year as a professor at Southeastern, a pastor from Virginia told the true story about a little boy who came to the evening service at his church. The pastor waxed unusually long that evening, and the child became restless.

"When will he be finished, Mom?" he asked.

"Quiet!" snapped his mother.

Soon the little boy inquired again, "Mom, when will he be done?"

The mother again replied, "Son, sit still and be quiet, or I'll take you out and spank you."

Finally, after the pastor had preached almost an hour, the boy had all he could stand. "Mom," he pleaded. "Just take me out and spank me, please!"

The boy thought a whipping was better than the preaching he was hearing! Evangelistic preaching should be marked by effectiveness, earnestness, and biblical fidelity—and it shouldn't be boring.

In a 1996 lecture at Southeastern Seminary, Haddon Robinson spoke of four worlds the preacher must know in order to communicate the message to any generation. He should know the world of the Bible, which includes a thorough exegesis of the text. He should also know the current culture in which we live. The third world is the preacher's own, personal world—his strengths and weaknesses. The final world is the immediate world of his local church or the congregation that he is currently addressing. By knowing these worlds and exercising some serious study, preachers can apply the gospel to any generation.

In Jonathan Edwards's day, a literate culture required depth of thought and profound images. In our day, influenced by television, illustrations play a larger role than ever. Communicating to this generation requires an understanding of relationship, which is such a vital part of our culture. That said, the exposition of the Word of God must serve as the foundation of our preaching.

Evangelistic preaching must be passionate, biblical, urgent, and relevant. We can learn from others, but we must receive our message from God. Then we will proclaim a word from God, not an echo from another preacher. Note the following insights from great preachers:

- Charles Spurgeon: "A burning heart will soon find for itself a flaming tongue."[6]

- Jerry Vines: "I milk a lot of cows, but I make my own butter."

- Martyn Lloyd-Jones: "Preaching is theology coming through a man on fire. . . . What is the chief end of preaching? It is to give men and women a sense of God and His presence."[7]

- E. M. Bounds: "It takes twenty years to make a sermon because it takes twenty years to make the man."[8]

THE GOSPEL INVITATION

Central to the evangelistic service is the public invitation. Because of extremes by a few evangelists who are manipulative and insincere, some preachers have moved away from the open invitation. I believe the invitation is essential to effective evangelistic preaching.

BIBLICAL EVIDENCE FOR THE INVITATION

Some people question whether the public invitation is a viable or even a biblical way to call people to salvation. In his outstanding book *The Effective Invitation,* Alan Streett argued the New Testament consistently demonstrates the necessity of a public call. Streett also recognized the consistent call of God to open obedience in the Old Testament. Further, he cited the ministry of Jesus as it relates to the invitation. Beyond the narratives of Jesus and his call of the disciples, Lazarus, and others, the use of the Greek word *parakaleo* is significant in this discussion. Paige Patterson describes one way this word, meaning "to come alongside," can be translated:

> I have frequently translated it as "give an invitation." Any time you come across the word *exhortation* on the pages of the New Testament, you have, in effect, an appeal made for people to come and stand with the speaker in whatever it is that he is doing. This, of course, could take many patterns. . . . In any case, it is an invitation to decide.[9]

Streett noted that five times *parakaleo* is related to evangelistic preaching. Other expressions of this meaning range from the analogy of sowing and reaping to the call for open acknowledgment of Christ in Romans 10:9–10. Thus, the New Testament teaches the importance of a public call to Christ.

THE PUBLIC INVITATION IN HISTORY

Public calls for the converted to proclaim their faith in Christ openly persisted until the time of Constantine, according to Streett.[10] For more than a millennium following Constantine, the emphasis shifted from salvation by grace through faith in Christ to the sacramental system of the Catholic church. During this era, the public invitation disappeared. Occasionally preachers such as

Bernard of Clairveaux would issue a call for some type of public response, but this was the exception, not the rule.

During the Reformation, the Anabaptists were consistent "in calling men to repent of their sins, place their faith in Christ, and present themselves for rebaptism (since their infant baptism was null and void)."[11] In the First Great Awakening, Jonathan Edwards met with persons privately after they responded to his preaching. George Whitefield and others followed this pattern of calling people to repent, then meeting with them privately about their spiritual needs. Sometimes Whitefield could not sleep or eat because of the many people seeking counsel.

Howard Olive discusses four ways John Wesley utilized a public invitation: (1) he used personal workers who sought anxious souls; (2) he called upon seekers to attend a service in the midweek to demonstrate their faith; (3) he invited seekers to step out publicly for church membership; (4) he used the mourner's bench or anxious seat.[12]

Separate Baptists continued the trend of a public call, but Charles G. Finney made the greatest impact in the modern era. He used the mourner's bench, or the anxious seat, and implored people to come forward and kneel at the altar. With mass evangelists such as D. L. Moody, Billy Sunday, and Billy Graham during the past 150 years, the evangelistic invitation has become a staple in the evangelical diet. Moody used inquiry rooms, Sunday exhorted sinners to "hit the sawdust trail," and Graham calls people to come openly "just as they are."[13]

How to Give an Effective Invitation[14]

I have been in a few services where the evangelist seemed more interested in a large response than the work of the Spirit. Such abuses should not prevent us from extending the gospel invitation.

1. *Give it with a spiritually prepared mind.* At the point of the invitation, the preacher is dependent on the Holy Spirit, so we must be sensitive to his movement.

2. *Give it expectantly.* Believe God will honor the faithful preaching of his Word.

3. *Give it dependently.* Depend on the Holy Spirit.

4. *Give it clearly.* Be specific in the appeal. Often people do not respond because they are unclear as to what they are called on to do. Do not rush through the invitation; allow time for clarity, and give enough time to it to allow people to respond.

5. *Give it courteously.* Be direct, but don't manipulate the people.

6. *Give it confidently.*

7. *Give it urgently.*

Methods can include giving an invitation:

• To come forward to confess Christ;

• To come forward to go to a counseling or inquiry room;

• To raise their hands, indicating a desire to follow Christ;

• To pray at one's seat; or

• A combination of the above.

The best way to learn to give an effective invitation is by observing effective evangelists.

CONDUCTING AN EFFECTIVE EVANGELISTIC MEETING

HOSTING A GUEST EVANGELIST

One of the most haphazard activities in the local church is the hosting of a guest evangelist. My colleague Daniel Forshee offers the following suggestions for hosting an evangelistic team. If you are the host pastor, here are some practical things to do:

Secure an evangelist whom you know to have integrity. Whenever possible, secure a vocational evangelist. Ask if he has a music evangelist whom he can recommend. If possible, secure the musician as well, since music plays an important role in a successful meeting.

Set the date. The best times for a fall revival meeting are August through November; for a spring revival, March through May. It is better to select the speaker you desire, then set the date. Setting a date and then finding someone who fits the calendar is a poor way of selecting a speaker.

Secure a thorough preparation manual. Some evangelists provide you with a manual. The North American Mission Board (SBC) provides outstanding materials for such meetings. I have used these materials and have found them effective.

Begin preparations three to six months in advance. Share with the church council, deacons, teachers, and other key leaders with excitement!

Organize a revival planning team to help with preparations. Most preparation manuals guide this process.

Pastor, be enthusiastic! You are the key to the involvement of your people.

Select a theme for the meeting. Some possibilities are "Shine Jesus Shine," "New Life in Christ," "Freedom in Christ," and so on. This will help in your promotions and publicity.

Use budgeted money for incidentals. The church should budget for travel, lodging, meals, pianist, organist, and so on. *Never* tell the evangelist that the love offering will be given to the team, and then take expenses for the meeting from the offering. This lacks integrity, but it happens too often. House the team in a decent hotel. Reimburse the team for mileage if they drive. Surely we can treat the called of God on the same level as the IRS does when it comes to reimbursement for mileage!

Be clear with the evangelistic team about finances. Provide mileage expense, airfare, and related costs (parking, meals en route). I know from experience how much travel costs. Quality begets quality!

Extend a thoughtful, prepared request for the love offering in every service, especially Sunday morning. Use Scripture, illustrations, and personal example. Do not treat the offering haphazardly. Explain that the evangelists are being paid with no set amount—strictly on a love offering basis. Emphasize to your congregation the joy of giving.

Have special love offering envelopes available in every service, including Sunday morning. I know one pastor who used envelopes for registering attendance as well as the offering. He had all the people put their names on the envelope, indicating that no one had to give. But he encouraged those who desired to worship through giving to enclose a gift as well. There was no high pressure, only encouragement. The love offering was extremely high for a church of its size. Give people the opportunity, teach them to give out of love for God, and they will give!

Introduce the team each night. Guests need some introduction. It is best to do this during the welcome time early in the service.

Schedule some fun—golf, for example. If you pastor First Baptist Church of Grand Canyon, then you know where to take your guests!

Have trained counselors available, especially for youth night. This is a *great* time to get laity involved in evangelism. Besides, God is pleased when people prepare for his blessings!

Pastor, extend the invitation. Often the response is greater after an additional appeal by the pastor, since the people know him. For example, say, "When Dr. Hunt used the illustration about the young boy, God convicted my heart . . ."

Be a gracious host. Make sure that the only concerns the evangelists have are preaching the gospel and leading worship.

PREPARING FOR AN EVANGELISTIC MEETING

There are two keys to conducting an effective mass evangelism crusade. One is practical or organizational. The other is spiritual.

Organizational preparation. A mass evangelism meeting should work from an updated, cultivated *prospect list.* If the meeting is to be a harvest event and not a cultivating event, there must be people in the services who are unsaved. They should have already heard the gospel and should be ready to respond to its claims. This will take some time in the months and weeks before the meeting.

You will reach some people before the meeting starts if you begin about six weeks ahead. For example, in a church which I served, we saturated the community with copies of the New Testament, we used radio, we updated our prospect list, and we visited many people. The week before the meeting began, our church saw someone come to Christ.

The very Sunday morning the meeting began, a young woman who had not been to church since she was about twelve gave her life to Christ and was baptized that night. This happened because we had met her and established a relationship.

During an evangelistic meeting, make specific appointments with unsaved people for the pastor and the evangelist to visit. If you take the initiative to set such appointments, you will probably win several whom you visit as the Holy Spirit moves in their lives.

In addition, organizational preparation for a meeting requires *publicity*. Use every avenue you can. We tried to touch our community with different approaches: visitation, door-to-door New Testament distribution, door-to-door flyer giveaway the day before the meeting, phone calls, radio spots, and an ad in the newspaper. In one case, our revival meeting was part of the simultaneous crusades that we periodically have sponsored as Southern Baptists. There were television spots as well and a direct-mail flyer available to us. We targeted specific people to visit. Many people in our community were touched by a small, struggling church. As a result, many came to Christ, and we continued to baptize others after the meeting was over.

The third organizational concern for a revival meeting is *attendance*. Sometimes, we don't get the church people to attend. Monday night is notorious as a weak attendance night, for example. Another problem is that we don't get lost people to attend. How can they come to Christ if they're not present to hear the gospel? A key to attendance night is sponsoring special emphases. In previous days in rural churches, pack-a-pew night was a big hit. Groups, classes, or individuals would compete to see who could pack the most pews or pack the pew with the most people. This approach doesn't work as well today, but other emphases are good possibilities. The most significant special emphasis today is youth night.

Spiritual preparation. How do you prepare the church spiritually for revival? First, provide a list of unsaved people to the evangelist several weeks before the meeting. This will allow him to pray specifically with the church during your preparation. It will also encourage him to see that the church is serious about reaching people!

Second, organize focused prayer for the church. This includes praying for the meeting in every Sunday school class, each service, and each meeting, beginning at least six weeks before the meeting. God's blessing is often equal to the level of our expectancy. All-night prayer meetings or seasons of fasting and prayer can be effective.

Finally, encourage special times of prayer during the week of the meeting. Prayer walks through the community are increasingly used as a means to mobilize believers to pray. Have prayer times before each service, and enlist individuals to pray during the service.

Evangelistic meetings are an excellent time to deepen the commitment of the church to prayer!

INNOVATIVE EVANGELISTIC MEETINGS

Some evangelists are using innovative approaches to share the timeless gospel message. Kelley Green has an approach called Frontliners. Each summer he leads crusades at night and involves youth groups from across the country in evangelistic outreach during the day. This combination of a youth mission trip and a harvest meeting has proven fruitful.

Wayne Bristow uses Total Life conferences in churches with non-traditional worship services. These conferences target young adults in communities where it is difficult to sustain attendance for four or five days, and where traditional revival meetings are no longer successful. Total Life events include evangelistic dinners and luncheons; special events for young people, older children, senior citizens, and young adults; and mixed audience rallies.

Words such as *revival* and *crusade* are confusing or even intimidating to unchurched people. Wayne recognizes these terms have lost much of their meaning, so he uses other terminology. He calls his meetings Total Life conferences. Changing the terminology can change the emphasis in some settings. But this may not be appropriate or workable in every church.

EVENT EVANGELISM

Thom Rainer's book, *Effective Evangelistic Churches,* contains several surprises. For example, Ranier found that event evangelism seems to have little impact. This is true, if we define success or effectiveness in terms of conversions. But we need to remember that evangelism is more than harvesting, although this is our ultimate goal. We must plant and cultivate as well as harvest. Event evangelism can be effective in giving people an opportunity to hear the gospel—particularly people who might not hear it in any other way.

For example, a neighborhood block party will present Christ to those for whom the doors of the church are not readily accessible. An evangelistic concert in the church building at Christmas or Easter may draw people who might not come at other times to hear the

Word of God preached. We should not judge such events strictly on how many people are converted.

The lost and confused people of your community aren't likely to fall into your church in large numbers asking for answers. Thus, we must take the message to them in creative ways. This can be done through what is known as "event evangelism."[15]

By being sensitive to your community, its needs, and its activities, you can use existing events or develop some new ones to introduce people to Jesus Christ. Is your town having a parade? Have the church build a float, then let members walk along the parade route passing out tracts.

Valentine's Day, Halloween, Christmas, and New Year's provide opportunities for your church to create an event that draws the unchurched. Then you can tactfully share Jesus with them. In developing an evangelistic event, remember that you're trying to attract the unchurched, not the church! This may mean doing things a little differently than fits your style, but this is OK as long as you don't compromise the gospel. It may also mean having the event somewhere besides the church building. Furthermore, in advertising, it may mean focusing on the event or the personality rather than the church. You're not hiding the church or acting ashamed of the gospel; you're just being crafty in your presentation.

The following A-B-C method of evangelism event development and execution was devised by Toby Frost, manager of event evangelism for the North American Mission Board. These guidelines should help you get a handle on the idea.

A stands for attraction. No matter how dynamic your event, how glorious your music, and how engaging your speaker, evangelism cannot take place without an audience of unchurched people! Plan an event that will attract the unchurched. Be sure to try to capture the interest of the community when you promote the event. And remember that promotion must be accompanied by enlistment. Members of your church should bring their friends, neighbors, relatives, and coworkers to the event.

B *stands for bridge.* Provide a nonthreatening, relational bridge for sharing Jesus. This could be a meal, special music, group-building fellowship activities, evangelistic film, or any number of other elements to bring people together to hear the message of Christ.

C stands for communicate the gospel. There is no point to your event without this! The gospel must be clearly and convincingly expressed to your audience. Plan to share Christ with as much care and detail as you use in planning all the other elements of your event. Follow-up is crucial. You must record and follow up on all those who surrender their lives to the Lord.

SPORTS EVANGELISM

A specialized type of evangelistic event is sports evangelism. Eddie Fox, head of world evangelism for United Methodists, says that the roads of Rome carried the gospel in the first century, but sports is the means of carrying it today. The evangelist of the future may look more like Reggie White than Billy Graham. The kingdom of God is awakening to the fact that sports evangelism can be highly effective.

Following is a general breakdown of the types of sports evangelism, although it can take many other forms.

Major event-centered sports evangelism. This includes potentially thousands of events per year in the United States, including most pro sports and many major college events, as well as the one-time events such as the Olympics. Most churches in most cities don't realize what an evangelistic gold mine is right before them almost every weekend. Using these events to reach the lost is not difficult and complicated; it's a matter of motivating, educating, and enabling our people!

Personality-centered sports evangelism. This approach is using a famous athlete to draw a crowd. During the meeting, he shares his testimony and the way of salvation. A thread of this runs through all types of sports evangelism, as it is almost always the persona of an athlete or athletes that draws the audience. Networking with churches and associations on whom to use, and how, is crucial. Personality-centered sports evangelism can work in a variety of ways. The athlete may appear live or on video. Tracts with his or her testimony could be prepared specifically for the sport or event.

Competition-centered sports evangelism. This is based around nonprofessional, club-level league competition, such as ongoing ministry in the adult men's basketball league, in Little League, etc. This has commonly been called recreation ministry. We should be sharing the gospel through written materials and events formed around recreation play all across the nation.

The variations go on and on. Groups such as Athletes in Action and Fellowship of Christian Athletes have long been involved in this type of ministry, but even the smallest church can get involved.

Cheryl Wolfinger of the International Sports Federation (ISF), which sends sports evangelism teams around the world, reports that her organization is swamped with domestic requests for sports evangelism teams. This is happening, although ISF makes no effort to procure domestic requests. Wolfinger uses these increased requests to highlight the interest in sports evangelism throughout the United States.

Mark Snowden, media and sports evangelism consultant for the International Mission Board of the Southern Baptist Convention, confirms Wolfinger's analysis of the burgeoning requests for sports evangelism development in the United States. He reports that the IMB continues to use sports evangelism to get into hard-to-reach countries. Snowden said the IMB is beginning to appoint full-time sports missionaries instead of relegating this work to short-term missionaries, as it has in the past.

Tom Felten is publisher of *Sports Spectrum*, a national Christian sports magazine that is a vital tool for reaching athletic-minded lost people. Felten says, "What we're seeing right now is more and more parachurch groups and denominations adding full-time sports evangelism personnel to their staff. The growth is phenomenal. An indication would be our Super Bowl Outreach Kit. We started it six years ago with 2,100 churches involved. This year we will have 6,000 to 7,000 churches holding evangelistic Super Bowl parties. Sports evangelism has been and continues to erupt."

Churches must see the big picture and make specific application of the sports evangelism possibilities within the United States. Courtney Cash, Wolfinger's associate, says some churches are taking advantage of sports evangelism, but that the percentage is low. "They are hosting clinics, organizing leagues, supplying chaplains, providing tournaments in multi-housing units, and playing pick-up games with youth in the inner city," Cash says. "However, even though there are almost one hundred sports ministries in the United States, there [are few] networks to help churches utilize the existing new tool, teach them how to reach sports people, or connect them with the necessary materials to be completely successful in their efforts."

If mass evangelism has been neglected in your church, consider planning an evangelistic meeting, or an event, in your church. Such a meeting brought a renewed focus on evangelism in the church I served as pastor. It could do the same for your church.

BIBLIOGRAPHY

Douglas, J. D., ed. *The Work of an Evangelist: International Congress for Itinerant Evangelists. Amsterdam, The Netherlands.* Minneapolis: World Wide Publications, 1984.

————. *Equipping for Evangelism: North American Conference for Itinerant Evangelists, 1994.* Minneapolis: World Wide Publications, 1996.

Frost, Toby, Bill Sims, and Monty McWhorter. *Special Evangelistic Events Manual.* Atlanta: North American Mission Board, 1995.

Hamilton, Thad. *Evangelistic Block Party Manual.* Alpharetta, Ga.: North American Mission Board, 1991.

Streett, R. Alan. *The Effective Invitation.* Grand Rapids: Kregel, 1995.

16

Church Evangelism: Biblical Church Growth

A total of 6,700 SBC churches baptized no new converts in 1995. That's one out of seven Southern Baptist churches and missions. C. E. Matthews, who led the convention in evangelism in the 1950s, said a church that baptizes no one in an entire year has sufficient cause to put on sackcloth and ashes and proclaim a time of fasting and humiliation.

The church is not a vacation spot for saints; it's an emergency room for sinners. We must teach people that the primary place of ministry for the church of the Lord Jesus Christ is outside the church building. The most evangelized, the most reached area in your community is the building in which your church meets on Sunday. There's only one problem: this is also the place where the fewest number of lost people are likely to be. Large numbers of lost people never enter a church building, even for a funeral. According to Roy Fish, the "church building is not to be the primary *place* of witness in ministry, it's to be the primary *base* of witness in ministry."

"The church," said William Temple, "is the only institution on earth raised up to exist for its own nonmembers."[1]

Church growth has become a popular topic in evangelicalism in recent years. This chapter will focus specifically on evangelistic growth—true church growth in the biblical sense. The church in Jerusalem added three thousand people in one day at Pentecost; then converts were added daily. Soon the number of men stood above five thousand; then priests came to the faith, and eventually the numbers were so great that Luke couldn't report them (Acts 4).

Some people complain about an emphasis on numerical growth in the church. I like to remind them that one book of the Bible is called Numbers! Seriously, one can be too zealous for numbers, but those who criticize an emphasis on numbers usually do so because their numbers are few. I agree that one cannot measure church growth by numbers alone. Let's assume that a church in a rapidly growing area is growing at the same rate as a church in a declining population area. Is it as effective as the second church? What about retaining members? Is a growing church effective if it baptizes one hundred people annually but grows in attendance by only a dozen per year?

Suffice it to say that under normal circumstances a church ought to grow. Rick Warren has it right when he says the critical issue is not church *growth* but church *health*.[2] A healthy, Christ-honoring church is more likely to grow than a divided or spiritually dead congregation.

THE CHURCH GROWTH MOVEMENT

We can't discuss growing churches without considering the impact of the church growth movement over the past generation. Churches have been growing since the first century. But the Church Growth *Movement* refers to the specific phenomenon arising out of the influence of Donald McGavran, and continuing through the ministry of such men as Peter Wagner, Win Arn, Elmer Towns, and many others. It is most clearly seen today in the professional organization known as the American Society for Church Growth.

HISTORY

Church growth began in the Book of Acts, but the Church Growth Movement began in 1955 with the publication of Donald McGavran's *Bridges of God*. This movement began overseas and was imported to the United States. McGavran (1897–1991) is the founder of the movement. His parents and grandparents were missionaries.

He was ordained by the Disciples of Christ in 1923 and received his Ph.D. from Columbia University in 1936. He served as a missionary in India. McGavran asked, "Why do some churches grow while others don't?" His book, *Bridges of God*, was published to address this and other important questions.

C. Peter Wagner (b. 1930) served as a foreign missionary in Bolivia, South America, for sixteen years. In 1971 he began teaching at Fuller Seminary. He has written numerous books and articles: *Church Growth and the Whole Gospel, Our Kind of People, Leading Your Church to Growth,* and others. Rainer writes,

> Although McGavran was the pioneer of the Church Growth Movement, C. Peter Wagner has been its best salesperson, teaching, speaking, serving in key positions, and traveling worldwide. His most important work, however, has been his writing. He began his writing ministry in 1956, and published his first book in 1966. Wagner has published over seven hundred works since 1956, including almost forty full-length books.

Other leaders of church growth and church growth advocates include Ralph Winter, Arthur Glasser, Charles Kraft, Win Arn, John Wimber, Kert Hunter, George Hunter, Elmer Towns, John Vaughn, Rick Warren, C. Kirk Hadaway, Thom Rainer, and Gary McIntosh.

There are other influential voices in the area of church growth outside the specific Church Growth Movement. Influential pastors include Rick Warren, Bill Hybels, Leith Anderson, and Chuck Smith. Thom Rainer has become increasingly significant as a leader, particularly among Southern Baptists, but among evangelicals as well. Rainer has been particularly influential in balancing all the interest in innovative approaches with more traditional churches that also grow. Further, Rainer has reminded church growth leaders that we should measure growth by evangelistic impact above anything else.

The Church Growth Movement has offered many helpful contributions to evangelistic church growth. For example, this movement has noted there are different levels of evangelism.

Types of Evangelism According to the Church Growth Movement[3]

E-0 evangelism: Evangelizing unsaved persons within the congregation.

E-1 evangelism: Evangelism that crosses barriers related to the church building or the perception of the church in the mind-set of the unsaved.

E-2 evangelism: Evangelism that crosses ethnic, cultural, and class barriers.

E-3 evangelism: Evangelism that crosses linguistic barriers.

Wagner summarized the Church Growth Movement in six presuppositions:

1. Nongrowth displeases God.

2. Numerical growth of a church is a priority with God and focuses on new disciples rather than decisions.

3. Disciples are tangible, identifiable, countable people who increase the church numerically.

4. Limited time, money, and resources demand that the church develop a strategy based on results.

5. Social and behavioral sciences are valuable tools in measuring and encouraging church growth.

6. Research is essential for maximum growth.[4]

The findings of the Church Growth Movement have been helpful in assisting churches to grow. Some of the findings or emphases have proven controversial. For example, its emphasis on pragmatism (emphasizing results to an extreme) may lead to lack of attention to biblical truth.

Few aspects of the Church Growth Movement provoke more controversy than the homogeneous unit principle. The principle states that people typically come to Christ "without crossing racial, linguistic, or class barriers."[5] Wagner says, "The rationale upon which a homogenous unit is determined is a group which can 'feel at home.'"[6]

The problem with the homogeneous unit principle is in its application. Used as a description, it can be helpful. We will reach people who are most like us. One need not be a rocket scientist to see this. But this is far different from being *prescriptive,* or saying we should *only* reach people like us.

MODELS FOR EVANGELISTIC CHURCH GROWTH

One of the significant shifts in church growth at the dawn of a new century is the movement from specialists who analyze trends as the leaders of church growth to effective pastors who model such growth. This is true in denominational leadership as well. The old paradigm emphasized the development of new tools, methods, and strategies coming from denominational leaders and think tanks. In the future, effective tools and strategies for church growth will be birthed on the field. Denominational leaders will shift to the position of discovering and announcing proven methods in churches rather than discovering or creating them. Growing churches, not professors or specialists, will set the pace for effective church growth.

Rather than listing a few principles of evangelistic church growth, I want to examine two models developed by local churches that may be used by other congregations. These are Total Church Life, developed by Darrell Robinson in several pastorates, from small church starts to megachurches; and the Purpose Driven Church of Rick Warren. After a brief overview of these approaches, I will demonstrate why they are helpful for our day.

TOTAL CHURCH LIFE

I launched into a seminary pastorate in 1985 with tremendous zeal. Unfortunately, I could best be described at that time as ignorance on fire! I had learned many wonderful things in seminary. But faced with the regular grind of pastoring, I discovered it was difficult to translate the seminary lessons into the laboratory of the local church. After that experience, I came to the conviction that we needed tools to assist in translating the seminary experience into practical ministry. Then I read *Total Church Life* by Darrell Robinson. The simple truths in this book would have helped me in moving from seminary to church field.

Total Church Life is a simple, holistic approach to ministry that gives proper focus to the purpose of the church. The strategy was developed by Darrell Robinson in pastorates at First Baptist Church, Pasadena, Texas, and Dauphin Way Baptist Church, Mobile,

Alabama. The strategy has been popularized under Robinson's leadership as head of evangelism of the SBC Home Mission Board (1989–97).

I like to refer to Total Church Life as "gospel boot camp," or "Church Growth 101." It is not a program or method; it is a strategy, a philosophy of ministry. It is especially effective for more traditional churches that have lost their understanding of the nature of the New Testament church.

Over two thirds of evangelical churches are plateaued or declining. This is true of four fifths of all Protestant churches. This is an abomination before a holy God, who deserves more than saints who sit and stew. It is just cause for a time of national fasting and humiliation. Robinson offers help to those churches that seek to move off the plateau, comparing what he calls a strategically focused church (similar to Warren's Purpose Driven model) with a programmatically focused church. Most churches in the second category are declining churches.[7] (See Figure 16.1 and 16.2.)

Robinson compares the dilemma of plateaued and declining churches with the church at Ephesus in the late first century A.D. This church had a phenomenal start, but it was in trouble by the end of the first century, and it ceased to exist later (see Rev. 2).

Total Church Life is based on the belief that any local church has three essential functions:

1. *Exalt the Savior.* This is accomplished through Christ-honoring worship, united fellowship, mobilized praying, and a healthy organization.

2. *Equip the saints.* This task emphasizes the importance of involving laity in ministry through the Sunday school and other organizations.

3. *Evangelize sinners.* This is done by leading the church to fulfill the Great Commission.[8]

The most helpful aspects of Total Church Life for evangelism are these:

• It places the evangelistic outreach of the church within the larger church life; too many churches see evangelism as one more program or emphasis without realizing it is critical to the very nature of the church.

Figure 16.1

The Strategically Focused Church

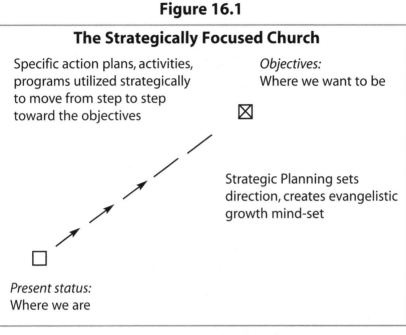

Specific action plans, activities, programs utilized strategically to move from step to step toward the objectives

Objectives:
Where we want to be

Strategic Planning sets direction, creates evangelistic growth mind-set

Present status:
Where we are

Figure 16.2

The Programmatically Focused Church

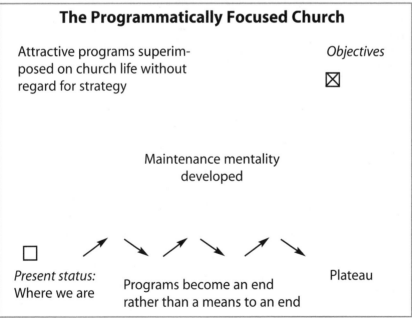

Attractive programs superimposed on church life without regard for strategy

Objectives

Maintenance mentality developed

Present status:
Where we are

Programs become an end rather than a means to an end

Plateau

- Total Church Life emphasizes the responsibility of the church to reach its church field. The twofold approach of *total penetration* of a church field through *total participation* of its members is overlooked in many churches.

- It offers a practical approach to developing a holistic evangelistic ministry. The approach gives three key decisions related to effective evangelism:

    1. A *time* decision: calendar planning;

    2. A *money* decision: budgeting; and

    3. A *people* decision: involving the laity.

Figure 16.3
Total Church Life Evangelism Strategy Planning Calendar

Year _____

Church Name_____

Year _____	Equipping Activity	Evangelistic Event	Target Group
JANUARY			
FEBRUARY			
MARCH			
APRIL			
MAY			
JUNE			
JULY			
AUGUST			
SEPTEMBER			
OCTOBER			
NOVEMBER			
DECEMBER			

- Calendar planning is a central part of the strategy. The calendar runs on two simultaneous tracks: event planning and equipping opportunities. Southern Baptists in particular are experienced in events: revival meetings, friend days, etc. We are not as effective with process. By emphasizing both events and equipping, we teach the laity to see evangelism as an ongoing part of the process of being the church of the Lord Jesus rather than occasional special events. (See Figure 16.3.)

- *Total Church Life* provides invaluable aid in leading a congregation to develop a succinct statement of purpose. I have seen more than a few churches adopt the "Exalt, Equip, Evangelize" theme as their vision. Some churches have this concept in mind while using different terminology. The church where I am a member illustrates this tripartite thesis in its mission statement: "*Find* those who need Jesus, *feed* all on the Word, until we are *fully* established in Christ."

PURPOSE DRIVEN CHURCH MODEL

A second approach to building an evangelistic church is the Purpose Driven Church model of Rick Warren, lived out in the Saddleback Community Church in Southern California. Warren's book, *The Purpose Driven Church,* is must reading!

After nearly 16 years of meeting in schools, country clubs, warehouses, tents and even mental hospitals, Saddleback Valley Community Church moved into its own facility on September 17th, 1995. Nearly 12,000 people filled the three dedication services of the Lake Forest, California, congregation.

Saddleback has used 79 different facilities, in five different cities, to house the burgeoning congregation's various ministries since beginning in Warren's home in 1980 with seven members. "If you could figure out where we were each week, you got to come!" joked a member.

The event included the baptism of 384 new converts in Saddleback's outdoor baptism pool on the patio of the new facility. Worshipers watched some of the baptisms projected live onto three large video screens included in the new building. "We wanted to keep the focus on the theme of our church: *changed lives,*" said Warren. The church led the Southern Baptist Convention in baptisms in 1995.

The following week, members held a grand opening of the building for the community. Members brought hundreds of unchurched neighbors to the services resulting in 210 professions of faith and another 64 baptisms.

In June of 1995, Saddleback was recognized in a study by Liberty University, Lynchburg, Va., as the fastest-growing Baptist congregation in American history, growing from one family to over 11,000 attenders in 16 years.

You can attribute the church's growth to Warren's philosophy of ministry, called *"the Purpose Driven Church,"* which places a greater emphasis on building people rather than erecting buildings. "We've wanted to prove to the world that the church is *people* not buildings, and that you don't need buildings to grow a church. I think we made our point," said Warren.[9]

Warren's strategy focuses on moving from secondary issues, such as programs, finances, buildings, events, or seekers, to the primary issue: a biblical, purpose-driven focus. "Absolutely nothing will revitalize a discouraged church faster than rediscovering its purpose,"[10] he contends. He cites a familiar survey in which church members were asked, "Why does the church exist?" Some 89 percent responded: "The church's purpose is to take care of my needs and my family's needs." Only 11 percent said winning the world to Christ is the church's purpose. Ninety percent of pastors who were asked the same question said the church exists to win the world to Christ, and 10 percent said it exists to care for members.[11]

The slogan for Saddleback comes directly from the New Testament: "A great commitment to the great commandment (Matt. 22:37–39) as the great commission (Matt. 28:19–20) will grow a great church."[12]

Five key words are used to summarize the five purposes of the church in the Purpose Driven Church model:

1. *Worship.* "Love the Lord your God with all your heart" (*magnification*).

2. *Ministry.* "Love your neighbor as yourself" (*ministry*).

3. *Evangelism.* "Go and make disciples" (*mission*).

4. *Fellowship.* "Baptize them" (*membership*).

5. *Discipleship.* "Teach them to obey" (*maturity*).

Warren also describes the fivefold purpose of the church with the words *edify, encourage, exalt, equip,* and *evangelize.* Notice the last three are the key terms used in the Total Church Life approach. Certain principles are timeless and unchanging!

Saddleback is not a church with a nice purpose statement that is never displayed in the life of the church. The entire organizational structure is built around the five purposes. First, there is a recognition of the need to move people from where they *are* to where they *need to be.* Warren calls this moving people from the community to the core.

The life development process is tied directly to the purposes of the church (see Figures 16.4 and 16.5).

The goal of the church, according to the baseball diamond diagram, is not to get them on first base but to get them around the bases into active ministry and evangelism. Warren argues that *everything* in the church should be done on purpose: assimilating new members, programming, education, small groups, staffing, structuring, preaching, budgeting, calendaring, and evaluating progress.

I am convinced that the Saddleback Community Church is the most viable model of a church intentionally growing by reaching unchurched people. It also plants other churches, which adds to its strength.

We cannot discuss church growth without focusing on one of the best-known contemporary models: Willow Creek Community Church near Chicago. Pastor Bill Hybels has a deep, sincere burden for reaching the unchurched. Several aspects of Willow Creek are encouraging: (1) its mission is "to turn irreligious people into fully devoted followers of Jesus Christ;" (2) the church has a definite plan and strategy for reaching the lost with the gospel of Jesus Christ; (3) its vision is to produce a "biblically-functioning community," and

Figure 16.4

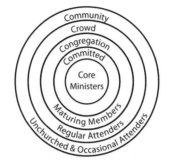

(4) its desire is to seek "excellence in all we do for God." Finally, Hybels gives an excellent example of how important it is for a church to have a clear vision and stick to it.

However, I cannot affirm Willow Creek as the best model for contemporary evangelistic church growth. I have been to Willow Creek on more than one occasion and have been blessed in its services; however, the long-term impact of this model is open to debate.

Figure 16.5

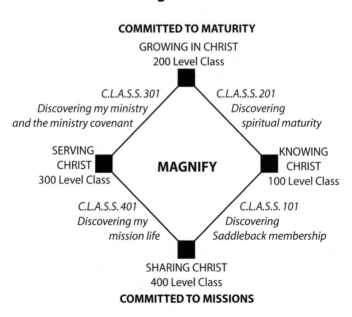

There is always the danger of crossing the line when relating Scripture to culture. When we are driven by culture rather than Scripture, the long-term result is usually unhealthy. Beyond this, focusing too much on *one* model has its hazards. For example, in a given week, Willow Creek has no more people in attendance than First Baptist Church, Jacksonville, Florida; Bellevue Baptist Church, Memphis, Tennessee; Second Baptist Church, Houston, Texas; or Saddleback Community Church in the Los Angeles area. Still, Willow Creek is getting most of the national headlines. The Willow Creek model is sweeping across the evangelical community.

Let me be clear: I love much of what Willow Creek is doing. Most of us are so pathetic at reaching unchurched people that we should be ashamed. But our desire to reach the unreached must be built on a solid foundation. Willow Creek's ecclesiology must be examined as closely as its methods and service style. Danny Akin of Southern Seminary has noted this: How one becomes a member of Willow Creek is not at all clear.[13]

In the fall of 1996 at its leadership conference, Pastor Hybels acknowledged that numerous ministerial staff were not even members of the church. Further, Willow Creek has shown an extremely ecumenical approach to the ordinance of baptism, immersing annually and sprinkling twice a year. Akin also noted an overemphasis on pragmatism and feminism as concerns. We must build churches out of theology or a doctrine of God, not out of anthropology, the doctrine of man. A God-centered, purpose-driven church is the need of the hour.

REVITALIZING THE STAGNANT CHURCH

If most churches are not growing, how do we get them to grow again? Books have been written on this subject. Suffice it to say that the most critical element is the presence of God in the midst of a renewing church. Jesus said, "*I* will build *my* church" (Matt. 16:18). Stagnant churches must redirect their purpose. Critical to this is leadership, which is addressed in the final chapter. Let me give an example of one church that turned from stagnation to growth.

A Case Study for Evangelistic Church Growth: FBC, Corinth, Texas

Can a declining, rural church become a growing church? First Baptist Church of Corinth, Texas, was a small country church north of Dallas, in what was becoming suburbia. The church had declined slowly for more than a decade. No one had been baptized for the previous eighteen months, and the church had not baptized as many as ten people in more than a decade. Like many churches, FBC struggled to adapt to its changing environment.

The building where they met on Sundays was sagging. Originally constructed from concrete blocks that had been taken from old army barracks, the structure was in some disarray—nothing more so than the baptistry.

The baptistry had been constructed out of sheet metal. Though no one had been baptized for many months, there was a slow drip from the faucet. The steady drip had caused the drain to clog shut. In the bottom of the baptistry were two or three inches of filthy, rusty water. When a young woman trusted Christ as Savior (the first convert), the church had a problem. How would they baptize someone in that rusty, old baptistry? Listen to what pastor Munton did:

"As best I could, I mopped out the filthy water. I filled the baptistry with water (there was no need to plug the drain!). After giving the young lady a tetanus shot (just kidding!), we baptized her, the church's first convert in more than a year. The excitement was great! But for the next several months, I was forced to siphon the water out of the baptistry with a garden hose!"

For the first few years the Sunday school growth and evangelistic outreach resulted mainly from personal visitation by the pastor and a few committed laypeople. There were high attendance days, revival meetings, Vacation Bible School, and special events. Growth in both Sunday school attendance and evangelism was steady, though not spectacular. More laypeople began to gain an enthusiasm for outreach. New staff with a passion for reaching people were added. Commitments to grow and reach people were strengthened.

The church, however, faced some important obstacles. Space problems became critical. Many Sunday school classes began to meet off-campus. The church decided to relocate from the one-acre parcel they had occupied for decades. Eventually, the church began to meet in a local school for Sunday services. Although the changes caused a few people to leave the church, their numbers were more than matched by enthusiastic new Christians.

Over time the church developed a more seeker-sensitive approach to Sunday morning services. Many young couples were drawn to music with a contemporary flavor and practical, yet expository sermons. Sunday mornings became times of evangelistic harvest.

Traditional methods were used as well. Evangelistic meetings proved very successful. Vacation Bible School was always successful. Evangelism programs were utilized, though the church never saw great results from them. Most of the new converts were people who had been invited by friends. Often they came to worship services, and even Sunday school classes, for several weeks before coming to faith in Christ. Many of them trusted Christ during worship services.

The church became unusually effective at reaching the unchurched. Approximately 65 percent of the congregation was from an unchurched background. New believers became the most effective evangelists.

Evangelism training was a constant challenge. Small-group classes for evangelism training were held regularly. Special evangelistic training classes connected to evangelistic crusades were offered. At least once a year, a Sunday night was devoted to teaching people how to share their faith using the Roman Road plan of evangelism.

Eventually, a strong youth program was developed. Many teenagers came to Christ, and evangelism among teenagers was particularly effective. Often the teens themselves shared their faith at their schools and at church activities.

During the spring of 1995, the church was deeply touched by a time of genuine revival. Students from Howard Payne University, already experiencing revival, shared with the congregation on a Sunday evening. The next months resulted in brokenness, deepening faith, spiritual vitality, and evangelistic fervor. First Baptist Church of Corinth, Texas, which a decade earlier had averaged thirty people, now regularly had more than three hundred people in worship and baptized more than two hundred people in four years.

Evangelism at FBC Corinth was caught more than taught. Programs were rarely more than mildly effective, though evangelistic crusades continued to be effective, especially among teenagers. But the commitment of church members to invite their unchurched friends and to witness through their personal relationships made the real difference. The enthusiasm for reaching people and the commitment and sacrifice of lay leaders set the pace for church growth and evangelism.

Here is the statistical growth for FBC, Corinth, Texas:

Average Sunday School		
	Attendance	Baptisms
Prior to Munton's Coming		
1985	31	0
After Coming		
1986	54	10
1987	76	15
1988	85	17
1989	97	15
1990	124	18
1991	148	21
1992	177	56
1993	220	58
1994	234	46
1995	222	60

The key to the growth was the practical leadership of Doug Munton. This is *always* the case (see chapter 18). Munton was patient in implementing change, and he changed only what was necessary to bring growth. The worship format changed dramatically, but the Sunday school organization remained basically intact. The focus shifted from maintenance of believers to reaching the lost, but the sermons continued to be biblical, expository, and relevant to both believers and seekers. Prayer became a greater priority as well. A small, dying church *can* live again!

Approaches to Help Revitalize a Stagnant Church

Sunday School

Eddie Gibbs of Fuller Seminary was converted at age 16, in a very unchurched area. His parents did not go to church but did send him to Sunday school. Gibbs later mused, "I am the last of the Sunday school-attending generation." This may be true in England but not so in the United States. The Sunday school as an institution is not dead;[14] but the way in which the Sunday school is implemented *should* be buried in many churches. Churches with untrained workers with an introverted focus in their Sunday school classes cannot survive—nor should they.

Still, there are scores of churches—in fact, the majority of growing churches in the SBC—that grew predominantly through the Sunday school. The Sunday school is critical both in evangelism and in the assimilation of new believers.

The Green Forest Community Baptist Church, an African-American congregation in Decatur, Georgia, has grown from 25 members in 1980 to 4,500 in 1997 under the leadership of pastor George McCalep. One of the critical factors in the growth of the church has been the Sunday school.[15]

I believe in the Sunday school. I thank God that when I was in seminary I learned about Sunday school principles and the Growth Spiral.[16] I learned about the importance of Sunday school enrollment, tracking enrollment, and starting new classes. One of the stats I heard was that if you start a new Sunday school class and focus on outreach, within a year it will enroll an average of twenty-six new people. When I tracked that in two churches as a pastor and as a minister of education, we averaged exactly twenty-six people for every adult class we started! These two churches, both of which grew dramatically, one doubling in a year, grew organizationally through the Sunday school.

We took the Growth Spiral concept, which focuses on such issues as Sunday school enrollment, outreach, and new units, and adapted it to our church by scaling it down and simplifying it. Our people had no clue about Sunday school enrollment. They thought that if you didn't attend three weeks in a row, you ought to be dropped from the roll. It was a major struggle to get them to see you should keep people on the roll!

Sunday school is about reaching people as well as teaching. In the churches where I have served, we had to reorient our people to the true purpose of Sunday school. Most people think that Sunday school exists to teach the Bible. When the Sunday school movement began in Southern Baptist life, the Sunday school had a threefold purpose: (1) to teach the Bible, (2) to reach people with the gospel, and (3) to minister to the body of Christ. We had worker meetings, and we elevated evangelism through the Sunday school. We even drew up a covenant and had our Sunday school teachers sign it. It included a commitment to make weekly contacts and to set the pace for others. The teachers did not have to come to visitation every week, but they committed themselves to make contacts. In the past, as many as 80 percent of converts came through the Sunday school. This is changing because the front door, the worship service, is becoming a more significant factor in reaching unreached people.[17]

How do we get Sunday school teachers involved in outreach? Weekly worker meetings are essential. The next step is to secure a layperson who is teachable to be Sunday school director. A teachable spirit is absolutely critical.

I enlisted a director like this and took him and two or three other leaders to a Sunday school conference. They got such a vision for Sunday school outreach that I had to calm them down a bit! I didn't want them to run ahead too fast because they would get beat up by the other laypeople. Gradually, over a year's time, we began to implement some of those changes. If your Sunday school is not evangelistic, it may take a year or two to change it. Find those teachers who are open to outreach and work with them. Encourage everybody. As you change, love everyone, but move with the movers.

You must also close the back door in Sunday school. Having observed numerous churches with strong Sunday schools, I'm convinced this is crucial. We had excellent retention of new Christians in the last churches I served, and it was because we were a Sunday school-based church.

HIGH ATTENDANCE DAY

Set an attendance goal for the church and Sunday school classes. By setting a total class goal that equals more than the church goal, you increase the likelihood of reaching the church goal. For example, if your High Attendance Day goal is 120, set the total Sunday school class goal at around 140. It is essential that Sunday school workers be ready to enroll and visit those who come on High Attendance Day the following week. The day is especially successful if attendance goes up in the weeks following this emphasis.

SOUL-WINNING COMMITMENT DAY

In Southern Baptist circles this emphasis has been especially effective in maintaining a focus on evangelism. Many churches from other traditions have a similar evangelism day emphasis. I'm convinced that, even as the nation of Israel had certain annual days of consecration, the church should be called to a public commitment to evangelism annually.

Southern Baptists observe this day in October, with the North American Mission Board providing outstanding support materials. This day is *successful only* when you follow it with witness training. Nothing frustrates people more than being told they *should* do something without being told *how*.

I have preached during many of these days with great success. Here are some practical steps to make Soul-Winning Commitment Day effective:

1. *Make the day a matter of serious prayer in the church.*

2. *Promote the day vigorously.* The North American Mission Board provides good resources that any church or denomination can use.

3. *Enlist key leaders to make commitments.* During the two or three weeks before the effort, say to the legitimizers, such as the deacons and Sunday school division leaders, "We will have Soul-Winning Commitment Day in a couple of weeks. Would you pray about the commitment God would have you make as a leader?" Particularly enlist those whom you know to be sensitive to evangelism.

4. *Use commitment cards like "My Soul-Winning Commitment."*

My Soul-Winning Commitment

I,_____, surrender myself to Jesus Christ, my Lord, to share the gospel by doing the following:
(Check one or more):

❏ I want to receive Jesus Christ, the Light of the world, into my life as Lord and Savior.

❏ I will pray regularly for the evangelistic ministry of our church.

❏ I will attempt to share the gospel with a lost person.
  ❏ daily   ❏ weekly   ❏ monthly
  ❏ at least once

❏ I will enroll in witness training.

❏ I will seek to share Christ with the following people.

_____   _____
_____   _____
_____   _____
_____   _____

Give one of these cards to each teenager and adult. Early in the service, state that you are calling the church to a public commitment. Note that anyone can commit to pray and, as they will, commit at whatever level they will honestly support. As you begin the message, have the people then put their name on the card at that point so they will be able to check the appropriate boxes during the invitation.

Have tracts laid out at the altar when people make their commitment. Ask them to kneel in prayer, consecrating themselves to God, then take the tracts to share with others in their evangelistic contacts.

Provide simple training for church members who commit to soul-winning. Make sure the training comes quickly following the commitment. The training should include going out to visit. Simple training linked with servanthood evangelism is a great first step.

Take all the commitment cards and

• Write a general letter to all.

• Put them into a computer system and write a personalized letter, noting each specific commitment. Then write a second letter one, three, and six months later. With a computer, this can be done easily. Follow-up enhances the effort greatly.

Allow testimonies during weeks to come from people who took a step further in their commitment to evangelism.

CHURCH PLANTING

We cannot discuss church growth without dealing with the subject of church *planting*. Tom Wolfe said there are two conversion blockers in the American church. The first is our lack of vision for the task to reach all peoples. In addition, the vision of the congregation is wrong. Wolfe argues that we must think of church planting as *essential* to church growth.[18]

Statistics indicate that Wolfe's exhortation is valid. In the past decades, Protestant churches declined 9.5 percent while the American population increased about 11 percent. Eighty-one percent of Protestant churches are declining. Each year in the United States, 3,500 to 4,500 churches close, while 1,100 are planted.[19]

The most significant example of a growing congregation is one that reaches people in its own field but also plants other churches. In class students often ask me to describe the "model" church. While there are many viable models (just look at the different types of churches in the New Testament!), I describe the model church as one that is biblically grounded and unashamed of the Word of God. Further, this church understands how to present the timeless truths of Scripture in a timely way. It is a color-blind church, with a passion for God, a burden for the lost, and a heart as big as the world.

The model church seeks to share Christ with every person in its area. But it does not stop there. This church is committed to *planting* other churches as well. Listen to Rick Warren's advice: "I believe that you measure the health or strength of a church by its *sending* capacity rather than its *seating* capacity."[20] Such a church is mobilized to fulfill the Great Commission at home and beyond.

The most pressing need to be addressed in the new millennium is the place of church planting in the major urban areas. Consider Los Angeles as one example. Greater Los Angeles is the second largest Hispanic city on earth. It is the second largest Chinese and Japanese cities and the largest Vietnamese, Philippine, and Korean cities outside these respective nations. More than 81 percent of African-Americans live in the city, as do 88 percent of Hispanics and

90 percent of Asian-Americans. Yet, only 25 percent of white Americans live in the city.[21]

Elmer Towns has noted the reason we have not evangelized the cities and thus why there is such a need for church planting: We typically see people in the cities as *undesirable* because they are poor, illiterate, or foreign. We see them as *unwanted* because they are unlike people in the typical Anglo congregation. They are *unseen* because we Anglos typically overlook people who are not like us. Towns offers five principles for church planting.[22]

New Principles for Church Planting in America

1. Recognize that traditional American church methods that are geared to American suburbia and rural areas will not generally work in urban America.
2. View the United States as a secular mission field and develop an urban strategy that is local to national, not the reverse.
3. Apply successful foreign church growth concepts to urban United States.
4. Develop a church planting strategy that encourages creativity in methodology, yet is biblical in principle.
5. Give general permission to deliver the gospel (unchanging principles) in an innovative fashion (new methods) that is effective in each localized urban setting.

We must reach the cities. In 1870, 10 percent of the United States population was urban, 90 percent rural. It is estimated that by the year 2005, 90 percent of the population will be urban and 10 percent rural. The church has lagged behind in addressing this need.

APPLICATION

Using the following simple chart in the Total Church Life strategy, list all your current church ministries and emphases, determining which, if any, of the categories they fit. Remember, it is God who is the Author of evangelistic church growth.

Figure 16.6
Total Church Life Evaluation Sheet

MINISTRY	EXALT	EQUIP	EVANGELIZE

BIBLIOGRAPHY

Rainer, Thom. *The Book of Church Growth*. Nashville: Broadman & Holman, 1994.

Robinson, Darrell. *Total Church Life*. Nashville: Broadman & Holman, 1996.

Terry, John Mark. *Church Evangelism*. Nashville: Broadman & Holman, 1997.

Warren, Rick. *The Purpose Driven Church*. Grand Rapids: Zondervan, 1995.

17

Worship Evangelism: Linking the Glory of God to the Gospel

A woman from a free congregational tradition visited a liturgical service. She continually punctuated the message of the pastor with "Praise the Lord!" Finally, a member of the church turned around and said to the guest, "Excuse me, but we don't praise the Lord in the Lutheran church." A man down the pew corrected the member: "Yes, we do," he said, "It's on page 19."[1]

The revolution in worship services in contemporary evangelicalism is obvious. More than 25,000 congregations use overhead projectors as an aid to singing contemporary choruses each Sunday. The church where I attend regularly incorporates drama in its services. Thousands of other congregations sing only the old hymns of the faith. Many use some sort of "blended" style to meet the needs of their members and to make the services palatable for the unchurched. Radical changes in corporate worship have led to "worship wars"[2] in more than a few congregations.

R. W. Dale said, "Let me write the hymns and the music of the church, and I care very little who writes the theology."[3] He understood the powerful impact that worship has on the church. The corporate worship of a local church also affects its evangelistic growth.

Martin Luther understood the power of music in worship. "I really believe, nor am I shamed to assert," said the Reformer, "that next to theology there is no art equal to music."[4] Luther further recognized, "Experience proves that next to the Word of God music deserves to be extolled as the mistress and governess of the feelings of the human heart."[5]

Most questions about worship deal with style rather than substance. But more about that later. Let us begin with a theology of worship from the pages of Scripture.

BIBLICAL WORSHIP

A common Hebrew word for worship, *shachah,* means "to prostrate oneself." Worship for the Hebrew meant to come before the Lord in humility. Hebrew worship focused on giving offerings to the Lord. A number of terms in the New Testament denote worship. *Latreuo* is one of many that emphasizes veneration of God. The familiar word *proskuneo* means "to kiss toward," focusing on one's allegiance to the Lord. To state it simply, worship is to be God centered. Much of what we do in church is a means to a greater end. Worship is an end in itself. Worship relates directly to the emotions; however, true worship goes deeper.

True worship of the ancient Hebrews was predicated on the activity of God in history—in particular on the initiative taken by God to reveal himself to his people. Thus, Abraham was called by God (see Gen. 12). In response, Abraham built altars of worship. God revealed to Noah the coming judgment on humanity. Noah responded in obedience by building the ark, and he worshiped God by building an altar after the flood. Ultimately, an elaborate process of worship developed through the tabernacle and the temple. Too often the people of God missed the genuine relationship with God in their ritual, so prophets like Amos exhorted the people to true worship. The Psalms provided songs for worship, while national festivals reminded the people to seek the Lord. Eventually, the synagogue service became the heart of Jewish worship.

The New Testament worship services patterned themselves after the synagogue. However, Phifer noted key differences in the worship services of the early Christians.[6] The New Testament writings, particularly Paul's letters and the Gospels, soon became a prominent part of the services. To the Psalms were added Christian hymns, some of which are probably included in Paul's epistles (Phil. 2:5–11). Paul encouraged the singing of "psalms and hymns and spiritual songs" (Eph. 5:18–19). Baptism and communion were added features of Christian worship. Zeal characterized the services. The resurrection emphasis led to a celebrative spirit. Christian worship moved from the Jewish Sabbath to the Lord's Day, commemorating the resurrection of Jesus.

Ralph Martin reminds us that, although we can gain a general knowledge about worship in the early church, "there is, of course, no place in the New Testament which clearly states that the church had any set order of service, and very little information is supplied to us about the outward forms which were in use."[7] By the early second century, the *Didache* gave evidence of a greater sense of structure in worship.

This means that the *style* of worship is not prescribed in the New Testament but the *substance* of worship is—in particular, the celebration of the risen Lord. Just as evangelism must keep a proper tension between the changeless message and changing methods, worship must give attention to a biblical focus while avoiding the temptation to prescribe one form of worship. This tension is borne out in history.

CHRISTIAN WORSHIP THROUGH THE AGES

The ritualism of the Middle Ages mitigated against true worship. Even more foreboding was the theological shift away from an emphasis on a regenerate church, leading to multitudes who observed the liturgy without a personal knowledge of the One whom they worshiped. Only a dramatic theological restructuring could rescue worship.[8]

The Reformation brought such a restructuring. Martin Luther returned the Bible and the hymnal to the people. Luther introduced hymns with more familiar tunes that were theologically rich and written in the language of the common man. Donald P. Hustad commented, "Worthy lyrics sanctify the secular melody."[9] Jesuit Adam Conzenius complained that "Luther's hymns have destroyed more souls than his writings."[10] If only the contemporary church could grasp as Luther did the dynamic of biblical lyrics and a winsome melody! Calvin emphasized the singing of the Psalms in his services. The Pietists of the late seventeenth and early eighteenth centuries began writing subjective hymns, reflecting their emphasis on religion of the heart. At this same time, British pastor Isaac Watts began composing hymns. Such hymns as "When I Survey the Wondrous Cross" and "We're Marching to Zion" set a new standard for English church songs, thus his title "the father of English hymnody." By the turn of the nineteenth century, over 130 hymn collections had been printed.

Franklin Segler wrote that "a religious awakening has always been accompanied by a revision of the liturgy."[11] More recent centuries have witnessed the increasing role of music in the evangelistic mission of the church. One can trace the roots of music used for evangelistic purposes to the Evangelical Awakening and the ministry of John and Charles Wesley. Charles Wesley wrote more than six thousand hymns. These were crucial to the theology of early Methodism. His brother John preached biblical sermons that emphasized the application of the text to life. To these Charles wed hymns utilizing secular tunes.

The impact of the songs of the Wesleys is hard to overestimate. To a largely illiterate population the hymns taught doctrine and supported Christian experience, combining "the revivalist's fervor with the cooling elements of disciplined poetry and biblical theology."[12] Further, early in the Evangelical Awakening the wide use of singing, particularly the singing of groups of young people along the cities and roads of the countryside, had a profound impact. Thousands of nominal Christians were caught up in evangelistic fervor that shattered old forms and traditions and opened new channels of spiritual growth for entire congregations.[13]

The camp meetings of the Second Great Awakening were characterized by simple, emotional hymns, many with evangelistic appeals. The camp meeting songs developed into the gospel hymn, marked by a verse and chorus. *The Southern Harmony,* a collection of camp meeting songs published in 1835, sold six hundred thousand copies over twenty-five years.

Charles Finney worked closely with local churches in urban centers, so a different type of revival song was needed to reach the people in the cities. The church hymnals set too high a standard for some tastes, but the typical camp meeting songbook's standards were too low. Thus, he utilized Thomas Hastings, who published an early hymnbook, as a musician in the urban setting.

The first true music evangelist to be widely recognized was Ira D. Sankey (1837–99), who teamed with evangelist D. L. Moody. Sankey led congregational songs and sang solos. Sankey served as an emerging model for music evangelists. "The Ninety and Nine," "Jesus of Nazareth Passes By," and others made a great impact on believers and unbelievers alike. Lord Shaftersburg did not exaggerate when he said, "If Moody and Sankey had done nothing else but teach us 'Hold the Fort,' their visit would have been worthwhile."[14] He and Philip P. Bliss published *Gospel Hymns and Sacred Songs* in 1875. This collection included hymns which they, Fanny Crosby (1823–1915), and others had penned. Between fifty thousand to eighty thousand copies were sold by 1900.

Sankey was followed by scores of other musicians who teamed with evangelists. These included Charles Alexander, partner with J. Wilbur Chapman and R. A. Torrey; Homer Rodeheaver, who teamed with Billy Sunday; and more recently Cliff Barrows, with the Billy Graham team.

In the twentieth century, music on the radio, Stamps-Baxter gospel quartet music, and revivalistic Southern hymns have added to evangelistic music. With the rise of evangelistic music, a tension developed between music designed to worship God and music primarily aimed at reaching the lost.

RECENT CHANGES IN CORPORATE WORSHIP

The Jesus Movement during the late 1960s and early 1970s laid the groundwork for a significant shift in the corporate worship of the American church. The charismatic movement added to the growing awareness of a need for freedom in worship.

Charles E. Fromm noted that for several decades the church resisted change in worship, leading up to the revolution that occurred in the 1960s and beyond:

> By the mid-sixties, it was generally acknowledged that if God had ever spoken at all through music, it had only been in the cherished hymns and psalms of the forefathers; that all things musically modern

were, at best, tainted and unprofitable; and that spiritual song was best left safely locked up in the sanctity of ceremony.[15]

The changes in musical forms were influenced by young people who came to Christ in the Jesus Movement. The innovations served to present a new freshness in worship *and* were useful in reaching others as a result. In fact, the primary focus of much of the new music was evangelistic. Donald Hustad stated that "it should be obvious that the motivation behind all the pop-gospel phenomena of our day is evangelism."[16]

The rise of contemporary Christian music and the accompanying explosion of Christian radio stations after 1970 laid the groundwork for dramatic changes in worship services. Two streams merged to create the genre known today as contemporary Christian music. Folk music, especially as it was expressed in the youth musical, eventually merged with the rock sound of the Jesus Movement coffeehouses to form what is easily recognized today as contemporary Christian music.

The youth musical became a powerful medium for attracting young people to the gospel message in the late 1960s and early 1970s. Such musicals came out of the sixties and the increasing popularity of the folk song and such personalities as Bob Dylan, Joan Baez, and Peter, Paul, and Mary. "Do Lord," "Give Me Oil in My Lamp," and "I've Got the Joy, Joy, Joy, Joy down in My Heart" became part of church youth fellowships.

The first widely used youth musical was *Good News*. The evangelistic focus of the musical is evident in its title. Ralph Carmichael and Kurt Kaiser then wrote *Tell It Like It Is*. Others included *Celebrate Life* by Buryl Redd and Jimmy and Carol Owens' *Come Together*. Soon youth choirs became the heart of many youth groups, while youth choir tours covered North America.

Contemporary Christian music began in the coffeehouses and youth fellowships of the period and mushroomed into a five-hundred-million-dollar industry annually by 1990. John Styll, president of the Gospel Music Association in 1993 and publisher of *Contemporary Christian Music* magazine, summarized the advent of the genre:

Contemporary Christian Music was born out of the counterculture movement of the 60s. Disillusioned hippies who found the answer in Christ used their most natural means of expression—music—to proclaim the joy of their salvation and to share Christ with others. It wasn't organ music either. It was the music they understood.[17]

Dozens of "Jesus rock groups" had begun playing in Southern California. Larry Norman, called the "poet laureate" of the Jesus Movement by some, was one of the best known leaders. His simple ballad about the second coming of Christ, "I Wish We'd All Been Ready," was a signature song of the movement. Chuck Girard and Love Song were referred to as the "Beatles of the Christian music world" by some. Nancy Honeytree, Don Francisco, the Second Chapter of Acts, Barry McGuire, Keith Green, Eddie DeGarmo, Dana Key, Petra, Amy Grant, Brown Bannister, and Dogwood sprang from coffeehouse and similar ministries in the early 1970s. Jesus music festivals provided another forum for musicians to share their songs.

Contemporary Christian music was effective in evangelism through mass rallies, high school assembly programs, and festivals. Richard Hogue stated that the voice that young people listened to in the early seventies was not the athlete, but "the musician and the intellectual."[18]

The music of the Jesus Movement endured because of its close relationship with a major reason the movement began in the first place. Positively, the Jesus Movement was experiential and evangelistic, emphasizing a relationship with Christ. Negatively, it was a protest movement against the institutional church. The music gave a spiritual compass to a generation that felt disenfranchised due to the "generation gap."

Morgenthaler observed, "In the 1970s and 80s, much of the evangelical church experienced a *worship revolution:* an upheaval of traditional worship forms brought on by a belated, yet significant, 'cultural awakening.'"[19] The new musical styles among the youth gradually gained favor in many churches. But favor was not universal, as Carol Flake observed:

> Not all evangelicals were cheered by the success of CCM [contemporary Christian music]. The rock of ages they clung to did not roll with the times. Not surprisingly, Ralph Carmichael's first concert at the

National Religious Broadcasters convention stirred few amens. The growth of contemporary Christian music and the opening of the gates between sacred and secular genres stirred up a long-simmering controversy over the devil's role in rock and roll.[20]

Instruments associated with pop music, such as guitars, electric keyboards, and drums, stormed into many churches with the new songs. Such instruments became more acceptable in some churches because of their use in youth gatherings. The idea of an electric guitar in a worship service caused a virtual apoplexy to many, as illustrated by one pastor's observation: "I'll never forget the first Sunday they had all those guitars in there. [Some members] just went nuts."[21]

Bob Burroughs, a worship leader and composer, linked the Jesus Movement with revivalism of the past by stating that contemporary music, with guitars, amplifiers, and so on, was "the biggest thing to hit Christian music since Ira Sankey joined D. L. Moody!"[22] Added to the rise of contemporary Christian music was the advent of praise and worship choruses, developing out of the Jesus Movement but receiving significant impetus from the charismatic movement. Publishing houses such as Maranatha! Music and Sparrow Records emerged during this period.

Choruses became the inroad into the mainstream of worship services. Such songs gave a new and needed sense of freedom, emphasizing the experiential side of the faith. However, the Jesus Movement was also characterized by a simplistic and even self-centered theology, which also crept into worship. Unfortunately, this focus added to the shift in our consumer-driven culture to receiving a blessing from God rather than giving an offering to God.

To summarize, worship in the Bible focused on the character of God. Throughout history, music and worship styles have changed with the growth and expansion of the church. In the modern era, musical changes often paralleled times of spiritual awakening and renewal. Over the past century, a distinction has developed between music focused on worship and music designed for evangelistic services. Added to this are the experience-oriented choruses of the Jesus Movement and the charismatic movement, resulting in services that focus on meeting contemporary needs without demonstrating a true understanding of worship. How can we keep the best of contemporary worship without abandoning the biblical focus?

IMPLICATIONS FOR WORSHIP FROM SCRIPTURE AND HISTORY

We must affirm the *vital role of theology* in all we do, particularly worship and church growth. Theology matters, but too often we don't emphasize its role. Our focus on modern methods to help churches grow has opened the evangelical church to criticism on theological grounds. Sally Morgenthaler makes the point well:

> In the 90s we are getting quite good at target practice—honing in on the lifestyles, habits, wants, and needs of particular people. Yet in our zeal to hit the bull's-eye, we have forgotten that *God grows the church through spiritual power.*[23]

Morgenthaler further cites Barna, who has discovered that the key thing unchurched people are looking for in a church is not a certain worship style but specific doctrinal beliefs. She adds, "To replace doctrine with style is to totally misinterpret the message our culture is sending."[24] Barna also says,

> We have 325,000 Protestant churches, 1,200 Christian radio stations, 300 Christian television stations, and 300 Christian colleges. . . . During the last eight years, we in the Christian community have spent in excess of $250 billion in domestic ministry and have seen a 0 percent increase in the proportion of born-again adult Christians of this country. Are we concerned about this? Do we feel any accountability for this picture?[25]

Most churches are so introverted that they are not concerned about honoring God through the worship experience or about bearing fruit through new believers. The sad truth is, we born-again Christians are an insulated, narcissistic subculture, involving ourselves with very few people outside our own churches. How can we witness to the lost if we do not know anybody who fits that description? "Some churches have perfected the art of draining other churches."[26]

We must remind ourselves that our primary object in life is to glorify God. Our adoration of God must transcend any other object of

ministry, including our desire to see churches grow. There is no better way to glorify God than to bring a lost sheep to the Shepherd
(Luke 15).

Morgenthaler gives a PASS formula to test songs for worship.
"Personal—they related someway to people's everyday lives and
involved their whole being, including their emotions. Attractive—
they hold people's attention. Straightforward—both Seeker Bob and
Saintly Bill can understand and latch onto them quickly.
Substantive—give a thoroughly biblical message that is faithful to
the whole counsel of scripture."[27]

We must recognize the difference between *worship services* and
evangelistic services. An evangelistic service, ranging from contemporary seeker services to traditional mass evangelism, can include
elements of worship, but its purposes are different. Many church
leaders fail to distinguish between a seeker service, which is evangelistic by design, and a seeker-sensitive worship service, which
welcomes the unsaved. Evangelistic services are needed, but not to
the neglect of worship services. Os Guinness put it well: It is "per-
fectly legitimate" to "convey the gospel in cartoons to a nonliterary
generation incapable of rising above MTV. . . . But five years later,
if the new disciples are truly won to Christ, they will be reading and
understanding Paul's letter to the Romans."[28]

Weekly services dedicated to the worship of God *can* have an
evangelistic impact. George Hunter and others have stated that our
culture is becoming more like the apostolic era. Our postmodern,
post-Christian era demands genuine worship by radically changed
believers who honor God with their lives. Such worship not only
glorifies God but also draws the attention of unbelievers (Ps. 126;
Acts 2:47; 16:25ff; Rom. 15:9–11; 1 Cor. 14:23–25).

Worship leader Tommy Coomes came to Christ because of the
genuine, dynamic worship at Calvary Chapel, Costa Mesa,
California, the mother church of the Jesus Movement. It was the
worship that drew him to Christ. He later observed, "There is a spiritual dynamic going on in authentic worship that can't be reasoned
away."[29] Don McMinn said it well:

> Music is not the power of God for salvation, and
> neither is the media of writing, speaking, or sign lan-
> guage. The gospel is the power of God to salvation,

and when it is presented, regardless of *how* it is presented, lives will be changed.[30]

We should give proper attention to *celebration* in our worship services—not celebrating our experience but the resurrected Lord. Hustad has warned that "the 'new enjoyment' may lead to a worship hedonism which is another form of idolatry—worshiping the experience instead of worshiping God."[31] Confession and brokenness are necessary for honest worship to occur;[32] still, celebrating the resurrection of Jesus Christ should be the focus of our worship. When he is our focus, we are reminded that Christianity is not primarily fun; it is *essential.*

We should *dismiss false dichotomies* as unacceptable: such generalities as "Boomers don't like hymns" or "Boomers don't like church to look like church" are inaccurate. Such dichotomies lead to a reductionism that fails to distinguish between the timeless and the trendy, the contemporary and the faddish. Some people sing choruses because this is the music they like, with little thought given to the issue of worshiping God. Others hold to a more historic, traditional approach because in their minds, it demonstrates authentic worship. Perhaps the truth is that they just don't like change!

Style and substance are both vital, but substance must guide stylistic concerns. We must never make "either-or" that which is actually "both-and." There is no one all-encompassing worship style that will reach the multitudes or exalt our great God.

The best recent book surveying evangelistically growing churches[33] is Thom Rainer's *Effective Evangelistic Churches.* The book reports the findings of a survey of 576 evangelistically growing Southern Baptist churches. In the chapter surveying worship styles, Rainer defined the following categories: Liturgical, Traditional, Revivalist, Contemporary, Seeker, and Blended (see Figure 17.1).[34]

The largest number of evangelistic churches (44.5 percent) are traditional. The second largest (31.2 percent) follow the blended format, while contemporary/seeker (21.3 percent, although the lion's share of these was contemporary) made the third group. True seeker services played a diminutive role in these churches. What important conclusions were drawn from this research?

1. *Various worship styles are effective.* In this survey, the *quality* of worship was seen as more important than the particular style.

2. *The atmosphere of the service is critical for reaching people.*

3. *The attitude of those leading the service played a bigger factor than the style:* "Leaders describe their worship services with such words as *warm, exciting, loving, vibrant, hopeful,* and *worshipful.*"[35]

We must keep a healthy balance between *new music* and *lasting songs.* Bob Burroughs, while affirming and writing many contemporary scores, feels that an overemphasis on singing choruses instead of hymns could become detrimental:

> The praise chorus music itself in some churches has taken the place of the hymnal, and the music is so shallow . . . that the great Hymnody of the church, which is a teaching aid also for theology, and for doctrine . . . is lost. When you sing "Alleluia, alleluia" over against "A Mighty Fortress" or "Savior, Like a Shepherd Lead Us," or some of those, the young people and the young adults really do miss out on some . . . great theology. [36]

The key to worship is not the songs we sing or the music's beat. The key is not style, although style does matter. The key is spirit. The key is *life.* Over the past decade I have been privileged to speak in some five hundred churches, mostly but not exclusively Southern Baptist, in over twenty states. I could share many stories of pathetic churches who are dying. The favorite song of such churches is "I Shall Not Be Moved" or "Take My Life and Let It Be," and they mean "let it be," as in "don't bother me!" These churches that have confused reverence with rigor mortis are legion. But I would rather note some other churches where life is contagious, where God is at work—big churches, small churches, new missions and some over a century old, rural and urban. Here are some examples:

- A church in Houston, Texas, in a blue-collar neighborhood, with hymns, no choruses, and special music with a southern gospel or country flair.

- An innovative, contemporary megachurch thirty minutes away from the one just mentioned, in an upwardly mobile area, blending old hymns with new hymns and choruses, incorporating drama, and using an overhead.

Figure 17.1
Worship Styles

Liturgical

Mood: Formal, solemn, majestic.

Music: Pipe organ, traditional hymns, classical anthems.

Purpose: To lead the church to give corporate recognition to the transcendent glory of God. Favors reverence over relevance.

Biblical Model: Isaiah 6.

Traditional

Mood: Orderly, majestic, contemplative.

Music: Organ and piano, traditional and gospel hymns, traditional and contemporary anthems.

Purpose: To lead the congregation to praise and thank God for his goodness and to hear him speak through his word. Geared for people with a religious background.

Biblical Model: Colossians 3:16–17.

Revivalist

Mood: Exuberant, celebrative, informal.

Music: Organ, piano, and taped gospel hymns, contemporary songs, and anthems.

Purpose: To save the lost and encourage believers to witness. More emphasis on evangelism than worship.

Biblical Model: Acts 2–3.

Contemporary

Mood: Expressive, celebrative, contemporary, informal.

Music: Keyboard, piano, and taped music, praise choruses and contemporary songs.

Purpose: To offer a sacrifice of praise to the Lord in a spirit of joyful adoration. Contemporary worship for believers, although some unchurched are invited.

Biblical Model: Psalm 150.

Seeker

Mood: Celebrative, contemporary, informal.

Music: Piano, taped, synthesizer and band; scriptural music and contemporary; little traditional congregational singing.

Purpose: To present the gospel in clear non-God-talk terms and modern forms. An upbeat, evangelistic service.

Biblical Model: Acts 17:16–34.

Blended

Combination of traditional and contemporary elements.

- A rural church in North Carolina, with a young pastor, singing traditional hymns as though they were written yesterday, filled with the love of Christ.

- A midsized congregation in the northeastern United States, using both familiar songs and new tunes, and occasionally some written by members, with a very free service order.

- A small-town congregation in South Carolina where *contemporary* means songs like "There's Just Something about That Name" and "His Name Is Wonderful." In other words, songs contemporary twenty-five years ago. But a church full of life and reaching people.

Many more churches could be cited, but my point is clear: No one style of worship is the exclusively biblical approach. The Bible, especially the New Testament, does not give specific instructions about the form of the worship service. This does not mean that anything goes in worship. "Decently and in order" is how Paul told the Corinthians to worship. Some form, tradition, or liturgy gives continuity from generation to generation. There must be an underlying theology of worship and a biblical ecclesiology.

What I am saying is that there is a need for traditional churches, for some people love church like Granny had. But churches that worship in a manner that honors Christ *and* relates to culture are also necessary.

OPEN WORSHIP AND EVANGELISM

People are passionate about what happens in worship services. We must teach our people that worship is not designed to please the congregation but to please God.

There is a tendency to make a strong distinction between worship services for the saved and evangelistic services or weekly seeker services. But there is ample biblical evidence for the concept of open worship—worship that focuses on exalting God, but that draws people into his presence. This includes drawing sinners to salvation. Today we are in the midst of a *worship reformation,* a movement that continues to address the issue of worship form (relevance) stretching beyond form to the core of worship itself—biblical substance. This is a worship movement with more life-reaching, life-changing potential than anything the evangelical church has seen in the last seventy-five years.

I am convinced that in the area of worship and evangelism—to quote a dc Talk song—"God Is Doing a New Thing." Actually, the new thing is an old thing. The Lord gave Moses clear instructions about worship: "And if a stranger dwells with you, or whoever is among you throughout your generations, and would present an offering made by fire, a sweet aroma to the Lord, just as you do, so shall he do" (Num. 15:14). So strangers were expected. Deuteronomy 26:10–11 also mentions how aliens worship. The psalmist declared, "Let everything that has breath praise the Lord. Praise the Lord!" (Ps. 150:6). The presence of unbelievers is also noted in the New Testament (see 1 Cor. 14:22–25).

Israel was to be a kingdom of priests and a light to the nations. Worship really is an encounter of God with his children. Lost people are potential children of God. The Bible indicates that there is none righteous, but it also says that those who seek God will find him if their search is genuine. In our worship we should not put unnecessary burdens on unsaved people who may be in attendance.

Morgenthaler asks rhetorically, "Just how does evangelism take place in a service that is 'fully worshiped'?" Her reply is worth considering: "It happens in two ways: first, as unbelievers hear the truth about God (through worship songs, prayers, communion, baptism, scripture [preaching!], testimonies, dramas, and so on); and second—and more importantly—as they observe the real relationship between worshipers and God."[37] This can be seen in Psalm 126 in the Old Testament and in the Acts narrative in the New Testament.

Some evangelists, including Franklin Graham and the Harvest Crusades of Greg Laurie, are moving toward a worship experience, even in their evangelistic crusades. Perhaps a miniature example of open worship would be Paul and Silas when they worshiped in the prison at Philippi and their worship drew the prison keeper to want to know Christ (see Acts 16). Gerrit Gustafson gives a definition of worship evangelism, the kind of evangelism that occurs in the context of open worship: "Wholehearted worshipers calling the whole world to the wholehearted worship of God . . . [and] the fusion of the power of God's presence with the power of the gospel."[38]

What then are the characteristics of worship evangelism? Morgenthaler is insightful:[39]

Nearness. Worship evangelism features a sense of God's presence.

Knowledge. The worship is centered on Christ. Our worship is not centered on seekers or on us; it is centered on the risen Lord. Some seeker services deny the gospel because they think seekers are offended by it. We should not be offensive in worship or at any other time, but we should not be surprised if the gospel is an offense to some people (see 1 Cor. 1)! The fear of offending people with the salvation message may indicate a much deeper problem: We may be willing to do whatever it takes to get unbelievers into church but not to bring them to Christ!

Vulnerability. This is an opening up to God. Lost people are not looking for perfect Christians; they are looking for people who are *real,* who open themselves before a holy God and make it clear that they are not God, that they are seeking to worship him. Perhaps we need to talk less about being seeker friendly and emphasize that we are sinner friendly. After all, Jesus was called a friend of sinners. The point of vulnerability is that worship ought to be about honesty. We're not perfect. We need to let the world know we make mistakes. But we have an anchor in Jesus Christ when our ship is adrift.

Interaction. Worship evangelism means participating in a relationship with God and others. How can we make the church and worship relevant? The key to relevance is not changing the gospel or our worship to make people happy. God desires not that we be happy—but holy. When we're holy, we find happiness. The only way to be relevant is to be real. The central issue is not to be *relevant* but to be *significant.*

"Contrary to popular belief," Morgenthaler adds, "it is not culturally relevant in turn-of-the-millennium America to throw out every single piece of historic Christian communication."[40] Morgenthaler cites a survey that discovered that 47 percent of unchurched people indicated they would like to sing some traditional hymns. Taking the older hymns and updating the music would communicate to the current day.

In Houston we were members of Sugar Creek Baptist Church, Sugar Land, Texas—a large, urban, contemporary megachurch. We would sing traditional hymns like "Blessed Assurance" but in a more contemporary style. "Leaning on the Everlasting Arms," for example, was sung while our worship leader played the acoustic guitar. It added just a little different sound to the hymn. It had the same words and content, but it was slightly different to fit with the worship context of that congregation.

APPLICATION

Take a few minutes to consider the corporate worship of your church. Does it exalt God? Is it a celebration of the resurrected Lord? Can lost people be saved by participating? Would they want to know the God represented in your worship?

Morgenthaler, whose book is by far the best I have seen on this subject, offers five rudders to guide worship evangelism.

1. Worship first, evangelize second.

2. Never sacrifice authenticity for relevance.

3. Add before you subtract.

4. Be committed to relevance based on your community's culture in the present and its meaningful religious past.

5. Customize your own worship methodology.[41]

I'm grateful for churches like Willow Creek that are seeker driven because such churches do reach people. Nevertheless, I must agree with Morgenthaler, who says, "I am of the firm conviction that if seeker-driven churches become first and foremost *worshiping* churches, they could have an incredibly vital role in re-energizing and reshaping evangelicalism as we enter the next millennium." She adds, "I disagree strongly with Willow Creek's contention that seekers and worship do not mix. If we truly understand what worship is, we would appreciate why worship services are an essential part of God's strategy for building the kingdom and drawing others into it."[42]

Our God is worthy of worship that exalts his great name and demonstrates to sinners the wonder of knowing him.

Bibliography

Dawn, Marva. *Reaching out without Dumbing Down: A Theology of Worship for the Turn of the Century Church.* Grand Rapids: Eerdmans, 1995.

Hustad, Donald R. *Jubilate! Church Music in the Evangelical Tradition.* Carol Stream, Ill.: Hope Publishing Company, 1981.

Morgenthaler, Sally. *Worship Evangelism: Inviting Unbelievers into the Presence of God.* Grand Rapids: Zondervan Publishing House, 1995.

White, James Emory. *Opening the Front Door: Worship and Church Growth.* Nashville: Convention Press, 1992.

Caught More Than Taught: Evangelistic Leadership

E verything rises and falls with leadership. This is true in sports, business, families, government, and in the church as well.

This book has been written for students, ministers, and laity—in fact, any believer who seeks to learn more about evangelism. However, this chapter is especially for pastors. Unless the pastor leads the church in its evangelistic fervor, the church's commitment will soon wane.

Philips Brooks was right when he said, "If God called you to preach, don't stop to be a king." On the other hand, Spurgeon was correct in admonishing if you can do anything besides preach, by all means do it. The call to be a pastor of a local church is indeed a high calling. The need of our day is for pastors who lead their churches in evangelism.

Paul used three words interchangeably to refer to the office of pastor. *Poimen,* or "pastor," denotes shepherding a flock. Hence, pastors are to feed, protect, and nurture a congregation. The word translated "bishop" or "overseer" is *episcopos.* The pastor is the leader of the church. Jesus is the sovereign head, but the pastor is the human leader. Finally, a pastor is a *presbuteros,* an "elder," or a mature example to the flock.

Unfortunately, some people have unrealistic expectations of pastors, thinking they should have a big "S" on their shirts. Note the following description of a perfect pastor:

> He preaches exactly 20 minutes and then sits down. He condemns sin but never hurts anyone's feelings. He works from 8 A.M. to 10 P.M. in every type of work from preaching to custodial service.

> He makes $60 per week, wears good clothes, buys good books regularly, has a nice family, drives a good car and gives $30 per week to the church. He also stands ready to contribute to every good work that comes along.

> He is 26 years old and has been preaching for 30 years. He is tall and short, thin and heavy-set, handsome. He has one brown eye and one blue; hair parted in the middle, left side dark and straight; the right, brown and wavy.

> He has a burning desire to work with teenagers and spends all his time with older folks. He spends all his time with a straight face because he has a sense of humor that keeps him seriously dedicated to his work.

> He makes 15 calls a day on church members, spends all his time evangelizing the unchurched, and is never out of the office.[1]

If I have learned anything about ministry and evangelism over the years, it is this: *everything* rises or falls with leadership. In the Bible, when God began to do a work, he set aside someone as the anointed leader—a person who understood humility and submission to God but was also bold and courageous.

The writer of Hebrews admonished, "Remember your leaders, who spoke the word of God to you. Consider the outcome of their way of life and imitate their faith. . . . Obey your leaders and submit to their authority. They keep watch over you as men who must give an account. Obey them so that their work will be a joy, not a burden, for that would be of no advantage to you" (Heb. 13:7, 17 NIV).

The apostle Paul told us,

> It was he who gave some to be apostles, some to be prophets, some to be evangelists, and some to be pastors and teachers, to prepare God's people for works of service, so that the body of Christ may be built up until we all reach unity in the faith and in the knowledge of the Son of God and become mature, attaining to the whole measure of the fullness of Christ. Then we will no longer be infants, tossed back and forth by the waves, and blown here and there by every wind of teaching and by the cunning and craftiness of men in their deceitful scheming. Instead, speaking the truth in love, we will in all things grow up into him who is the Head, that is, Christ. From him the whole body, joined and held together by every supporting ligament, grows and builds itself up in love, as each part does its work (Eph. 4:11–16 NIV).

In his last letter, Paul gave Timothy sound advice concerning leadership. In 2 Timothy 2:1–15 we can glean principles for leading in evangelism. Following a word of exhortation in verse one, Paul outlined to Timothy how to multiply leadership and thus the ministry. He followed the exhortation with three analogies for sound leaders, concluding with a testimony concerning his own example and a recognition of the faithfulness of God. The inspired words of Paul provide the perfect framework for developing principles of effective leadership.

LEAD WITH CONFIDENCE IN GOD'S CALL

Paul exhorted Timothy to "be strong in the grace that is in Christ Jesus" (2 Tim. 2:1 NIV). Timothy faced an awesome task, but one the Lord himself had ordained. Timothy was probably insecure about the task before him. He was neither the first nor the last church leader to struggle with such emotions.

One of the attributes of effective pastors whom I have admired is their ability to rest in the call of God on their lives. Adrian Rogers tells the story about when he was first called to ministry. He began to think, *God, you can't call somebody like me. I'll never be of any use to you. Why would you call someone like me?* He genuinely struggled with his call.

One night he went out into a football field to spend time with God. And he said, "God, unless you fill me with your Spirit and your power, you'll never use me; I'll never be of any use to you." He got on his knees before God. He felt he could not get low enough, so he laid down on the ground to humble himself before God, begging God to use him, to fill him, to empower him. He still didn't feel low enough, so he dug a hole and put his nose in it, getting as low as he could to the ground. God will never use us unless we realize that we are nothing apart from him.

As a leader, you must recognize that you will take abuse by virtue of your position. In his first pastorate, John Morgan was berated weekly by a lady in his church. After one occasion when she ripped the young pastor unmercifully, John and his wife retreated to their seminary housing. John's dad, himself a pastor, called that evening. John poured out his broken heart. The elder pastor gave sage advice to his son: "John, when you hang up, get a quiet place to pray. Then thank the Lord for the opportunity to preach. Thank God that you made it home tonight. Then thank God that you are not married to that woman!"

If God has called you to be a leader, you should be yourself. Don't copy others. Be strong in the grace of God. While in Houston, I observed closely the ministries of John Bisagno, pastor of First Baptist Church, Houston; and Ed Young, pastor of Second Baptist Church in that great city. These men lead two of the strongest churches in America, and they are only a few miles apart. But their leadership styles are dramatically different. Be yourself.

The church that John MacArthur serves grew through verse-by-verse preaching. Chuck Swindoll did the same with warmth and humor. Ed Young has grown a church reaching upwardly mobile Houstonians. John Bisagno has built a people's church, with more of a laid-back style. Get to know *who* you are in Christ, *like* who you are, and *be* who you are.

LEAD BY EQUIPPING OTHER LEADERS

"Great men lead people," Bill Bright of Campus Crusade for Christ says, "but greater men train leaders." Paul sounded this advice to Timothy when he declared, "The things you have heard from me . . . commit these to faithful men who will be able to teach others also" (2 Tim. 2:2). While serving in Indiana, I saw firsthand the reality that the greatest barrier to overcome in church growth is the two-hundred barrier in attendance. A primary reason for this is that, when a church grows to this size, a pastor must train leaders or employ more staff to facilitate further growth. The training of leaders has received too little attention. Paul mentored Timothy, and Timothy mentored others.

Mentoring is very popular today, and that is good. There are two kinds of mentoring: formal and informal. The formal style follows the example of Jesus and his disciples. A pastor or leader will gather regularly with a small group for teaching and accountability. When I was in college, a Presbyterian layman took three students through intensive discipleship, Scripture memory, and witnessing. This was an invaluable experience to me. I know pastors who effectively mentor key laymen; others mentor young men who have surrendered to the ministry. I spend specific, consistent time with certain students, particularly doctoral students, in a mentoring relationship.

Informal mentoring looks for opportunities to mentor on a more short-term or casual basis. We should not underestimate the teachable moments that arise spontaneously. Taking laity or students with you to conferences can be life changing.

There is also great value in peer mentoring. The greatest thing that ever happened to me in my seminary experience was the development of a mentoring friendship with four other men during our doctoral work. The five of us and our wives get together annually each summer, and we keep up through phone calls and letters during the year. These men, though my age, are my heroes, and they provoke me to good works.

Mentoring in evangelism is vital. As evangelism director in Indiana, I worked with a young man who was attempting to plant a church. He felt unprepared to witness and had become discouraged. I began to spend time with him and put him in contact with others who could encourage him. He attended an evangelism conference in Atlanta, where he stayed in the home of a soul-winning layperson, a member of the First Baptist Church of Woodstock, Georgia. He also received special evangelism training in Indiana. As a result, he began winning people to Christ. After a year of effective witnessing, his mission church led the state in baptisms by ratio!

The philosopher Aristotle, in his *Nichomachean Ethics,* described three kinds of friendships: (1) friendship of pleasure, based on pleasure in each other's company; (2) friendship of utility, based on usefulness derived from your association; and (3) friendship of virtue, derived from mutual admiration.[2] Perhaps mentoring is best done when all three of these elements exist and when it is founded on biblical teaching.

LEAD IN HUMILITY

Paul also told Timothy to be like a soldier (2 Tim. 2:3–4). A soldier understands the importance of serving others, both his commander and his country. Rather than leading in an autocratic matter, the servant-leader is the biblical model. Jesus said we are to be ministers or servants. He declared, "The Son of Man did not come to be served, but to serve, and to give His life a ransom for many" (Mark 10:45). The word *serve* means "to heal broken bones." It also means to "furnish a house."

Hear the sage wisdom of pastor John Morgan, who has built the Sagemont Church in Houston from a handful of people to a megachurch: "I lead by example. If we need satellite parking, I park the farthest away. When we eat, I never go first. Be low key. People call me 'Brother John.' If you have to tell people you are the pastor, that you answer only to God, and that God speaks to you, you are headed for trouble."

To demonstrate a servant heart, Morgan did the following: "We have Wednesday night suppers. I began bussing the tables, then some staff helped me. I didn't tell the deacons. After a year, the deacons joined in. Some members have tears in their eyes; they don't want me to do it!"

Being a servant means being human, being transparent. There is a difference between *vision* and *ambition.* Ambition's goal leans toward self-fulfillment, self-recognition, and self-gratification. Vision regards something we receive from God, not what we dream on our own. I often ask my students to identify the vision God has given them. Billy Graham has never strayed from God's vision for his life. Neither should we.

Fenton Moorhead, pastor of Sugar Creek Baptist Church near Houston, said, "We must admit our mistakes. If you make a mistake in public, apologize in public." He adds: "The little things are important. A nine-year-old wrote me, telling me she enjoyed the sermon, and made comments. I called her and gave her guidance. Her mom was thrilled that I called."

A principle of leadership: the leader must be able to handle power well. Lord Acton's dictum was, "Power corrupts and absolute power corrupts absolutely." Heed his warning. John Bisagno says, "You should never use all the power and the authority you have as a leader. As a leader, take more blame than you deserve and give more praise than is deserved—not in a manipulative kind of way but in a spirit of humility."

Demonstrate a servant attitude in the way you talk about God and other people. Rick Warren says there is nothing spectacular about a pastor who says, "I love to preach." What is much more significant, Warren argues, is the pastor who says, "I love my *people*." Your respect, your awe, your wonder that God has called you will say much to those who follow you. John Bisagno says, "Leadership must be granted by the people and earned by you."

LEAD OTHERS TO GREATNESS FOR GOD

Paul's second analogy is that of an athlete competing for a crown (see 2 Tim. 2:5). Observe the commitment of Olympic gold medalists—the sacrifices they endure for a temporal crown. Why the years of training for a few moments of glory? They have a passion, a vision for the prize.

I believe every person wants to make an impact. God has given each Christian a vision that he or she must fulfill. Your role as a leader is to help others catch the vision that God has for their lives. No one is less motivated than a person who is called upon to fulfill the goals of another person. But a visionary leader sees the potential in others that they do not see in themselves. Goethe said, "Treat a man as he appears to be, and you make him worse. But treat a man as if he already were what he potentially could be, and you make him what he should be."

Who knows but that you may have a missionary under your influence? a great pastor? a businessman whose success will mean millions of dollars contributed to the cause of Christ? Many are not involved in evangelism because they have no idea of the impact they can make. Give vision and hope to the people of God.

LEAD BY FAITH

Notice Paul's analogy of a faithful farmer (see 2 Tim. 2:6). A farmer works the ground, believing the harvest will come. The doubting farmer will give up on the harvest at the first sign of drought.

I love these words of Aristotle: "That which we learn with delight we never forget." Expectant, excited, encouraging leadership is found in most evangelistic churches. Take a moment and think of the one person who most influenced you in your walk with Christ. It was probably his or her *encouragement* that made the greatest impact. Faith is contagious. If you are an encourager, those whom you lead will grow in their own sense of expectancy. An optimistic leader, driven by faith in God, moves forward in confidence in God's desire to bless a church that pleases him. Such a leader does not jump on the bandwagon of every fad that comes along. An expectant leader's faith is in God, not his own ability, so he is not tossed to and fro by the latest craze.

We can have confidence in the gospel. We can *expect* God to honor a faithful church. Paul said that we should know the times, which means literally an intimate understanding of the society in which we minister (Rom. 13:11). Cultures change, demanding innovative, contextualized approaches to reach lost people. But our understanding of culture should lead us to address societal needs with a Christ-centered solution, not a culture-driven approach (Rom. 13:12–13). Let the "Elmo fads" come and go; let's keep the gospel paramount in our ministries. Toys will come and go, but eternity is for keeps.[3]

LEAD CONSISTENTLY AND BIBLICALLY

Paul offered himself as an example (see 2 Tim. 2:7–14). In verse 14, Paul summarized the previous verses by commanding Timothy to remind those whom he led of such vital truths. One of the most significant things a leader can do is to define what is real, what is truth, to those whom he leads. People with type-A, extroverted, charismatic personalities lead more easily as a rule, but leadership must be founded on the timeless principles of Scripture, not the force of one's personality.

Leadership is defining reality. Our understanding of reality comes from God's Word. Defining reality means confronting people who refuse to follow. It means standing firm in the face of the skeptical, the apathetic, or the indifferent. The epitaph on a hypochondriac's tombstone read, "I told you I was sick." You will constantly have to choose the hill on which you are willing to die. Some leaders lose their authority to lead by becoming involved in secondary decisions in the church. What would you give your job for in your ministry? If a church in its actions mitigates against evangelism, will you give in or defend the gospel? While many pastors lose their ministries for bad reasons, there are some things worse than losing your job. One is losing your convictions. We need leaders who will declare boldly the unsearchable treasures of Christ from a heart of love and without fear of the consequences.

LEAD BY THE STRENGTH OF YOUR CHARACTER

Leadership is influence. You must have integrity, conviction, and character. Without this, those whom you lead will recognize the emergence of the "Barney Fife" syndrome in your life. Remember Barney? He carried a gun, but it had no bullets. Having a badge without bullets is like being in a leadership position with no respect. If you have to tell people you are the leader, you are not the leader!

If your present ministry is just a stepping-stone for your ambition for the future, people will figure that out. More importantly, God has already figured it out. But if you demonstrate a genuine love for God and a love for the people to whom you minister, more than a few will follow you. Love *everyone,* but move with the *movers.* Over time, they will follow. Your burden for lost people will become their burden.

I learned this in Indiana. When I went there—first as associate, then as evangelism director—I knew I was getting in over my head. So I asked two people for advice: Carlos McLeod, evangelism director for the Baptist General Convention of Texas; and Malcolm McDow, my professor at seminary.

Both gave me great advice. They told me that I should not go to the churches in Indiana promoting my programs or plans. They advised me to preach the Word of God and let the people sense my passion for Christ and the gospel. When the people sensed my love for God and a desire to help the churches rather than convincing them to use my programs, they would follow my leadership.

These leaders were exactly right. I knew little about Indiana and less about denominational leadership. But the Lord gave me a great burden for the lost people and the churches in Indiana, and he honored my ministry there more than I could have asked or dreamed.

Pastors often complain about the seven words that kill churches: "We've never done it that way before." It is difficult to get people to change. But if we are to lead people to be open to change, we must demonstrate that we are open to change. Model the truth that change is normal, not the enemy. If you love contemporary worship but are in a traditional church, you will have to change as much as the people at first, meeting them where they are. Are you as excited about changing yourself as you are about changing others?

As a church grows, leadership styles change. Leading a church of one hundred people is different from leading a congregation of three hundred, five hundred, or one thousand. Many pastors never lead a church beyond two hundred people in attendance, not because there are no more people to reach, but because the pastor must change his style of leadership. He must relinquish responsibilities (read: power) to laypeople and eventually to other staff. He must move from being a shepherd to serving as a rancher.

APPLICATION

"No Christian leader is the person of God that our Lord wants him to be unless day after day the consuming desire of his heart is that people come to Christ."[4] These words from Wesley Duewel demonstrate the importance of linking leadership in ministry to evangelism. As a leader, ask yourself: Are those I am leading more excited about evangelism because of my leadership? Are they more effective in sharing their faith?

A person who thinks he is leading when no one is following is only taking a walk. Take a minute to say to the Lord, "Make me the kind of leader that people want to follow so the Great Commission will be fulfilled to a greater degree because of my leadership."

BIBLIOGRAPHY

Barna, George. *The Power of Vision*. Ventura, Calif.: Regal, 1992.

Ford, Leighton. *Transforming Leadership*. Downers Grove, Ill.: InterVarsity, 1991.

Conclusion

I t's not where you are; it's where you are headed." I have made this statement before in this book, and I repeat it ad nauseum to my students. Each day you and I sow seeds that will affect where we will be in the days to follow. What am I building in my life today that will affect eternity? I pray this book has encouraged you to head toward excellence in evangelism. William Carey said we must attempt great things for God and expect great things from God. This is still true today.

President Teddy Roosevelt epitomized the challenge of stepping out of our comfort zones to make a difference: "Far better it is to dare mighty things, to win glorious triumphs, even though checkered by failure, than to take rank with those poor spirits who neither enjoy much nor suffer much, because they live in the gray twilight that knows neither victory nor defeat."[1]

One of the things I tell my students is that sermons are meant to comfort the afflicted and to afflict the comfortable! I hope this book has done a bit of each—comforting some of the fears you have about evangelism while convicting you of any negligence you have toward this task.

After about fifteen years of marriage, certain things begin to need replacement (I *don't* mean your spouse!). Our refrigerator, battered from so many moves, died this year. About the same time, my wedding ring broke. I would like to blame it on the ring company, but I think the twenty or more pounds I have gained since college is the culprit! I had taken the ring off only a couple of times during all of those years, and I missed it while it was at the jewelers for repair. I was happy to be married, and I wanted people to know it!

It was great to have the ring back. I was no more married when I put it on again than I was when it was being repaired, but it still made a difference. Evangelism is like that. You can be a Christian and not consistently share your faith, just as you can be married without a ring. But evangelism is the very thing that, above all others, identifies us as the proud, grateful, purchased possession of Christ. You will never feel right about your relationship with Jesus without openly telling others about him.

I pray this book has been a spiritual "trip to the jewelry store" for you to get things fixed. Let the light of the Son shine through the gem of your changed life.

After a speech, pro-life activist Penny Lea was approached by an old man. Weeping, he told her the following story:

> I lived in Germany during the Nazi holocaust. I considered myself a Christian. I attended church since I was a small boy. We had heard the stories of what was happening to the Jews, but like most people today in this country, we tried to distance ourselves from the reality of what was really taking place. What could anyone do to stop it?
>
> A railroad track ran behind our small church, and each Sunday morning we would hear the whistle from a distance and then the clacking of the wheels moving over the track. We became disturbed when one Sunday we noticed cries coming from the train as it passed by. We grimly realized that the train was carrying Jews. They were like cattle in those cars!
>
> Week after week that train whistle would blow. We would dread to hear the sound of those old wheels because we knew that the Jews would begin to cry out to us as they passed our church. It was so terribly disturbing! We could do nothing to help these poor miserable people, yet their screams tormented us. We knew exactly at what time that whistle would blow, and we decided the only way to keep from being so disturbed by the cries was to

start singing our hymns. By the time that train came rumbling past the church yard, we were singing at the top of our voices. If some of the screams reached our ears, we'd just sing a little louder until we could hear them no more. Years have passed and no one talks about it much anymore, but I still hear that train whistle in my sleep. I can still hear them crying out for help. God forgive all of us who called ourselves Christians, yet did nothing to intervene.

Now, so many years later, I see it happening all over again in America. God forgive you as Americans for you have blocked out the screams of millions of your own children. The holocaust is here. The response is the same as it was in my country— Silence![2]

While Lea applied this tragic story to the abortion holocaust in America, it also speaks to the negligence of the church to seek to save lost souls from hell. May our generation not be so busy spending time in activity that we miss the cries of the hurting. Tell someone about Jesus, won't you?

Appendix
Using the New Technology

This morning, as I began writing this section, I was sitting in a rocker typing on my notebook computer while my nine-year-old son played a game via CD-ROM on the desktop computer. My poor daughter, only four, was stuck with the primitive VCR. At least she has her own CD-ROM games! Recently my brother visited us. A Ph.D. chemist, Austin was amazed to watch his four-year-old niece crank up the Aptiva, slide in her disk, and go to town on her educational game.

Technology can dazzle us or deceive us. This is especially true with the Internet. Information both good and bad is only fingertips away when a person has access to the World Wide Web. In the same way, the chat rooms online give people opportunities to meet others while remaining somewhat anonymous; in some cases, however, liaisons have formed that have brought broken homes and even death. How can we fulfill the Great Commission by reaching out with this new technology?

SHARING CHRIST IN THE CHAT ROOMS

America Online has scores of chat rooms in which millions of people from around the world talk with one another. If you have a computer and a modem, you can chat with an Israeli about aviation or a Brit about education. Room topics abound. Some are completely ungodly. For instance, the homosexual presence is apparent in the number of chat rooms featuring their views. There are rooms

341

for paganism, Wicca, Mormonism, and New Age interests. This ungodliness must cause believers to make a difference in the online world. Thankfully, there are multitudes of Christian chat rooms from "Bornagainers Online" to "Christian Fellowship." There are also rooms such as "Married with Children" with pleasant people.

Here are some suggestions about sharing Christ in the chat rooms.

First, some chat rooms should be avoided. The sexual content and the rampant ungodliness of some can be oppressive. If you are a radical witness and determine to go to the darker rooms (like some people I know who witness boldly in topless bars in New Orleans), do not go unless you have another Christian with you online and in that room. Words are powerful, and they can cause you to stumble.

Second, as you enter a chat room, begin by general conversation. I go into a "family and careers" room, and I do not go just to mark on my belt how many times I witness. I talk about my family and my hobbies. Inevitably, someone asks what I do, and I tell them I teach students preparing for ministry. I can tell by their reaction who is open to talk. In fact, they usually come to me because I am *friendly*, and many people are *searching*. Jesus was a friend of sinners (note: *not* a friend of sin), and I want to be also. The fact that I am a Christian who cares enough to ask such simple questions as "How many children do you have?" opens doors to share Christ.

What is so wonderful about this technology is that I have won to Christ people who have *no* Christian background—people so secular they would never let anyone in their house to talk to them or go to church. I have also met people who dropped out of church years ago.

The power of testimony is essential. I share my testimony with people regularly. Here is another helpful feature of Internet evangelism: If you are shy, the people with whom you talk can't see you! They don't even know your name, unless you tell them. This anonymity can give you boldness. You might send your testimony to people by E-mail, asking for their response.

Many of my students are very effective at witnessing online. Timothy Abraham, a former Muslim now radically saved, is a great example.

I asked Timothy to share key points he has learned about online evangelism:

- Remember we are talking to real people, not a machine or someone in the world of imagination.
- Christ must remain central to everything we do online.
- Online chatting can be fun, and there is no more enjoyment than sharing the love of Christ online.

When Timothy witnesses, he normally spends more time listening than talking. The online world is filled with lonely, hurting people. After chatting online, he will often ask to call the people and pray for them on the phone. This further opens a door to share Christ. He particularly shares his conversion from Islam, and he advises: "I make sure I address a woman as sister to eliminate any possibility of flirtation which would therefore give no glory to God." Timothy has won people to Christ in the United States and overseas.

EVANGELISTIC WEB SITES

Christian groups are developing web sites specifically aimed at sharing Christ. The following information is the best I have seen, and in fact comes from the web site at *http://www.soon.org.uk.* This is the site of SOON gospel literature, an evangelistic ministry in the United Kingdom. It provides wonderful advice about the Internet in general and evangelism in particular. You might begin here to investigate how to share Christ online, particularly if you are new at this method.

Following is a list of other helpful sites for Christians to learn about evangelism.

- *Jews for Jesus.* Evangelizing Jewish people: *www.jews-for-jesus.org/*
- *Ron Hutchcraft Ministries.* Evangelistic web site of evangelist Ron Hutchcraft: *www.gospelcom.net/rhm/*
- *Jesus and the Intellectual.* A site produced by Campus Crusade for Christ: *www.ccci.org/intellectual/*
- *EvangeLinks.* Designed to assist believers in online evangelism: *www.cfore.com/EvangeLinks/*

- *Celebrate Jesus 2000 Home Page.* A web site related to this multidenominational evangelistic effort: *www.celebratejesus2000.org*
- *The Good News.* Produced by the North American Mission Board, SBC: *www.thegoodnews.org*

The SOON web site notes that every other ideology is "evangelizing" online, and Christians must do so as well. At Southeastern Seminary we are launching an evangelistic web site that will allow students (actually, we will require them!) to spend time weekly at dedicated terminals in our Center for Great Commission Studies. Explore the online world as a viable and necessary place to confront people with the gospel.

Notes

PART 1

1. Taken from a chapel sermon by John Avant at Southeastern Baptist Theological Seminary, December 3, 1996.

CHAPTER 1

1. Darrell Robinson, *People Sharing Jesus* (Nashville: Thomas Nelson, 1995), 21–2.
2. Darrell Robinson, *Total Church Life* (Nashville: Broadman & Holman, 1997), 177–8.
3. *Reference: Commission on Evangelism* (Westminster, England: The Press and Publications Board of the Church Assembly, 1944), 1.
4. Lewis A. Drummond, *The Word of the Cross* (Nashville: Broadman & Holman, 1992), 9.
5. See D. T. Niles, *That They May Have Life* (New York: Harper and Brothers, 1951), 96.
6. "Evangelism: P-1, P-2, P-3," in Elmer Towns, ed., *Evangelism and Church Growth* (Ventura, Calif.: Regal Books, 1995), 212–16.
7. Delos Miles, *Introduction to Evangelism* (Nashville: Broadman Press, 1981), 138.
8. Ibid., 141.
9. Booth, Pierson, and Smith quotes are from Wesley Duewel, *Ablaze for God* (Grand Rapids: Zondervan, 1989), 108, 111, 116.
10. Adapted from Charles R. Swindoll, *Growing Strong in the Seasons of Life* (Portland: Multnomah Press, 1984), 87–8.

11. Max Lucado, *The Applause of Heaven* (Waco: Word, 1996), 74.
12. David Lockard, *The Unheard Billy Graham* (Waco: Word, 1971), 13.

CHAPTER 2

1. Drummond, *Word of the Cross,* 67.
2. See John Avant, "The Relationship of Changing Views of the Inspiration and Authority of Scripture to Evangelism and Church Growth: A Study of the United Methodist Church and the Southern Baptist Convention in the United States Since World War II" (Ph.D diss., Southwestern Baptist Theological Seminary, 1990).
3. Adapted from Swindoll, *Growing Strong,* 34–35.
4. Robert E. Coleman, *The Master Plan of Evangelism* (New York: Fleming H. Revell, 1972), quotes taken respectively from 27, 42, 51, 61, 71, 72, 79, 89, 97.

CHAPTER 3

1. Michael Green, *Evangelism in the Early Church* (Grand Rapids: Eerdmans, 1970), 13.
2. F. F. Bruce, *The Spreading Flame* (Grand Rapids: Eerdmans, 1995), 24.
3. Ibid.
4. To my knowledge, Leighton Ford was the first to use the terminology that follows. Roy Fish has taught the concepts for almost a generation, and Darrell Robinson has popularized the approach in his book, *Total Church Life.*
5. Roy J. Fish and J. E. Conant, *Every Member Evangelism for Today* (New York: Harper and Row, 1976), 11.
6. Green, *Evangelism,* 172.
7. Ibid., 175.
8. Robert H. Gundry, *A Survey of the New Testament* (Grand Rapids: Zondervan, 1981), 75.
9. Green, *Evangelism,* 66.
10. Charles R. Swindoll, *Improving Your Serve* (Waco: Word, 1981), 92–3.
11. *The Ante-Nicene Fathers,* Alexander Roberts and James Donaldson, eds. vol. 1: "The Epistle of Polycarp to the Philippians," 89.
12. Ibid., 90.

13. Ibid., 94.

14. Ibid., "Introductory Notes to the First Apology of Justin Martyr," vol. 1, p. 297. Italics added.

15. Green, *Evangelism*, 274.

16. Mendell Taylor, *Exploring Evangelism* (Kansas City: Nazarene Publishing House, 1964), 77.

17. Green, *Evangelism*, 275.

CHAPTER 4

1. Swindoll, *Growing Strong,* 71–3.

2. Ibid., 95.

3. N. E. Schneider, *Augustine of England* (New York: F. M. Barton Co., 1944), 126.

4. Kenneth Scott Latourette, *A History of Christianity: Beginnings to 1500,* rev. ed., vol. 1 (New York: Harper and Row, 1975), 349.

5. Piero Misciattelli, *Savonarola* (New York: D. Appleton and Company, 1930), 46.

6. Taylor, *Exploring*, 154–55.

7. John Mark Terry, *Evangelism: A Concise History* (Nashville: Broadman & Holman, 1994), 82.

8. For an elaboration of the material in this section, see Malcolm McDow and Alvin L. Reid, *Firefall: How God Shaped History through Revivals* (Nashville: Broadman & Holman, 1997).

9. Much of the following material is adapted from Alvin L. Reid, "The Zeal of Youth: The Role of Students in the History of Revivals," in *Evangelism for a Changing World*, Timothy Beougher and Alvin L. Reid, eds., (Wheaton: Harold Shaw, 1995).

10. Fortress Press continues to publish the book, illustrating its status as a classic in Christian spirituality.

11. Earle E. Cairns, *An Endless Line of Splendor: Revivals and Their Leaders from the Great Awakening to the Present* (Wheaton: Tyndale House, 1986), 34.

12. See David Howard, "Student Power in World Missions," in *Perspectives on the World Christian Movement* (Pasadena: William Carey, 1981), 211–14.

13. Jonathan Edwards, "Narrative of the Surprising Work of God," in *The Works of Jonathan Edwards,* ed. Sereno E. Dwight (Edinburgh: The Banner of Truth Trust, 1834), I:348.

14. McDow and Reid, *Firefall,* 222.

15. For further information on the life of George Whitefield, see Arnold Dallimore, *George Whitefield,* 2 vols. (Edinburgh: Banner of Truth, 1970).

16. For further information on the life of John Wesley, see Nehemiah Curnock, ed., *The Journal of John Wesley,* 8 vols. (London: The Epworth Press, 1938); John W. Drakeford, ed., *John Wesley* (Nashville: Broadman Press, 1979); Robert G. Tuttle, *John Wesley: His Life and Theology* (Grand Rapids: Zondervan, 1978).

17. John Wesley, *The Journal of John Wesley,* Nehemiah Curnock, ed. (London: Epworth, 1938), I: 475–76.

18. Daniel Dorchester, *Christianity in the United States* (New York: Hunt and Eaton, 1895), 316.

19. Benjamin Rice Lacy, *Revival in the Midst of the Years* (Hopewell, Va.: Royal Publishers, 1968), 70.

20. Quoted from Hill's biography in Arthur Dicken Thomas, Jr. "Reasonable Revivalism: Presbyterian Evangelization of Educated Virginians, 1787–1837," *Journal of Presbyterian History* 61 (Fall 1983): 322.

21. See Lacy, *Revival,* 68ff; also Thomas, "Reasonable Revivalism," 322ff.

22. See Chauncy A. Goodrich, "Narrative of Revivals of Religion in Yale College," *American Quarterly Register* 10 (Feb. 1838): 295–96.

23. Cairns, *An Endless Line of Splendor,* 92.

24. See Gardiner Spring, *Memoir of Samuel John Mills* (Boston: Perkins and Marvin, 1829); Thomas Richards, *Samuel J. Mills: Missionary Pathfinder, Pioneer, and Promoter* (Boston: Pilgrim Press, 1906); Cairns, *An Endless Line of Splendor,* 261–62.

25. *Connecticut Evangelical Magazine,* vol. 1, 100–05.

26. See John B. Boles, *The Great Revival 1787–1805* (Lexington: The Univ. of Kentucky Press, 1972), 68; and Hank Hanegraaff, *Counterfeit Revival* (Dallas: Word, 1997), 117–21.

27. From *The Autobiography of Charles G. Finney* (Minneapolis: Bethany House, 1977), 159.

28. J. Edwin Orr, *Fervent Prayer* (Chicago: Moody Press, 1974), 11–12.

29. Cairns, *An Endless Line of Splendor,* 177, gives the priority to the Pentecostal movement in characterizing the significance of what he calls a "global awakening" beginning in 1900.

30. J. Edwin Orr, *Revival Is Like Judgment Day* (Atlanta: Home Mission Board, 1987), 9.

31. For further study, see Alvin L. Reid, "The Impact of the Jesus Movement on Evangelism among Southern Baptists" (Ph.D. diss., Southwestern Baptist Theological Seminary, 1991).

32. Billy Beachem, Student Discipleship Ministries, Fort Worth, Texas, to Alvin L. Reid, Indianapolis, Indiana, 8 January 1990, Transcript in the hand of Alvin L. Reid, and *Quarterly Review* (July-August-September 1972): 20–21.

33. "Baptists among 80,000 Attending Explo '72," *Indiana Baptist* (5 July 1972), 5.

34. Ibid.

35. Billy Graham, *The Jesus Revolution* (Grand Rapids: Zondervan, 1971).

36. Robert Coleman was on the faculty at that time and edited a history of the revival entitled *One Divine Moment* (Old Tappan, N.J.: Fleming H. Revell, 1970).

37. Henry C. James, "Campus Demonstrations," in *One Divine Moment,* 55.

38. "Texas Baptist Church Sets New SBC Baptism Record," *Indiana Baptist* (15 December 1971), 5. The highest number the year before was only 395.

39. Dallas Lee, "The Electric Revival," *Home Missions,* June/July 1971, 32.

40. There are too many to name, but some examples of those who were touched by or provided leadership to the Jesus Movement were evangelist Jay Strack; Ohio evangelism director Mike Landry; HMB evangelism section staffer Jack Smith; Glenn Sheppard, who became the first to lead the Office of Prayer and Spiritual Awakening at the HMB; and many others. This writer, whose dissertation was on the Jesus Movement, was amazed to discover how many people today testify to the enduring positive impact of the Jesus Movement on their lives.

41. See John Avant, Malcolm McDow, and Alvin L. Reid, *Revival!* (Nashville: Broadman & Holman, 1996), for a detailed account.

42. Hanegraaff, *Counterfeit Revival.*

CHAPTER 5

1. Adapted from Lucado, *Applause*, 121.

2. For evidence on the veracity of Scripture as the unique revelation of God, see Drummond, *Word of the Cross*, 16–63.

3. In particular, I would note Drummond, *Word of the Cross*.

4. John Avant recently displayed the specific relationship between one's view of Scripture and evangelism. See Avant, "The Relationship of Changing Views of the Inspiration and Authority of Scripture to Evangelism and Church Growth."

5. See, for example, F. F. Bruce, *The New Testament Documents: Are They Reliable?* (Grand Rapids: Eerdmans, 1943).

6. Space does not allow a thorough treatment of such critical issues as the infallibility and inerrancy of the Bible. See Drummond, *Word of the Cross*, 43–63.

7. Ibid., 62.

8. Ibid., 98.

9. R. B. Kuiper, *God-Centered Evangelism* (London: The Banner of Truth Trust, 1966), 13.

10. For a discussion of the sovereignty of God in evangelism, see J. I. Packer, *Evangelism and the Sovereignty of God* (Chicago: Inter-Varsity Press, 1961).

11. See Millard J. Erickson, *Christian Theology* (Grand Rapids: Baker, 1984), 781–823, for a discussion of views of the atonement.

12. Drummond, *Word of the Cross*, 142, italics his.

13. Erickson, *Christian Theology*, 822–23.

14. David P. Wells, *No Place for Truth* (Grand Rapids: Eerdmans, 1993), 53.

15. Ibid., 58.

16. Ibid.

17. Timothy Beougher made this quote while presenting an unpublished paper for a meeting of professors of evangelism for Southern Baptist Seminaries, May 10, 1997, in Dallas, Texas. The author is thankful for insights gained from Beougher, which helped in the development of this chapter.

18. A good source for further study on pluralism is D. A. Carson, *The Gagging of God* (Grand Rapids: Zondervan, 1996).

19. Ronald H. Nash, *Is Jesus the Only Savior?* (Grand Rapids: Zondervan, 1994).

20. Woodfin, Yandall, *With All Your Mind* (Nashville: Abingdon, 1980).

21. David Lawrence Edwards and John R. W. Stott, *Evangelical Essentials: A Liberal-Evangelical Dialogue* (Downers Grove: Inter-Varsity Press, 1989).

22. James Davison Hunter, *Evangelicalism: The Coming Generation* (Chicago: Univ. of Chicago Press, 1987), 35.

23. Nash, *Is Jesus the Only Savior?* 103.

24. See Stephen D. Kovach, "Christ as Community: Inclusivism and the Theological Method of Stanley J. Grenz," Paper presented to the Evangelical Theological Society, 21 November 1997, Santa Clara, California.

25. Clark H. Pinnock, *A Wideness in God's Mercy* (Grand Rapids: Zondervan, 1992), 112.

26. Charles R. Swindoll, *Living above the Level of Mediocrity* (Waco: Word, 1987), 236–38.

PART 2

1. Robert Reccord, Southeastern Baptist Theological Seminary chapel service, October 16, 1997.

2. Duewel, *Ablaze for God,* 103.

3. Ibid., 107.

CHAPTER 6

1. Leighton Ford, *The Power of Story: Rediscovering the Oldest, Most Natural Way to Reach People for Christ* (Colorado Springs: NavPress, 1994), 10.

2. Duewel, *Ablaze for God,* 68.

3. Ibid., 88.

4. Charles H. Spurgeon, *Lectures to My Students* (Grand Rapids: Baker, 1977), 9.

5. G. Campbell Morgan, *Preaching* (London: Revell, 1937), 36. Italics added.

6. Duewel, *Ablaze for God,* 56.

7. *Christian History,* vol. XIII, no. 2, 3.

8. Ibid.

9. Roland H. Bainton, *Here I Stand: A Life of Martin Luther* (Nashville: Abingdon Press, 1950), 144.

10. Jonathan Edwards, "Thoughts on the Revival," in *The Works of Jonathan Edwards,* ed. Sereno E. Dwight, vol. 1 (Edinburgh: Banner of Truth, 1834, reprint, 1987), 424.

11. McDow and Reid, *Firefall,* 172.

12. Duewel, *Ablaze for God,* 28.

13. Ibid., 29.

14. Ibid., 108, 121.

15. John Pollock, *To All the Nations* (San Francisco: Harper and Row, 1985), 41.

16. From the Paul-Timothy conference mentioned earlier.

CHAPTER 7

1. Dallas Willard, *The Spirit of the Disciplines* (San Francisco: HarperSanFrancisco, 1988), 1.

2. Ibid.

3. Richard Foster, *Celebration of Discipline* (San Francisco: HarperSanFrancisco, 1988), 2.

4. Willard, *Spirit of the Disciplines,* 9.

5. Donald S. Whitney, *Spiritual Disciplines for the Christian Life* (Colorado Springs: NavPress, 1997), 13.

6. Foster, *Celebration,* 62.

7. Ibid., 64–66.

8. Whitney, *Spiritual Disciplines,* 32.

9. Ibid., 152.

10. Polycarp, *Epistle to the Philippians,* 77.

11. Whitney, *Spiritual Disciplines,* 153–54.

12. Foster, *Celebration,* 55.

13. Ibid., 17.

14. Spurgeon, *Lectures,* 314–15.

15. Whitney, *Spiritual Disciplines,* 112–17.

16. Ibid., 97.

CHAPTER 8

1. Duewel, *Ablaze for God,* 212.

2. Foster, *Celebration,* 33.

3. Ibid., 34.

4. Ibid.

5. Chris Schofield, "Biblical Links Between Prayer and Evangelism," Th.M. Thesis, Southeastern Baptist Theological Seminary, May 1995, 11.

6. Whitney, *Spiritual Disciplines*, 62.

7. R. A. Torrey, *How to Pray* (Pittsburgh: Whitaker House, 1983), 81.

8. Andrew Murray, *With Christ in the School of Prayer* (Springdale: Whitaker House, 1981), 115.

9. Ralph Herring, *The Cycle of Prayer* (Nashville: Broadman Press, 1966), 62–63.

10. Calvin Miller, "Praying without Ceasing," in *Evangelism*, Beougher and Reid, eds., 40.

11. Ibid., 47.

12. Foster, *Celebration*, 42.

13. Charles R. Swindoll, *Living Above the Level of Mediocrity* (Waco: Word Books, 1987), 113.

14. Ibid., 44.

15. E. M. Bounds, *The Necessity of Prayer* (Springdale: Whitaker House, 1984), 31.

16. Thom S. Rainer, *Effective Evangelistic Churches* (Nashville: Broadman & Holman, 1997), 11–17.

17. Chris Schofield, "Linking Prayer and Bold Proclamation: An Exegetical Study of Acts 4:23–31 and Ephesians 6:18–20 with Implications for Contemporary Church Growth," *Journal of the American Society of Church Growth* 8 (Winter 1997): 67.

18. Ibid., 71.

19. W. Stanley Monneyham, "Getting More Hooks in the Water Is Not Enough," *Christianity Today*, XXV, No. 16 (18 Sept. 1981): 20.

20. J. G. Hallimond, *The Miracle of Answered Prayer* (New York: The Christian Herald, 1916), 69–71.

21. *Praying Your Friends to Christ* (Alpharetta, Ga.: North American Mission Board, 1998).

22. Diane Ginter and Glen Martin, *Power House* (Nashville: Broadman & Holman, 1994), 16.

23. Ibid., 17. This book offers many resources on specific prayer ministries.

24. Spurgeon, *Lectures*, 42–43.

25. Leonard Ravenhill, *Revival Praying* (Minneapolis: Bethany Fellowship, 1964), 174–75.

CHAPTER 9

1. Miles, *Introduction to Evangelism,* 199.
2. Duewel, *Ablaze for God,* 27.
3. Ibid., 79.
4. Ibid., 273.
5. Drummond, *Word of the Cross,* 188.
6. Andreas J. Kostenberger, "What Does It Mean to Be Filled with the Spirit? A Biblical Investigation," *Journal of the Evangelical Theological Society* 40, no. 2 (June 1997): 235.
7. Schofield, "Linking Prayer and Bold Proclamation," 68.
8. Ibid.
9. Kostenberger, "What Does It Mean to Be Filled With the Spirit?," 239.
10. Ibid.
11. See C. Peter Wagner, *Your Church Can Grow* (Ventura, Calif.: Regal, 1984), 86–87, 89–90. Wagner uses the expression *evangelist,* while others use *evangelism.*
12. C. H. Spurgeon, *Twelve Sermons on the Holy Spirit* (Grand Rapids: Baker, 1973), 137.
13. David Baroni and John Chisum, "O, Mighty Cross," in *Firm Foundation* (Mobile: Integrity Music, 1994).
14. Taken from *Adult Roman Road Witness Training Teacher's Guide,* copyright 1993, North American Mission Board, SBC (formerly Home Mission Board). Used by permission.

CHAPTER 10

1. Miles, *Introduction to Evangelism,* 194–95.
2. Beougher and Reid, eds., *Evangelism.*
3. Delos Miles offers excellent guidelines related to the spiritual autobiography. The following is taken from Miles, *Introduction to Evangelism.* Used by permission.
4. I have included the spiritual autobiography of Miles, my predecessor at Southeastern, to illustrate. From Miles, *Introduction to Evangelism,* 167–75.

PART 3

1. Bennett, *Book of Virtues,* 493.

CHAPTER 11

1. James F. Engel and H. Wilbert Norton, *What's Gone Wrong with the Harvest? A Communication Strategy for the Church and World Evangelism* (Grand Rapids: Zondervan, 1975), 45.

2. Herschel Hobbs, *New Testament Evangelism* (Nashville: Convention Press, 1960), 114.

3. I am indebted to my friend Tim Beougher of Southern Seminary for this model.

4. Continuing Witness Training, Home Mission Board, Atlanta, Georgia. Used by permission.

5. Waylon B. Moore, *New Testament Follow-Up* (Grand Rapids: Eerdmans, 1963), 17.

6. Ibid., 29–36.

CHAPTER 12

1. Part of the following is taken from Alvin L. Reid and David Wheeler, "Servant Evangelism," *SBC Life* (May 1997). Used by permission.

2. The term was coined by a pastor, Steve Sjogren, in Cincinnati, Ohio. Sjogren, pastor of the Cincinnati Vineyard Church, describes the concept in his book *Conspiracy of Kindness* (Ann Arbor: Servant, 1993).

3. Charles Roesell, *Meeting Needs, Sharing Christ* (Nashville: Convention Press, 1996).

4. C. Kirk Hadaway, *Church Growth Principles* (Nashville: Broadman & Holman, 1991), 21–22.

5. Taken from John Mark Terry, *Church Evangelism* (Nashville: Broadman & Holman, 1997), 106.

6. Taken from Rick Warren, "The Purpose Driven Church Conference," notes, May 15–17, 1997. Saddleback Community Church, Lake Forest, California.

7. Miles, *Introduction to Evangelism,* 187.

CHAPTER 13

1. Green, *Evangelism,* 199.

2. My training in Continuing Witness Training taught me this approach.

3. R. A. Torrey, *How to Bring Men to Christ* (Pittsburgh: Whitaker House, 1984), 33.

4. Ibid., 59.

5. Brooks Alexander, "What Is a Cult?" *Spiritual Counterfeits Project Newsletter* 5, no. 1 (January–February 1979).

6. J. K. Van Baalen, *The Chaos of the Cults* (Grand Rapids: Eerdmans, 1938).

7. I am indebted to Calvin Miller's lecture "The Way to Narrative Preaching" at a conference in Illinois, August 11–12, 1997, for insights on this subject that follows.

8. Ibid.

9. George Hunter, *Church for the Unchurched* (Nashville: Abingdon, 1996).

10. George Hunter, "The Rationale for a Culturally Relevant Worship Service," *Journal for the American Society of Church Growth* 7 (1996): 137–38.

11. Kevin Graham Ford, *Jesus for a New Generation* (InterVarsity Press, 1995), 37–39.

12. Ibid., 69.

13. Ibid., 70.

14. Ibid., 91.

15. Ibid., 114–17.

16. Ibid., 136.

17. Ibid., chapters 9–11.

18. Ibid., 174.

19. I am indebted to Roy Fish for helping me to think along these lines.

CHAPTER 14

1. Green, *Evangelism*, 219.

2. Thom S. Rainer, *The Bridger Generation* (Nashville: Broadman & Holman, 1997).

3. Roy Fish, *Introducing Children to Christ,* TC1794, Southwestern Baptist Theological Seminary, 1997. Unless otherwise noted, all references to Fish in this chapter are from this excellent audiotape.

4. Miles, *Introduction to Evangelism,* 325.

5. Ibid., 325.

6. William Hendricks, "The Age of Accountability" in *Children and Conversion,* ed. Clifford Ingle (Nashville: Broadman Press, 1970), 97.

7. William Hendricks, *A Theology for Children* (Nashville: Broadman Press, 1980), 15.

8. Fish, *Introducting Children to Christ.*

9. Ibid.

10. Ibid.

11. I am indebted to Fish; Miles, *Introduction to Evangelism;* and Jim Eaves for these principles.

12. Jim Elliff, "Childhood Conversion," *Heartland* (Summer 1997), 4.

13. Miles, *Introduction to Evangelism,* 328.

14. Some of this material is adapted from Reid, "The Zeal of Youth."

15. Edwards, "Narrative of the Surprising Work of God."

16. Ibid.

17. Jonathan Edwards, "Some Thoughts Concerning the Present Revival of Religion."

18. W. W. Sweet, *The Story of Religion in America* (New York: Harper and Brothers, 1930), 140.

19. George Whitefield, *George Whitefield's Journals* (Edinburgh: Banner of Truth, 1985), 354.

20. Cairns, *An Endless Line of Splendor,* 42.

21. Bennett Tyler, ed., *New England Revivals as They Existed at the Close of the Eighteenth Century and the Beginning of the Nineteenth Centuries* (Wheaton: Richard Owens Roberts, 1980).

22. John Pollock, *Moody* (Chicago: Moody, 1983), 34.

23. Ibid.

24. W. T. Stead, *The Story of the Welsh Revival* (London: Fleming H. Revell, 1905), 42–43.

25. See J. Edwin Orr, *The Flaming Tongue* (Chicago: Moody Press, 1975), 3–7; Stead, *Welsh Revival,* 66–67; Bob Eklund, *Spiritual Awakening* (Atlanta: Home Mission Board, 1986), 31.

26. Llewellyn Brown, "The Torrey Mission in Cleveland," *Watchman* (14 February 1907), 32.

27. Ibid., 63.

28. Fred W. Hoffman, *Revival Time in America* (Boston: W. A. Wilde Co., 1956), 164. See also Cairns, *An Endless Line of Splendor,* 213.

29. Clifford E. Olmstead, *The History of Religion in the United States* (Englewood Cliffs, N.J.: Prentice-Hall, 1960), 590.

30. This term was coined in Rainer, *Bridger Generation.*

31. Ibid., 14.

32. Thus the group was described on their official web site at www.Hansonline.com.

33. Rainer, *Bridger Generation,* 54–56.

34. A. J. Broomhall, *Time for Action* (Downers Grove, Ill.: Inter-Varsity Press, 1965), 132, italics added.

CHAPTER 15

1. Part of this chapter is taken from my article, "Observing 'Mass' in the Southern Baptist Church," *SBC Life* (October 1996).

2. Winthrop Hudson, *Religion in America* (New York: Charles Scribner's Sons, 1981), 143.

3. Arthur Skevington Wood, *John Wesley: The Burning Heart* (Grand Rapids: Eerdmans, 1967), 97.

4. Rainer, *Effective Evangelistic Churches,* 33.

5. Susie Hilsman, "A Map of Words in the Magazine," *Worldwide Challenge* (March–April 1986), 45–46.

6. Spurgeon, *Lectures,* 148.

7. Duewel, *Ablaze for God,* 22.

8. E. M. Bounds, *Power through Prayer* (Grand Rapids: Baker, 1972), 8.

9. Cited in R. Alan Streett, *The Effective Invitation* (Grand Rapids: Kregel, 1995), 63.

10. Ibid., 81.

11. Ibid., 87.

12. Howard G. Olive, "The Development of the Evangelistic Invitation," (Th.M. Thesis, Southern Baptist Theological Seminary, 1958), 24–25.

13. For further elaboration, see Streett, *Effective Invitation,* 98–130.

14. Adapted from Roy Fish, "Preparing for Invitations in a Revival Meeting," in *Before Revival Begins,* ed. Dan Crawford (Fort Worth: Scripta, 1996).

15. I am indebted to Victor Lee for the following material. Lee writes much of the material used by the North American Mission Board on this subject.

CHAPTER 16

1. Quoted by George Hunter, "'Doing Church' to Reach Secular, Urban, Pre-Christian People," Address to the Annual Meeting of the American Society for Church Growth, November 22, 1997.

2. Rick Warren, *The Purpose Driven Church* (Grand Rapids: Zondervan, 1995), 17.

3. See Towns, ed., *Evangelism and Church Growth*, 206.

4. Ibid., 78.

5. Donald McGavran, *Understanding Church Growth* (Grand Rapids: Eerdmans, 1980), 223.

6. C. Peter Wagner, *Our Kind of People* (Atlanta: John Knox Press, 1979), 75.

7. From Robinson, *Total Church Life*, 3. Used by permission.

8. A similar strategy is seen in Gene Mims, *Kingdom Principles for Church Growth* (Nashville: Convention Press, 1995).

9. Press release, attached to a letter from Warren to the author, 10 September 1995.

10. Warren, *The Purpose Driven Church*, 82.

11. Ibid.

12. Ibid., 102. The following material is condensed from pages 102–9.

13. Daniel L. Akin. "Willow Creek Community Church: Driven by Culture or the Scriptures?" *National Liberty Journal* (May 1997).

14. See Ken Hemphill, *Revitalizing the Sunday School Dinosaur* (Nashville: Broadman & Holman, 1996).

15. Olivia M. Cloud, "Growing a Church through Sunday School," *Facts and Trends*, November 1997, 45.

16. See Andy Anderson, *The Growth Spiral* (Nashville: Broadman Press, 1993).

17. See James Emory White, *Opening the Front Door* (Nashville: Convention Press, 1992).

18. Tom Wolfe, "Postmodernism," Annual Meeting of the American Society for Church Growth, 20 November 1997.

19. Charles Arn, "The State of the Church in the 21st Century," Annual meeting of the American Society for Church Growth, 20 November 1997.

20. Warren, *The Purpose Driven Church*, 32.

21. Elmer Towns, "Church Planting in the Urban Setting, the Key to Reaching America," *American Society for Church Growth,* November 22, 1997.

22. Ibid.

CHAPTER 17

1. Paul Anderson, "Balancing Form and Freedom," *Leadership,* Spring 1986, 24. Portions of this chapter are taken from Alvin L. Reid, "Substance, Style, and Spirit: A Theology of Worship and Church Growth," *The Journal of the American Society of Church Growth* 7 (Fall 1996).

2. Elmer Towns, *Putting an End to Worship Wars* (Nashville: Broadman & Holman, 1997), considers this issue in detail.

3. R. W. Dale, *Nine Lectures on Preaching Delivered at Yale, New Haven, Connecticut* (London: Hodder and Stoughton, 1952), 271.

4. Preserved Smith, *The Life and Letters of Martin Luther* (New York: Barnes and Noble, 1968), 346.

5. Roland Bainton, *Here I Stand* (Nashville, Abingdon, 1947), 267.

6. Kenneth G. Phifer, *A Protestant Case for Liturgical Renewal* (Philadelphia: Westminster, 1965), 23.

7. Ralph P. Martin, *Worship in the Early Church* (Grand Rapids: Eerdmans, 1974), 134.

8. The historical material is adapted from Alvin L. Reid, "Evangelistic Music," in *Evangelism and Church Growth,* ed. Elmer L. Towns (Ventura, Calif.: Regal, 1995).

9. Donald R. Hustad, *Jubilate! Church Music in the Evangelical Tradition* (Carol Stream, Ill.: Hope Publishing Co., 1981), 127.

10. Steve Miller, *The Contemporary Christian Music Debate: Worldly Compromise or Agent of Renewal?* (Wheaton: Tyndale, 1993), 115.

11. Franklin M. Segler, *Christian Worship: Its Theology and Practice* (Nashville: Broadman Press, 1967), 46.

12. Hugh McElrath, "Music in the History of the Church," *Review and Expositor* 69 (Spring 1972): 156.

13. Donald Paul Ellsworth, *Christian Music in Contemporary Witness* (Grand Rapids: Baker, 1979), 86.

14. Mendell Taylor, *Exploring Evangelism:* Kansas City: Nazarene Publishing House, 1984), 326.

15. Cited in Reid, "Impact of the Jesus Movement," 99.

16. Donald R. Hustad, "Music in the Outreach of the Church," (Southern Baptist Church Music Conference, 9–10 June 1969), 48.

17. John W. Styll, "Sound and Vision: 15 Years of Music and Ministry," *Contemporary Christian Music* (July 1993), 42. By 1981 contemporary Christian music was the fifth leading category of music, ahead of jazz or classical. In 1983, 5 percent of all record sales were gospel music, the majority of which was contemporary Christian music. Also, by the early 1980s, there were over 300 exclusively Christian music radio stations. See Carol Flake, *Redemptorama: Culture, Politics, and the New Evangelicalism* (Garden City: Anchor Press, 1984), 175–76.

18. Reid, "Impact of the Jesus Movement," 119.

19. Sally Morgenthaler, *Worship Evangelism: Inviting Unbelievers into the Presence of God* (Grand Rapids: Zondervan, 1995), 282.

20. Flake, *Redemptorama*, 178.

21. Reid, "Impact of the Jesus Movement," 124. Also Elwyn C. Raymer, "From Serendipity to Shindig!" *Church Recreation,* July/August/September 1968, 22.

22. Bob Burroughs, "What Did You Say?" (Southern Baptist Church Music Conference, 4–5 June 1971), 43; Forrest H. Heeren, "Church Music and Changing Worship Patterns," *Review and Expositor LXIX* (Spring 1972): 190.

23. Morgenthaler, *Worship Evangelism*, 36, italics added.

24. Ibid., 29.

25. George Barna, "How Can Today's Churches Minister More Faithfully?" *Growing Churches* (January–March 1992), 18.

26. Morgenthaler, *Worship Evangelism,* 27–28.

27. Ibid., 213. See also Marva Dawn, *Reaching out without Dumbing Down* (Grand Rapids: Eerdmans, 1995), 202.

28. Os Guinness, *Dining with the Devil* (Grand Rapids: Baker, 1993), 28–29.

29. Morgenthaler, *Worship Evangelism,* 92. This book is must reading for anyone interested in the relationship between worship and church growth.

30. Don McMinn, "The Practice of Praise" (Word Music, 1992), 129.

31. Hustad, *Jubilate!* 164.

32. The growing movements of revival characterized by open confession of sin demonstrate the need for this in our day. See Avant, McDow, and Reid, *Revival!*

33. Unfortunately, not all statistical analyses of church growth emphasize evangelistic or conversion growth.

34. Rainer, *Effective Evangelistic Churches,* 101. These are descriptive, not prescriptive.

35. Ibid., 116, italics added.

36. Reid, "Impact of the Jesus Movement," 134–35. Burroughs did not oppose contemporary music as a genre. He composed several contemporary youth musicals, including the first that used accompaniment tracts and computer-generated accompaniment.

37. Morgenthaler, *Worship Evangelism,* 88.

38. Gerrit Gustafson, "Worship Evangelism," *Psalmist* (February–March 1991), 50.

39. Ibid., 102–28.

40. Morgenthaler, *Worship Evangelism,* 128.

41. Ibid., 284.

42. Ibid., 45–46.

CHAPTER 18

1. R. G. Puckett, "The Perfect Pastor," *Biblical Recorder,* February 1, 1997.

2. Bennett, *Book of Virtues,* 332.

3. The above was adapted from Alvin L. Reid, "The Elmo Enigma," *SBC Life,* February 1997, 6–7.

4. Duewel, *Ablaze for God,* 105.

CONCLUSION

1. Bennett, *Book of Virtues,* 474–75.

2. From the brochure, "Sing a Little Louder," by Penny Lea.